THE

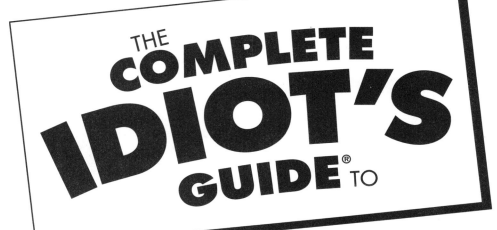

COMPLETE
IDIOT'S
GUIDE® TO

Stepparenting

by Ericka Lutz

ALPHA

A member of Penguin Group (USA) Inc.

This book is dedicated to the steps in my life: Aaron Sonnenschein, Rachel Sonnenschein, and Jack Olsen.

ALPHA BOOKS

Published by the Penguin Group

Penguin Group (USA) Inc., 375 Hudson Street, New York, New York 10014, U.S.A.

Penguin Group (Canada), 10 Alcorn Avenue, Toronto, Ontario, Canada M4V 3B2 (a division of Pearson Penguin Canada Inc.)

Penguin Books Ltd, 80 Strand, London WC2R 0RL, England

Penguin Ireland, 25 St Stephen's Green, Dublin 2, Ireland (a division of Penguin Books Ltd)

Penguin Group (Australia), 250 Camberwell Road, Camberwell, Victoria 3124, Australia (a division of Pearson Australia Group Pty Ltd)

Penguin Books India Pvt Ltd, 11 Community Centre, Panchsheel Park, New Delhi—110 017, India

Penguin Group (NZ), cnr Airborne and Rosedale Roads, Albany, Auckland 1310, New Zealand (a division of Pearson New Zealand Ltd)

Penguin Books (South Africa) (Pty) Ltd, 24 Sturdee Avenue, Rosebank, Johannesburg 2196, South Africa

Penguin Books Ltd, Registered Offices: 80 Strand, London WC2R 0RL, England

©1998 by Ericka Lutz

THE COMPLETE IDIOT'S GUIDE TO and Design are registered trademarks of Penguin Group (USA) Inc.

International Standard Book Number: 0-02862407-6
Library of Congress Catalog Card Number: 98-85118

07 06 05   11 10

Interpretation of the printing code: The rightmost number of the first series of numbers is the year of the book's printing; the rightmost number of the second series of numbers is the number of the book's printing. For example, a printing code of 98-1 shows that the first printing occurred in 1998.

Printed in the United States of America

Note: This publication contains the opinions and ideas of its author. It is intended to provide helpful and informative material on the subject matter covered. It is sold with the understanding that the author and publisher are not engaged in rendering professional services in the book. If the reader requires personal assistance or advice, a competent professional should be consulted.

The author and publisher specifically disclaim any responsibility for any liability, loss, or risk, personal or otherwise, which is incurred as a consequence, directly or indirectly, of the use and application of any of the contents of this book.

Most Alpha books are available at special quantity discounts for bulk purchases for sales promotions, premiums, fund-raising, or educational use. Special books, or book excerpts, can also be created to fit specific needs.

For details, write: Special Markets, Alpha Books, 375 Hudson Street, New York, NY 10014.

Contents at a Glance

Contents

Foreword

Did you know it has been estimated that by the year 2010 there will be more stepfamilies than any other type of family in the United States? That means a lot of people are already in need of information, support, and advice on becoming part of a stepfamily. If you feel as if you are putting together a giant jigsaw puzzle for which you have only a few pieces, don't just muddle through. Reach for this guide. It deals intelligently and sensitively with many of the realities of today's complicated families. Despite the title's tongue-in-cheek reference to *idiots,* please rest assured there are no stupid questions. All questions are valid, and this book answers many of them. It provides essential information that research has proven is helpful to stepfamilies during the early phases of togetherness.

We are always confronted by the gap between what we know from our life in the past and what we want to know about the world of remarriage. How in this world do stepparents go about making a positive contribution in managing conflict? Resolving differences? Setting clear boundaries? Minimizing chaos? Teaching responsibility? And building mutual respect and friendship?

For couples planning to remarry or those who have already taken on the title of stepfather or stepmother, this guide provides plenty of information on how it feels and what it means to be a stepparent. You can get a handle on stepfamily life by looking in these pages for information about

> Stepparent roles
>
> Daily life in a stepfamily
>
> Surviving the special challenges
>
> Building the extended family

From the first chapter it is clear that Ms. Lutz, sometimes witty and always passionate, provides the "heart" of a stepparent, along with her professional research. Self-help groups are popular but if you prefer to forage for information in private, you will find in these pages clear evidence that you are not "alone" and that successful stepparenting is a series of identifiable skills that can be learned. In some cases, the book will reinforce tips you've heard before—and there are times when confirmation of what you already know can be quite reassuring.

While the focus of this book is on stepfamilies with children at home, adult children in stepfamilies will find useful advice and insights here as well. Regardless of ages or length of remarriage, this book offers a deepened understanding of stepfamily riches for both parent and child. It won't solve all of your stepfamily quandaries, but it offers something very valuable: It will set you to thinking that being in a stepfamily is more than a sum of its parts. Being in a stepfamily is also a state of mind, a way of interpreting the world, and a pattern of behavior. For that understanding alone, the book is worth more than a glance. Read it before the wedding; you'll find it to be an indispensable reference book then and thereafter.

Margorie Engel, Ph.D.
President
Stepfamily Association of America

"To provide education and support for parents and children in stepfamilies."

Dr. Engel is an author, speaker, and media consultant specializing in families complicated by divorce and remarriage. For additional information, contact Stepfamily Association of America at 800-735-0329

Introduction

About half of all Americans are currently involved in some sort of step relationship. By the year 2010, more Americans will be living in stepfamilies than in nuclear families. You're in good company!

Bet you never planned to be a stepparent. For most of us, the role takes us by surprise. Despite how common a step living arrangement is, there's not a lot of information or advice out there, and what there is available is pretty scary.

Yet here you are, a stepparent (or contemplating becoming one). You've heard the horror stories and the stereotypes, and you're determined that you won't be wicked like Cinderella's stepmother or Hamlet's stepdad. Yet you're scared and you're frustrated—life at home is filled with tension. And to top it off, there's very little acceptance and support for what you're trying to do.

How will you make your way through the uncertainty, frustration, guilt, jealousy, and sheer logistics of it all?

Well, you're no idiot. You know that challenges are opportunities, and the scary bits of life are best met head on. You've picked up this book because you are determined to somehow steer yourself and your stepfamily safely through rocky shoals.

Greetings. I'm here to help you navigate your "Relation Ship" into smooth waters. I've been a stepparent myself for more than a decade. I'd never thought much about stepparenting when Aaron and Rachel came into my life 12 years ago. Then I fell in love with their father, and I was off on one of the most challenging and fascinating adventures of my life! As a stepmother, I've made mistakes (no stepparent is perfect), and I won't pretend that stepparenting is easy—hey, parenting of any kind is tough—but I believe that challenge is opportunity.

This book takes a positive approach to stepparenting for both women and men, for those considering stepping in, for those newly in step, and for those who have been stepparenting for a while and who could use some support and advice.

No matter who you are or where you are in the adventure, there's something for you. You'll find *The Complete Idiot's Guide to Stepparenting* packed with up-to-date information, advice, special tips, exercises, tools, stories, and encouragement from top parenting experts, as well as from real-life stepparents and stepkids.

Let's step on in!

What's in the Book?

The Complete Idiot's Guide to Stepparenting is divided into five parts, each covering a different area of stepparenting. You can read it cover-to-cover like a novel, or you can just dip in and out to grab the bits you need.

Part 1: Introducing...the Stepparent!

First comes love, then comes marriage.... Oops! Gotta meet the kids first! What does it mean to be a stepparent, anyway? This part of the book introduces you to stepparenting. These chapters will help you get used to being a stepparent (getting used to your new role takes some adjustment) and help you avoid some pitfalls along the way to forming your new stepfamily.

Part 2: The Stepfamily in Daily Life

Ah, life as a stepparent. For some, this may be your first experience dealing with children at close range. What's it like to be an Instant Parent? Lifestyles, living situations, chores, family structures, and your marriage are all new, all open for negotiation. Your stepkids need to get used to you, and you to them. This part ends with a chapter all about talking and listening skills, the most important tools any stepparent can possess.

Part 3: Special Stepparenting Challenges

Here's where we look at the hard stuff, the issues of stepparenting that keep you up at night. This part of the book gives suggestions about discipline issues, transitional periods during visits, and the joys and exasperations of grandparents.

Does the mere thought of talking to your partner's ex-partner give you the shakes? Turn here for help and a little hand-holding. You'll learn how to talk to your stepchild who comes from another culture, how to divvy up the holiday celebrations, and how to deal with society's hostility if you're a gay stepparent.

As this is the part of the book that looks at the serious issues, the final chapter gives information about what to do if your stepfamily is in a crisis, and how to find good outside help.

Part 4: Legal Schmeagle

It's law school time! This part of the book gives you the hard-core dirt on the legal details. What kind of rights and responsibilities do you have as a stepparent? (None!) How do you set up legal protections for yourself, your partner, and your stepchildren? There are details on how to find a lawyer, how to adopt your stepchild, how stepfamily money works and doesn't work, and more than you ever wanted to know about custody and child support.

Part 5: Putting It All Together

Is there a baby in your future? Now that we've dismissed the myths, what's it really like to be a stepmother? What are the top complaints of stepfathers? And where do you go from here? In the final chapter of the book, we'll look at the stepfamily from a larger perspective. This chapter puts it all together and teaches you how to extend your own family to include others, step by step.

If you need more information, turn to the back of the book. You'll find a list of other good things to read that will make you even more knowledgeable than you will be after you've finished this book! You'll also find tons of numbers for organizations and other useful resources.

Extras

As an added bonus, you'll find additional information and statistics, special tips, useful words to know, and warnings in little boxes throughout. Here's what they look like:

I Kid You Not!

Here you'll read statistics and humorous true-life stories about stepfamilies. To reassure you that you are not alone, you'll enjoy an occasional chuckle about famous stepparents in history, literature, and folklore.

Step-Speak

What's the lingo? In this box, you'll find special words, terms, and expressions related to stepparenting. They can all also be found in the glossary at the back of the book.

Stepping Stones

Stepping stones are designed to help get you over the muddy places. These stepping stones are extra bits of advice for specific situations to help you keep your feet clean and dry.

Don't Be Wicked

It's easy to mess up as a stepparent, but you don't want to be wicked, now do you? Here's the place for special warnings and cautions of things not to do.

A Special Note about Language Usage

The Complete Idiot's Guide to Stepparenting is designed for both stepmothers and stepfathers. Most examples and stories in the book can apply to adults and kids of either sex. In an attempt to use inclusive, nonsexist language, I've alternated gender pronouns and examples. Occasionally there are certain specific circumstances that apply to only one sex; you'll know what I'm talking about when you get there.

A Legal Disclaimer

Don't count on us! The legal information in *The Complete Idiot's Guide to Stepparenting* is not designed to lead you astray. We've tried to make it accurate, but we're not going to claim that we're perfect. The information in this book is designed to educate you about family law. But the first thing to know is that laws change constantly (just like the moods of stepchildren) and vary from place to place. So even though we're doing the very best we can, don't count on us. We're not liable, and you gotta talk to a lawyer to get the most accurate, up-to-date scoop on things.

Acknowledgments

Writing a book about stepparenting brings out the storyteller in everybody, and I could never have written this book without the input of almost everybody I spoke with during my research and writing. In addition to the many stepparents and stepkids who lent their (mostly anonymous) true stories to me, I want to single out a few individuals for special mention.

At the top of the list is my loving partner, Bill Sonnenschein, who not only leant his specific communication knowledge and sharp editorial eye, but stuck with me through the most grueling autumn of our lives together. Thank you, Bill—you know why. Here's a toast to next year in Bora Bora. Aaron and Rachel Sonnenschein are directly responsible for my expertise in this field and were so very understanding of my constant claim to the brown chair during their visits. A particular acknowledgment also goes to my own Annie, who is so sick of hearing the words, "Mommy has a deadline."

Special thanks to Andree Abecassis, Annie McManus, Ralph Manak, Mark Hetts, Naomi Baran, and Arthur, Karla and Jessica Lutz. Margorie L. Engel enthusiastically provided valuable resource information. Kay Pasley, of the University of North Carolina, Greensboro, graciously and speedily verified facts. My various editors at Alpha Books—Nancy Mikhail, Carol Hupping, Suzanne Snyder, and Krista Hansing were helpful, patient, and wise as they helped shape this book into its existing form.

Finally, a few words of gratitude and love for my personal save-my-emotional-butt network—Milo Starr Johnson, Ami Zins, Ailsa Steckel, Tilly Roche, and Carolyn Brown—the fab-five girlfriends who provided support, silliness, stories, sobs, and sass.

Special Thanks from the Publisher to the Technical Reviewer

The Complete Idiot's Guide to Stepparenting was reviewed by an expert in the field who checked for technical accuracy and provided a wealth of experience, valuable suggestions, and thoughtful insights. Our special thanks to Annie McManus.

Annie McManus has more than 15 years of professional experience working with children. She earned her master's degree in developmental psychology at San Francisco State University and worked in the San Francisco Bay Area as a parent educator, family crisis counselor, child advocate, and early childhood educator. Currently, Ms. McManus teaches psychology and early childhood education at Parkland College in Champaign, Illinois.

An avid world traveler, Ms. McManus studies children in their home environments while abroad, collecting their artwork and interviewing their parents and educators about child rearing and education practices abroad.

Part 1
Introducing...the Stepparent!

Becoming a stepparent? Welcome to a New You! Stepparenting is a role whose chal-lenges and glories you've probably never considered before. (Few of us grow up aspiring to be stepparents, yet here we are!)

If you're reading this book, you're probably either already a stepparent or you're thinking very seriously about joining the ranks of the fastest-growing family grouping in the United States.

Dating a divorcée with 12-year-old twins and wondering when's the best time to meet them? Moving in with a man and his every-other-weekend toddler daughter? Planning a church wedding and trying to negotiate four sides of the family? Trying to avoid being wicked?

This part of the book introduces you to the possibilities—and stresses—of beginning stepparenthood. A wide world of adventure awaits—step on into it!

Chapter 1

Stepparenting Myths and Realities

In This Chapter

➤ Understanding the myths of the stepparent, both good and bad

➤ Acknowledging your expectations and lowering your goals

➤ Redefining family roles

➤ How to take care of your emotional needs

Welcome! You're a member—or about to become a member—of one of the biggest demographics in the country. You're a stepparent, or you're thinking seriously about becoming one. Congratulations!

What is stepparenting like? The reality can be harder than you ever imagined. At times, you may feel completely alone, like the pilot on an explorer ship in uncharted waters. With pirates to the left and sharks to the right, you'll steer a dangerous path through frustrations, guilt, jealousy and anger.

Whoa! Relax! *It's not so bad!* Done right, with care, forethought, communication, and time, stepparenting can be a highly positive experience. It may be the biggest challenge you've ever faced, and (though it may sound like I'm looking *really* hard for a silver lining in a storm cloud) it will give you the biggest opportunities in your life—to form true relationships not based on bloodlines, overcome personal challenges, mold resistance and fear into warmth and joy, create a wonderful diverse family, and gain great personal satisfaction.

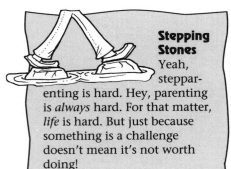

Stepping Stones
Yeah, stepparenting is hard. Hey, parenting is *always* hard. For that matter, *life* is hard. But just because something is a challenge doesn't mean it's not worth doing!

Step-Speak
A *family* is a group of related people (and how they're "related" is up to you). In a *natural family*, the children are the biological offspring of the adults. A stepfamily is a family where some members are *not* biologically or legally related to each other.

Stepparenting 101

The first and most important thing to remember about stepparenting is that it is *different* from biological parenting. It is less spontaneous, it requires more work, and people (the other biological parent, your friends, and the neighbor down the block) are watching you carefully to see how you do.

Part of the challenge is that the role of stepparent is fairly undefined. You don't know quite what to do about anything, and you're not sure what kind of role models to turn to for help. Sometimes it seems odd to put the word "stepparent" and you in the same sentence. As you start to really think about it, you realize you're not even sure what being a stepparent really means! In this chapter, we'll explore the general concepts of stepfamilies and stepparenting. First we'll look at what they are and are not. Then we'll begin to figure out how to get you into emotionally safer waters.

What Is a Stepfamily?

A stepfamily is, first and foremost, a family. Families come in all shapes and sizes. As a type of family configuration, stepfamilies have more similarities with other family configurations than they have differences.

Okay, now that I've said that, we'll spend the rest of the book focusing on what makes a stepfamily different and special from so-called "natural" families.

Stepfamily Configurations

No two step situations are the same. In this book, I'll use the broadest definitions possible—stepparenting is an emotional state more than a physical definition.

Here are some possible stepfamily configurations (and I haven't even begun to add in the pets: his dog, her dog, their dog….):

➤ His kids, but not hers

➤ Her kids, but not his

➤ His kids and her kids

➤ His kids, her kids, and their kids

➤ Stepparents with foster children, too

➤ Gay stepfamilies: his kids, him, and him; or her kids, her, and her

➤ Stepfamilies not defined by marriage, that is, living-together families

➤ Families where aunts, uncles, or grandparents take over primary parenting responsibilities

➤ Him, her and their adopted kids—sometimes. (Certainly yes, if the child has any memory of a previous parent or family grouping. Perhaps, if the child has a lot of contact with a bioparent. And yes, too, if you find yourself dealing with the issues explored in the book. While this book doesn't deal much with adoptive families per se, the situations, dilemmas, and advice may feel familiar. If so, use it! If not, there are many other wonderful adoption support groups and resources. See Appendix B for a start.)

Step-Speak
A *bioparent* is the natural, biological parent of a child. *Stepparenting* is parenting in a family with kids who are not biologically related to you.

Stepparenting: An Undefined Role

When you find yourself in a *stepparenting* relationship (that is, in a parenting role to children who are not biologically related to you), you'll find you're a bit like Alice in Wonderland, lost in a topsy-turvy world where none of the rules you *thought* should apply actually do.

Turn on the TV, go to a movie, or read a book. Okay, just look at a billboard! Listen to your neighbor whine! All around you are images and myths of stepparents that have influenced your thoughts and ideas about what a stepparent is and what a stepparent should be. Before you can decide what kind of stepparent you *want* to be, you gotta look at your own ideas about stepparenting. How your society looks at stepparenting affects how you'll see yourself in the role, so let's look at the myths for a moment. We'll also look at expectations, because what you *expect* to have happen in a situation can have an impact on what actually *does* happen (except when playing poker, alas). Once we discuss this, we'll be able to dismiss it and get on with real life.

Stepparenting Myths

Stepparents don't get a lot of credit. History and literature are filled with stepparents, from Snow White's jealous witch of a stepmom, to the pharaoh's daughter, who took Moses from the bulrushes and raised him as her own son.

The Wicked Stepmother

Many of the stepparents (especially stepmothers) in history and folklore are shown as wicked, cruel, and uncaring. They steal the father's affection from the children. They take the inheritance, they banish the princess to the cinder heap, or they're so jealous about her young beauty that they arrange to have her killed. (Sometimes, on a bad day, you might think you were the model for Snow White's stepmother. You don't *want* to be wicked, but what about those times when jealousy creeps in? Don't worry, we'll deal with that later on in the book.)

The Abusive Stepfather

In general, there's not a lot of mythology about stepfathers. What there is tends to portray stepfathers as abusive. The hard drinkin', flinty-hearted man who…well, whatever he does, it's negative. Stepfathers often complain that people assume the stereotype about them and automatically view the relationship as a disaster waiting to happen.

I Kid You Not!

Famous stepparent in literature: Hamlet's stepfather (the guy was also his uncle) was not a very caring man. He killed Hamlet's dad and then married his mother, grabbing the kingly throne for himself in the process!

The Dragon Slayer

Not all myths are negative. Sometimes the stepparent is looked on as a rescuer—the Able Woman, for instance, coming in to feed, clothe, and emotionally nourish the poor, feeble widower and his family of young children whom he loves but cannot care for. Then there's Super Stepmom, who mothers better than Mother ever did, baking cookies, driving the car pool, playing video games with the kids, and shopping with them. And then there's Big Daddy Moneybags, coming in with a whole lotta love and money to help save the starving young divorcee and her charming children.

Rescue fantasies are insidious. Very often it is the natural parent who believes strongest in the rescue fantasy, and that can be very seductive to the stepparent. "They want me, they need me," you feel. But if you or the people around you set you up to be the one to make it all better, you're gonna find yourself like Humpty Dumpty on that wall: sitting pretty but about to take a great fall. What happens when the family finds out that you aren't perfect? Yikes! What happens if they find out just how human you really are?

It's hard not to internalize some of these images, to take them on as your own. On a good day, you may think of yourself as the rescuer on a white horse, saving this family from the depths of their own ineptitude and giving them a proper father or mother. When it's a bad day (when you've blown it and screamed, when the kids look at you like you're a small ugly bug that crawled out of the wall and somehow ended up living with them), you may feel like a wicked stepmother or fear you are becoming an abusive stepdad.

I Kid You Not!

According to Paul Bohannan, author of *Divorce and After*, the terms "stepmother" and "stepfather" were first used to describe the "new" parent who *stepped* in after the "real" parent's death. "Today the stepparent is less often a substitute than he is an added parent."

Stepfamily Myths

Stepfamilies also have their own set of myths, which can be equally dangerous:

➤ **The Brady Bunch Family**   The term "blended family" is often used to describe two families, each with a parent and children, coming together. Perhaps the most famous blended family in media history is the Brady Bunch. He's got kids, she's got kids, and they all live together in a big house as a happy extended family. In the Brady Bunch, nobody has *issues*. (Highly unlikely!) If you buy into the Brady Bunch mythology (we'll deal more with it in Chapter 9, "New Family Structures"), you'll either spend a lot of time in denial about the real, unsmiling state of affairs, or you'll judge yourself harshly for not being able to create blended family heaven. To save ourselves a lot of grief, let's call these types of families "combined" families.

Step-Speak
The term *combined family* usually refers to a stepfamily with two sets of kids, one set provided by each love bird.

➤ **The Somehow Strange Sort of Family**   It's a dangerous myth that your family is somehow abnormal because it's "in-step" instead of "all-natural." It's also wrong: Statistics show that about half of all Americans are currently involved in some sort of step relationship. And while the year 2010 census statistics have not yet been

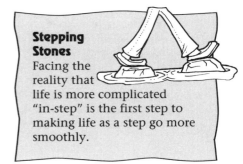

Stepping Stones
Facing the reality that life is more complicated "in-step" is the first step to making life as a step go more smoothly.

taken, the census bureau estimates that they will find more Americans living in stepfamilies than in nuclear families. Somehow, despite the facts, the mythology lives on, and as a result, stepparents often believe that their families aren't quite normal or aren't as good as biological families.

Common and Unrealistic Expectations

Just as getting rid of the ingrained societal myths can be hard, so can giving up your hopes and expectations about what marriage, partnership, parenthood, and family life will be for you. "Unrealistic expectations are the biggest risk," says Emily Visher, founder of the Stepfamily Association of America.

Have you ever heard yourself thinking of saying something along any of these lines?

➤ *Just you and me, and baby makes three.* (Hey, what about his older kids Bobby and Suzy over there in the corner?)

Don't Be Wicked
The stepfamily cannot function as does a "natural" family. It cannot, and it will not. If you try to make it do so, you will fail, flame out, bite the big one.

➤ *The kids won't live with us, so they don't really play a role in our lives.* (Whoa, Nellie. Hold on. What about summer vacation, family reunions, or if one of the kids gets into trouble with the law?)

➤ *My daughter always wanted a big brother to play with, and now she'll have him!* (Just because you're joining forces with another family doesn't mean the kids will automatically have a loving, close sibling relationship.)

➤ *I've always loved kids, and I'm great with them.* (Yes, but somehow it's different when you're "in-step." There's a lot more at stake and a lot more complications when you're romantically involved with the children's parent.)

The Built-In Family

Many expectations can be built up around the joys of family life. You love him or her as a parent, the children are an essential part of the whole seductive package, and the more time you spend around your Honey while he or she is actively parenting, the deeper you fall in love. You want to crawl into his or her life, curl up in the coziness of the family, and take a rest.

You've been seeing the family from the position of an outsider, unfortunately. Nothing is ever as smooth as it looks on the surface, and even if it has been fairly smooth, there is no way for you to slide into this still pond without rippling the waters.

No Infancy, Less Work

Hey, the stepparent-to-be thinks, this way I know what kind of kid I'm getting. She thinks: Hey, I get a kid (or more wonderful kids) without going through pregnancy and labor. He thinks: Full-fledged kids without all those months of screaming and diaper changes! All right! Alas, the intensive care of infancy and early childhood is matched in the intensity (if not time) of building a good relationship with an older stepchild. You're gonna have to work hard (possibly harder), depending on how old the children are and what their relationship is with their bioparent.

I Kid You Not

Famous stepparent in musical theater: Maria in the *Sound of Music*, was a warm and loving stepmother, though maybe just a little too sweet?

Insta-Love—Just Add Water and Stir!

This is one of the biggest and most brutal expectations of all, that everybody in the stepfamily will love each other, and that you'll gain (or regain) security, easy give and take, and love.

Love is not a requirement. The kids do not have to love you, and you do not have to love the kids. Let me say it again. *Love is not a requirement.* Go for "reasonable." Go for "content." Go for "we're working at it."

Don't Be Wicked
Many a stepparent has fallen into the trap of despairing that because things are terrible today, they'll be terrible forever. That's not necessarily so. Try to take a long-range view.

The insta-love expectation is particularly brutal because, as much as you want it to, it just won't happen that way. Remember, you chose your sweetheart and your sweetheart chose you, but the kids had little say over the matter. This is not *their* romance. And the person you fell in love with is the parent of these children. You may like the children, you may love the children, and they may like or even love you. But this is not a requirement for a functional, working stepfamily. Love takes time, and it must be earned.

How Stepfamilies Differ from "Natural" Families

Here's an easy-to-read chart adapted from Robert Adler's book, *Sharing the Children*:

"Natural" Family	Stepfamily
You meet, you fall in love, and you're a couple. It's all "you and me, baby, against the world."	You meet, you fall in love *but* one or both of you has some excess baggage and history—plus ex-spouses and some kids. It's all "you and me and Jimmy and Eliza against the world, and at least you and me against my Ex."
Love, love, and more love. You decide to have a child together. Now baby makes three.	You've been far more than a couple since the beginning. From day one, it's already a crowd.
The family is bonded through love and biology. That biology is strong stuff.	Yours, mine, ours—the kids are bonded (but also divided) by biology and history.
Each child has two loving parents.	Each child has two loving parents (who don't love each other), plus one or more other parents. Man, are there a lot of adults around, or what?
Family loyalty rules! Yeah, you fight, and, yeah, there are rivalries, but you are The Family.	Whoa—loyalty issues abound. Where do those loyalties lie? Watch out.
This is the kind of family that is featured in family values speeches, in Norman Rockwell pictures, and in Hallmark greeting cards. You are the model of the right way to be.	Your family is considered not quite acceptable, not quite as valuable. Hey, what's wrong here?

The Payoff: Surprise Pleasures

The stepfamily has its own dynamics, and they can be terrific! But first, rid thyself of the expectations that the stepfamily will ever be like that fantasy you had of the "natural" family. Redefine your expectations and lower your goals. As a stepparent, you have a remarkable opportunity—to enhance a child's life; to provide another opinion, another resource, possibly an ear and a strong shoulder; to provide a good role model; and to give the child the stability of a family structure that works.

As time passes, you will gain some treasures:

➤ Hugs and giggles

➤ The pleasure of your partner's child looking up to you and asking advice

➤ A sense of pride as you see the children mastering new skills

➤ A sense of belonging together

➤ Shared experiences and memories that make a family

> **Stepping Stones**
> Stepparenting can feel like a thankless task. When it feels like this, get Zen about it. Laugh a lot. Find the gratification in the acts themselves. When you rid yourself of expectations, pleasures will occur.

The Least You Need to Know

➤ Stepparenting is profoundly different from biological parenting.

➤ Stepparents tend to get a whole lot of negative press.

➤ There are stepfamilies, and there are stepfamilies; they come in a wide variety of configurations.

➤ Unrealistic expectations are the stepparent's biggest risk.

➤ Keep a long-range perspective. Big adjustments take time—something you'll want to remind yourself, your partner, and the kids when things get rough.

Chapter 2

Dating a Parent

In This Chapter

➤ Understanding the differences between parents and nonparents, and parents and stepparents

➤ Coping with a divorce survivor

➤ Salvaging your reputation

➤ Dealing with jealousy—yours and theirs

➤ What to do about sex

So you're seeing somebody—and this maybe-special somebody has kids. Then this is the chapter for you! Dating a parent—even casually—can be a little tricky, and it's vital to take care of your own emotional well-being. The first part of doing that is realizing what issues you may be dealing with when you date a parent. Not only is the scheduling a little complicated, but whether or not the little offspring are physically in the picture, they are a part of your new date's story. They affect his or her life, and they very well may affect your dates. If you've got kids of your own, they're going to affect your dates, too!

There are differences between parents and nonparents, as you'll see in this chapter. I'm talking about jealousy, reputations, competition, furtive sexual encounters, and all that good juicy stuff that literary novels are made of—but that isn't always so fun to encounter in real life.

Once a Parent, Always a Parent

Is there anything fundamentally different about being a parent? This question tends to make parents give each other knowing looks across the room, and to make *non*parents crazy, as though people are telling secrets behind their backs. It's easy enough to say— and I have—"Oh, the only difference is that parents never sleep—they lost the habit during their children's infancy, and now that Suzy *drives*, they spend their nights tossing and worrying." Yeah, I'm being flippant, but there's a grain of truth here. And it's only one of a few things that tend to make parenting (and active stepparenting) a different experience from living a childless life. Forgive me while I wildly generalize:

➤ It may seem apparent (ooh, I couldn't resist), but parents think about their kids often, even when they aren't around. (That's the sleepless stuff I mentioned above.)

➤ Parents tend to think they know it all and that nonparents don't know anything.

➤ Parents *don't* know it all, but there is a level of life knowledge that comes from the sheer acts of parenting or actively taking care of somebody else day in, day out, day in….

➤ Parents are instinctually protective of their children. Don't mess with Mama Bear, or she'll *charge* you.

➤ In a parent's heart, children always come first.

That last point is the most important! Somebody once said that having a child is like having a piece of your heart walking around outside your body. Nonparents may feel they are always in competition for a portion of a parent's love. In some ways, this is true (and if you're a parent yourself, I don't have to tell *you* this), so if you can't stand the heat….

Once Bitten, Twice Shy

Stepping Stones

Tip for parents: Try integrating your kids into your post-divorce social life. It's good for them to see you have friends and some life of your own. Getting the kids accustomed to your new social life will lessen the shock when you do meet that new Special Someone.

Dating a parent often means dealing with the survivor of divorce, one of life's more painful experiences. (Death of a spouse also wounds—we'll look at that in Chapter 8, "Your Marriage.") Divorce wounds can make another commitment difficult, or make the survivor withhold emotionally. Your date, the divorce survivor, may still be in an active state of grieving. Even if the divorce was long ago and the wounds are healed, there will be some scar tissue. Dating a parent *can* be like dating a callus (a callus is a type of scar tissue); it can be tough.

Think about the calluses on your heels and toes. They exist to protect the delicate tissue that keeps getting rubbed by your too-tight shoes. Calluses form over blisters. Just like a calloused foot, the parent you are dating may be less "open" to new possibilities of romance because he is protecting himself from ever, *ever* getting injured again. He may also be trying to protect his kids from harm—his kids may have calluses, too.

How Much Whining Can a Person Take?

Because the divorced parent may not be fully healed from the pain of the divorce, as you get closer and begin to form a deeper relationship, you will need to decide how much emotional venting you are willing to take. Only you can decide on your own tolerance level.

When Paul and Marilyn got together, he was barely a year out of his marriage, and though Marilyn didn't fully understand this at the time, he was still emotionally connected to his former relationship. He wasn't still in love with his ex, but he was still in the process of extricating his heart.

Heart extrication is pretty painful, and in their first few months together, Marilyn heard a *lot* about Samantha. Samantha, Samantha, Samantha. Marilyn was a good listener, a great ear. She held Paul when he cried about the death of the relationship. She hung in there when Paul talked about how scared he was of the possibility of getting deeply involved with someone new—and getting his heart stomped on again.

At a certain point, Marilyn told herself, "I'll give him another two months. If he hasn't shown any movement at that point, then we'll have to break up. I can't take this." In two months, it was evident that there *had* been progress, enough that Marilyn felt able to stay—and work—in the relationship.

Lucky Marilyn, and lucky Paul. It's not always so easy. Some people stay stuck in their old marriages. Tom was deeply attracted to Wanda, who had been divorced for four years, but after several months of dating he became convinced that Wanda was still in love with her ex and unable and unwilling to move on. He offered to go to counseling with her, and encouraged her to go alone as well. Wanda wouldn't. Eventually Tom felt he had to leave.

Commitment—or Commitable?

Are divorced people with children more or less likely to make a commitment to a relationship than single people? I don't have the facts on single people, but divorced people *do* tend to get remarried, and the time between divorce and remarriage averages less than three years. Despite this little factoid, people damaged by divorce tend to be a little gun shy—and for some very good reasons! (Hey, nobody should have to go through that pain once, let alone more than once!)

I Kid You Not!

Usually, divorce occurs within the first five years of a child's life.

Date Guilt (Who Am I to Have a Good Time?)

Parents are also likely to feel guilty about dating. Why are they "allowed" to have a good time when the kids are still so upset? They shouldn't feel guilty. In *The Official Parents Without Partners Sourcebook*, author Stephen L. Atlas says, "As a positive role model for children, a single parent's short-term relationships are no worse than a hostile marriage or long-term relationship." Atlas also stresses that having a parent who dates provides an opportunity for the child not only to see a parent's needs, feelings, and emotions but also to give that child the encouragement to form relationships that "meet one's needs, rather than to settle for what's available."

Don't Be Wicked
If you're a non-custodial parent, try not to date each and every time your kids visit. You need special time alone with your kids, plus, why add Date Guilt to the guilt you may feel as a non-custodial parent (you know, the terrible guilt of not always being there for your child, of not getting to spend enough time together…need I go on?).

Whether or not a single parent has reason to feel guilty about painting the town red with you, Date Guilt may be something you have to deal with. Here are some tips for coping:

➤ Be gentle. If your date is feeling protective of her family, don't push. You'll push her away from you.

➤ Be flexible about changes in plans.

➤ Point out that she *does* have a right to have fun in her life.

➤ Guard yourself a little, too. She may not be emotionally ready to date.

Date Guilt—It May Be For You, Too!

If you're also parent, you may need to wrestle with the grim specter of your *own* Date Guilt. Who are you to have a good time? Isn't it better to stay home and *mope*? A date with two parents suffering from Date Guilt may be a glum evening indeed. Hey, maybe you can work out a deal so that you take turns feeling guilty!

I Kid You Not!
Romantic? I don't think so…. Dates who are parents are more likely to "get casual" sooner than non-parents. Before too long, intimate familiarities begin as they kick off their shoes, scratch in private places, and forget to close the bathroom door. If it is mystery and romance you want, find a nonparent, somebody who doesn't *lose* it and yell, "Adam! Get in the car this instant, young man!"

Are You a Nymphet, a Harlot, or an Evil Black Knight?

When you date a parent, you very well may be crossing his or her ex's radar screen as a very large blip. The kids will talk about you. If you and the ex live in the same community, there may be chatty talk about your love life. How do you survive the gossip mill? And how do you avoid being cast in the ugly role of home wrecker, or worse?

Surviving Ex-Spouse Competition

You may or may not have the pleasure of knowing your new love's ex. In some ways it's easier to know him or her, and in some ways it may be harder. On the "pro" side, we all know that unseen people have a way of becoming gorgeous babes or ugly monsters. Seeing—and knowing—somebody reduces them to the human level. On the "con" side, you now have a real person to measure up against, and to potentially *deal* with. You may even like the ex—and that might make things even *more* complicated. Remember to keep these tidbits in mind:

➤ You are dating somebody who *wants* to be seeing *you*; they're *not* dating their ex.

➤ Keep in mind that people who know you both *will* be measuring you against the ex. You are not being paranoid. Concentrate on helping them learn who *you* are.

➤ Try to keep the competition external. Focus on valuing yourself for who you are rather than comparing yourself to the ex.

➤ The best way to maintain a good reputation is to take the high road and keep your mouth shut. Let *other* people judge the ex, not you.

I Kid You Not!

Famous stepparent in folklore: In the old Grimm's fairy tale, *Hansel and Gretel*, the father is rendered helpless by the force of the cruel stepmother. Remember how he was concerned about the kids, and how *she* sent them out into the forest? There's that cruel stepmother again! (And a wimp of a dad.)

"We Can't Go Out—I've Got Billy"

Dating a person who is in charge of children has its own scheduling complications. You may find yourself extremely frustrated when your hot date is canceled because the babysitter flaked out or because the little one has yet another summer cold. That little voice that whispers, "He only thinks of Junior, he never thinks of me," begins its steady yammer. It seems like the two of you never get any privacy.

Try to be sympathetic. Find out about your date's custody arrangements. And keep in mind that your new Sweetie may not be completely and utterly flexible about rearranging custody and visitation issues. Custody negotiations are sometimes the hardest part of divorce.

If you're not a parent yourself, dating a parent will give you a tiny taste of what having kids is like. The scheduling nightmares of dating a parent are only a forerunner to the crazy juggling that goes on *en famille*. Don't be frustrated, use it as a *learning* opportunity. These test cases provide brilliant opportunities for you to learn something about yourself— is this the life you want? Parents have children, and children take time. Children are not always convenient, and many times you have to change your plans. There's not much you can do about it. In matters of scheduling, children take precedence.

What about when the child is the only scheduling priority? If your needs are *never* met because the child is "in the way," you may be dating a Guilty Parent who may want—or need—to spend all possible time with the kid. This date may not *really* want to be dating. Or maybe she's unaware of your needs. Tell her. You can educate your "date" about how you like to be dated. You may need to offer to pay for a babysitter!

> **Don't Be Wicked**
> Nonparents don't always understand the babysitting thing with babies. "Get a sitter!" they say, as though it were that easy—logistically, or emotionally. Sometimes young babies and children *shouldn't* be left without a parent. Only the parent will know that.

Here's a special note: Don't be tempted to share your babysitter and bring all the kids together yet. When divorce turns a child's life topsy-turvy, the babysitter is often one of a child's few stable people. Asking a kid who is a divorce survivor to share her babysitter might be too hard. But what if you met your Sweetie through your kids? It happens more frequently than you think. I *still* say you should be careful about sharing a babysitter while you and your new honey paint the town red. Wait awhile until the new relationship has solidified.

Dating the Family

Dating a parent is one thing—when he's alone. But what about when the kids are along? On the one hand, the kids are important to him, and you should show some interest. If you're not interested in the important things in his life, why date him? (Must be that sex appeal.) On the other hand, you may like him but not want to get involved with the whole family. Good luck. Dating a parent *is* dating the child too—even if the child is not there at the time. Once you accept this, you'll have an easier time of it.

Presenting Your Date to Your Kids

If you are a parent, how you present your date to your kids is very important! Here are some suggestions for keeping your cool:

➤ Introduce your date as a friend, even if you have higher expectations for (or are in the middle of) a grand romance. Many relationships don't survive the first stages. Kids can feel very stressed out and threatened by a new partner on the scene, and there's no reason to upset them before you *know* it's serious.

➤ Try not to flutter around too much or get too cranky before the date. Kids will pick up on your stress. If they see you flipping out, they'll flip out too.

➤ Try not to pressure your kids too much to "behave." Expect your child to behave as she would with any guest, but don't force her to pretend to be someone she is not. A good but faulty impression will only lead to trouble later on. Plus, if you are too stressed about her behavior, she's likely to feel upset that you are dating. Some kids may even try to sabotage your new relationship!

Custody Battle Survival

Sometimes when a parent is in the middle of a custody battle, it is unwise for him or her to be—or be seen in—a dating relationship. We'll get more into custody issues later in the book, but there are a couple things to ask yourself for your own emotional welfare. Feeling hidden or "illicit" can be very hard on the self-esteem.

➤ If you are dating a man or woman who is hiding you from the "authorities," it is time to make a decision. Are you comfortable being "on the side?"

➤ Are you sure that the furtive quality of your date is really because of custody issues, or is he ashamed of you or uncomfortable (for other reasons) that somebody might find out he's dating again?

Until you are clear on the answers to these questions, you may have a hard time emotionally. Remember, you have a choice: If you are uncomfortable being the "lurking lover," you can wait until the divorce or custody battle is decided and the parent is free to acknowledge you in public.

Who Me? Jealous?

As you continue dating the parent, a strange emotion may occasionally course through your veins. One day you look in the mirror—your brown eyes are green! Poor baby, you're jealous. You've got the greatest new boyfriend, and the only problem is that he's spending all his time this summer with his kids. Who are you anyway, chopped liver? You want to do your bonding thing, and the kids are in the way.

Especially if you don't have children of your own, it's easy to feel jealous of the kids—they are, after all, "stealing" your time away from the one you want to hang out with. Or you may look at the attachment between them and want in. You may even see how lovely they are together and become jealous of the parent for having a child.

Stepping Stones

Sharing is hard. When a non-custodial parent's kids show up, the nonparent often gets shut down.

Don't be surprised at the intensity of the jealousy you feel. It's normal. But it's what you do with that jealousy that matters. This is an area where you're gonna have to bend or break up. The bond between parent and child *is* there, and it's appropriate that the child get to spend time with the parent. At the same time, yes, you should have the attention and time you crave.

Express your feelings to your boyfriend or girlfriend. The two of you should strive to find a balance that you're both happy with.

Sex! Sex! Sex! (and Love)

Are you having sex with a custodial parent? Keep in mind a few things:

➤ No double standards! If John is telling his teenage daughter to wait for sex until marriage and then he brings a woman home, Eleanor is going to see her dad as a hypocrite, and that wait-til-marriage idea will be out the window.

➤ Discretion is the better part of valor. You don't need to *hide* the fact that you're spending time with your boyfriend, but keep it out of sight. Seeing a man in bed with the mother can add to a child's insecurity (especially for a boy).

➤ Be prepared for the kids to be both upset, fascinated, and judgmental. (In other words, they may very well view a man as a hooded intruder and a woman as a loose slut.)

Love Impairs Judgment

So you're dating, and suddenly you're in love. Face it, you're a little bit ditzy right now. Your palms tend to sweat, your heart thumps, and you've got that stupid look on your face far too often. Making decisions while in love is a little like driving while drunk. Your judgment is impaired.

➤ When you are in love, all you want to do is be with the one you love. You'll scale mountains, ford rivers, fight dragons, and...oh yeah...put up with children, just to be near your lover's side.

➤ People in love tend to feel like they want to broadcast it to the world. "Look! We're in love!"

➤ People in love often can't keep their hands off each other—doesn't matter who is around.

Your job is to fight the hormones that are coursing through your veins and zinging up and down your nervous system. You have some decisions to make: Is this it, is this really love? Should we live together? Should we get married? Should I meet his kids? Should our kids meet each other? When? How? And those questions are just the beginning.

Ready to start? Hang onto your bobsled, Buddy, we're going on a ride. Next stop, adventure! Get ready to meet the cause of all this hoopla, the kids!

The Least You Need to Know

➤ A child's needs take precedence over a date's needs, every time.

➤ Your date is probably scarred by the divorce experience. Try to see what she's capable of right now. Then take care of your own emotional needs.

➤ Take the high road, don't gossip, and let your reputation take care of itself.

➤ When it comes to sex, be discrete around the children.

➤ Treat the children with respect, and don't *push*.

Chapter 3

Getting to Know the Kids

In This Chapter

➤ What you need to know before you meet the kids

➤ Getting started on the right foot

➤ Avoiding early trouble

➤ What to do when it doesn't go well

How do you get to be a stepparent? It's easy. Somewhere along the line you meet and "get together with" somebody who is a parent. And somewhere, usually a little further down the line, you meet the kids. Okay, so maybe it's not quite so easy, unless you're prepared! Here it is, the chapter that tells you what to plan for, how to avoid pitfalls, and how to survive if things don't go exactly as planned.

Having kids of your own can make meeting your new love's kids easier. After all, you know all about being a parent, right? You're *experienced*. But (I hate to break this to you) having your own kids can also make things doubly hairy. First of all, all kids are not alike. More importantly, the more people in a situation, the more complicated that situation is going to be. With your kids and your Sweetie's kids, you'll have to consider all that many more points of view, expectations, and sets of emotions. Ready to juggle? (You always *did* want to run away and join the circus, didn't you? Guess what? You just did!)

Getting Serious

Let's begin with romance. Scenario 1: You meet. Perhaps you see each other across a crowded room and stop, stunned. Eye-gazing, heart-thumping, beach-walking, and candlelit dinners follow. You tell your friends, "I think this is it; I think it's love." Maybe he talks about his daughters. Maybe you have to change a date because your son has to stay home from school one day. But in the hot charge of new love, many seemingly petty things—such as children—are initially swept aside, unconsidered, simply not much a part of the picture. But finally the day of reckoning comes, the initial emotional charge wears off, you look at each other and you both know it: The realities of life, your other friends, and the kids *do* need to be included in the relationship.

Now consider Scenario 2: Perhaps you're dating casually; you've been burned before. You know there are children involved, and before you take your relationship to the next level, you need to check out the kids—and you need to check out the potential love of your life as a parent. (And, to be equal about all this, she needs to check *you* out as a parent, too.)

No matter what the scenario, at some point, you, your new love, or both of you are going to decide that it's time to face the facts and meet the little rascals. And it's time to look at things with a whole new perspective, to look at the parent in your Sweet Baboo, and maybe for your Sweet Baboo to consider the parent in you, too!

The Time is Right

Meeting the kids can come at any one of a variety of points during the relationship. In some cases, you might even know the kids before you meet their parent, the partner of your dreams. In other cases, you might know the whole family casually before sparks of romance begin to fly. But for many people, the first time you'll meet the kids will be after things have gotten "serious." (In some situations, your sweetie's willingness to let you meet the kids is a sign that things *are* getting serious.)

Stepping Stones
How much, how often, or how soon a person talks about her kids is *not* a reflection of how much she loves them or how good a parent she is.

Did I Mention I Have Kids?

Remember the first time you heard Ms. or Mr. Maybe-Right talk about the children? When was it? Was it 10 minutes into your first date? Ten weeks later? Sometimes the subject just doesn't seem to come up, and sometimes you have a hard time getting past talking about the kids so you can move onto another subject of conversation. Whether or not your Hunny Bunny talks about the kids, it's important to remember that they are a part of his or her life. If you stick around, they're going to be a part of your life, too.

Egads! I'm Not Marrying the Kids!

You might have the attitude: "I'm not putting out any energy for some snot-nosed kid." Hey look, the nose may be snotty, but the kid is pretty important to the person you are dating. If you're going to be significant in your new sweetie's life, you're going have to deal with the kids. In fact, if you get married, you are marrying the *kids*, too. You don't have to love them— you don't even have to like them—but you will have to come to some sort of peace with them. It's a package deal. If you can't reach this middle ground, stepparenting is going to be even more difficult for you. Make it easier on yourself: Try to enlist the kids as *allies* in your life.

Step-Speak
An *ally* need not be a close friend or even somebody you love. An ally is somebody you trust to be there for you, somebody who is on your side.

The Resistant Bioparent

Okay, what if your love is resistant to your meeting the kids? It could be for a variety of reasons. Here are some things to consider—remember, every situation is different. In your new love's case, some, all, or none of the following could hold true.

➤ He's afraid of losing you the first time the kids turn into snarling demons.

➤ He's embarrassed that the kids' manners are so bad, and he feels they might reflect poorly on the job he is doing as parent.

➤ He wants to keep a little privacy in his life, something for just him.

➤ You provide a sanctuary of fun and irresponsibility for him. He doesn't have to be "Dad" with you.

➤ It's too soon, or there's no commitment or interest in commitment. (You could be one of many "Sweeties" on the scene, and he doesn't want to confuse, upset, or wrongfully raise the hopes of anybody.)

➤ The divorce was dreadful, the kids are still in pain, and he doesn't want to hurt them any further.

All these reasons reflect very real and very valid feelings. Try not to take it too personally; have some

Stepping Stones
If you've got kids, too, and you find yourself involved with a parent who is reluctant to meet the apples of your eye, it's time to find out why. Is she afraid of the impression she might make? Or maybe she's simply enjoying your adult company, and doesn't want to involve herself with other people's kids. No matter what the reason is, it's important that you know about it. Sit your Honey down for a little chat. Don't let your resentment build.

compassion, and don't push too hard. On the other hand, it is valid for you to want to meet the kids. It is important that you express your feelings about this, and it's vital to continue talking with your Dear Friend about when the appropriate time will be (and how the two of you will approach it). You don't want this to lead to your first fight, now, do you?

Scumbucket Alert!

But hey, what if you suspect that he's not introducing you to the kids (or is resistant to meeting your darlings) for other, less valid reasons such as these:

➤ He's ashamed of you—you don't meet some standard. (Dump him!)

➤ You're just one of a bunch of women he's dating, though he's not telling you that. (Keep a close watch on your emotions; remember that when the going gets tough, the smart ones go.)

➤ He's still with his wife. (If so, you're not in the running for Stepmother; you've been elected Mistress, and you'd better go read a different book.)

Stepping Stones
Try not to wait too long before meeting the kids or introducing them to their new stepparent-to-be. The longer you wait, the more the dread will build for all of you.

Meeting the Kids Post-Commitment

If your sweetheart's children (or your own little ones) live with their other parent out-of-state, you all may not have an opportunity to meet until right before the wedding, or after you've been living together for awhile. Ouch. This may present more of an emotional challenge to them, and to both of you. You're all going into that first meeting knowing that you are now "family" and knowing how much is riding on that fact. Don't despair: The meeting doesn't have to be a disaster. Breathe, think it through, plan, and prepare.

Getting Prepped

Whether it is early or later in the relationship, the "First Meeting" is an important event. For a most successful time—and let's define *successful* as an experience where everybody walks away feeling *more* comfortable, not *less* comfortable—I suggest some advance planning. Ideally you want the first meeting to *feel* casual but to be carefully orchestrated to avoid pitfalls. Before the first meeting, follow these tips:

➤ Define your expectations for the meeting, and lower your goals. (Remember Chapter 2.) It is not going to be love-at-first-sight, and it shouldn't be. Think of it in biological terms. You are encroaching on another animal's territory. Be polite and wary. This meeting is not about love or fun; it's about getting through it alive so you can live to see meeting #2.

➤ Think of meeting the kids for the first time as a blind date. What are the secrets to a successful blind date? According to my single pals, it's simple: Keep it short and safe. Try an activity that everybody will like, such as a park or a movie. Don't be over-ambitious: A full day at Great America will leave the kids (and you two already-stressed-out adults) tired, wired, and wasted. Keep it to a couple of hours at most. A meal isn't a bad idea, but you will be facing each other across a table for quite a while, and this may be too much for the kids to handle right away.

➤ Relax. (I know, it's not so easily done.) Consciously accept that this may be stressful, and take five minutes to let your tensions go. In Chapter 28, "Building the Extended Family," I'll give you some relaxation techniques for insta-relief.

➤ Work with your honey to fill out the following Parent Questionnaire.

The Parent Questionnaire

Doing your research ahead of time can pay off in a smooth, reduced-stress first meeting. Here, you'll find a number of questions designed to help you breeze on through. Enlist the help of your Sugar Pie on this one; after all, it's in his or her best interest that this first meeting go smoothly.

Before I took Bill to meet my extended family for the first time, I drew him a family tree, annotated with details about each relative's life, interests, and personality. Having that information helped him feel a little more comfortable amid the wild flock of family. Getting some details about the munchkins you are about to meet (and about the ones he'll be meeting, if you're a parent, too) is a good idea for the same reason—a little knowledge goes a long way. So grab your darling by the hand, sit down over a meal or a glass of wine, and let the questions fly!

Child's name (Let's say it is Petunia)

_____

_____

Why did you choose that name?

_____

_____

How does [Petunia] feel about her name?

_____

_____

Does [Petunia] have a nickname?

_____

_____

How old is [Petunia]? Age: _____

When is [Petunia's] birthday? Day _____ Month _____ Year _____

What have been your favorite ages for [Petunia]?

_____

_____

Why?

_____

_____

What does [Petunia] look like?

_____

_____

Favorite features?

_____

_____

Physical build?

_____

_____

Who does [Petunia] look like?

_____

_____

What is [Petunia] interested in?

_____

_____

Is [Petunia]: (circle your answers)

    high-/low-energy
    morning dove/night owl
    emotional/analytic
    outgoing/shy
    athletic/nonathletic

What are [Petunia's] favorite books?

_____

_____

What are [Petunia's] favorite toys?

_____

_____

What are [Petunia's] favorite TV shows?

_____

_____

Tell me a funny story about [Petunia]:

_____

_____

How has [Petunia] responded to the divorce (or death?):

_____

_____

What is [Petunia]'s relationship with her other bioparent like?

_____

_____

How do you think [Petunia] will respond to me?

_____

_____

Remember that these questions are only a starting point. The purpose of the Parent Questionnaire is to help avoid being blindsided by the unexpected. What you may find (as you munch fried calamari and quaff a pint in the local microbrewery) is that you're finding out as much about your boyfriend or girlfriend as a parent as you are about the kids. Hey, that's *good!*

I Kid You Not!

Famous stepparent in folklore: One of the most famous and most wicked stepparents in literature is Cinderella's Stepmother. After the death of Cinderella's father, she brought her own daughters into the marriage, took Cinderella out of the spotlight, and dressed her in rags because she wanted her own girls to look prettier while she also competed for attention for herself. This dame personifies all the jealous stepmoms through time: "Sweep up the ashes, little girl, I'm going out partying and *you can't come!*"

The Big Day

You've planned, you've plotted, and it's time for the big event. How's it gonna go? If you're like me, you're going to do a lot of worrying before the actual "date" begins. Before I met my stepkids Aaron and Rachel for the first time, I was a wreck. I was only 10 years older than Aaron, and I felt very young and vulnerable that day. The only saving grace was that I realized that from a 15-year-old's perspective, 25 was ancient—both a grown-up *and* an authority figure.

The Wardrobe

It may seem silly, but many people find themselves stressing over what to wear to meet the kids of the man or woman they're beginning to think they love. Here's what I suggest:

➤ Do choose something that's comfortable and "you."

➤ Don't try to dress like "kids these days" to show how cool you are. (If you've got older kids of your own, you know what I mean!)

➤ Keep in mind the nature of the event. Dress appropriately.

➤ Don't buy something new for the occasion. Crisp-and-clean is fine, but if it looks "too" new, you'll look like you are knocking yourself out trying to impress them. They'll either not notice (and all your efforts will be wasted), or they'll think you're trying too hard.

"Whoa! He's a Parent!"

During the first meeting, don't be surprised to find yourself sizing up what a good parent Lover Boy is. You may be considering this person as a potential spouse. That might mean a stepparent to your children and a parent to any kids the two of you might have together. How he handles conflict with his kids is a good key to how he'll handle conflict with you in the years to come.

At the same time, as you are doing your "sizing up," don't forget to give your love a break, too. He's probably nervous, and nervous people often make silly mistakes and say stupid things.

How to Use (and Not Use) the Parent Questionnaire

The Parent Questionnaire is what they call in the journalism biz "deep background." These are things you should know, things you want to know, but things you don't necessarily want the kids to know that you know. You don't want them to think that you're a little snoop.

One of the reason's you've been so nosy is because knowing certain details can help you a lot. For instance, the age, sex, and temperament of the child will impact how she or he will react during your meetings. We'll look at temperament in Chapter 11, but here are a couple of points about age and sex:

➤ Young boys have an initially more difficult time accepting their parents' divorce than do young girls (as time goes on, this evens out).

➤ Younger children are more accepting of change than are older children.

When You're Thrown Out in the Cold

Alas, it isn't always possible to plan. You may find yourself suddenly meeting the offspring of your new darling without any notice—no questionnaire, no planned activities. In that case, there's only one thing

Don't Be Wicked

Every child is unique, both in his reactions to you and your reactions to him. Don't lump them all together in your mind as "the kids." You'll be sorry!

Step-Speak

Temperament is the way a person approaches the world. Temperament is made up of at least 10 characteristics: mood, intensity, regularity, physical sensitivity, environmental sensitivity, energy level, first reaction, adaptability, persistence, and perceptiveness.

Don't Be Wicked

Be cool! Don't embarrass the child by saying, "Your mom has told me *so* much about you," or by letting on that you know the name of his old teddy bear.

31

Stepping Stones

It's easy—and normal—to feel jealous of your date's kids. Get it out in the open and discuss it with your love.

to do. Run! (No, just kidding!) Take a deep breath, remember that you are older and therefore *very* wise, look down at the small fry (or up at the hulking teenager), and politely say, "Hello!"

How Did It Go?

Good or bad, the first thing to do is take a deep breath, reach back and massage those aching neck muscles, and think to yourself, "Whew, well at least that's over."

Success!

Congratulations! You met and 10 minutes into it, you were wondering what the big fuss was all about. The kids are great: charming, warm, funny. You like them. They seemed to really like you. You laughed and enjoyed yourself. You're ready to throw this book out—obviously the author is a paranoid nay-sayer. Could be. I'm delighted it went well—that's the point of this chapter, after all. I contend that one of the reasons it went so well may be that you *were* prepared. You thought about it. You decided that it mattered enough to work on it.

When It Doesn't Go So Well

Stepping Stones

If you're in the middle of the first (or second or third) meeting and things aren't going so well, remember to breathe and exhale slowly. Don't overreact!

Unfortunately, it doesn't always go so well. There is a lot at stake here for the kids, as well as the parents. Try to remember three really important things:

➤ The child doesn't know you yet, and therefore his reaction to you is not personal.

➤ Don't confuse a child's first reactions with her "real" personality.

➤ Try not to take a child's personality or temperament personally. He or she might simply *be* shy, friendly, or rebellious.

Taking It All In

Here are some of the personalities and related reactions you might encounter at the first meeting with the kids, or observe in your own kids when they meet your sweetie for the first time. Some of these reactions are related to temperament—not necessarily the fact that they're meeting a "date." (More on temperaments in Chapter 11.)

➤ **The Shy Child** Some kids are just painfully shy. They avoid your eyes, they won't look at you, and they may not even talk to you. Think of the child as a small wild animal that you need to gently lure from its hidden lair. Take your time. Don't stare.

➤ **The Overly Welcoming Child** Some kids will leap on you, become immediately affectionate, and hold your hand. What a lovely child! Stay sensitive. This child may see you as no threat (yet!) or may be trying to disarm you. The child may simply be a friendly person, but a friendly person may still feel frightened or threatened.

➤ **The Resistant, Rude Child** A child who feels threatened may be very rude, sullen, or resistant. The bioparent may gaze at you with embarrassed eyes, as if to say, "This is not the charming Charley I know!" Try to keep some perspective on it. This kid would try to get rid of any perceived threat. Admire her fighting spirit.

➤ **The Suspicious Child** The kid may or may not know how serious the situation is (hey, *you* may not know!), but no matter what, he's suspicious. He eyes you like a cat meeting another strange cat. For a child (no matter how old), a parent represents security. You are the intruder infringing on that security. Your job is to show that you aren't a threat to his security and, at the same time, that you aren't going to let him be an *Alpha Dog*—that is, he isn't gonna be able to call all the shots here.

Stepping Stones
Children are like animals: They sense threats and smell fear. Stay calm. Approach your potential stepchild as if you're trying to get closer to a small wild animal. Move slowly, or the child will bolt.

Step-Speak
Alpha Dog is the dominant dog in the dog pack that all the others roll over for. In human-speak, the Alpha Dog is the one in charge, the Head Honcho, the Big Kahuna.

Stay Aware and Stay Wary

Don't confuse the child's personality with your ultimate acceptance. Sarah will never forget the first time she met her boyfriend Bob's kids. On the phone the night before Bob had prepared her: "Adam is going to love you. But Hannah is going to have a harder time."

Yet the minute Sarah met 15-year-old Adam and 12-year-old Hannah, the opposite situation came into play. Bob made the introductions as Sarah got into the car. Hannah bounced up and down with excitement. Adam stared out the window and mumbled a hello. They went out for pizza. Adam wouldn't meet her eyes and sat sideways on his

Don't Be Wicked
The first few meetings are not the time to start correcting manners, scolding, or attempting discipline of any sort. Bite your tongue!

chair, hunched so low that his hair drooped into the cheese. Giggly, bubbly, friendly Hannah insisted on sitting next to Sarah and held her hand until the food arrived. Throughout dinner, Hannah kept up a steady chatter. Sarah was taken aback. Was Bob really so out to lunch that he didn't know his kids?

Actually, Bob *did* know his kids—Adam was painfully shy but very accepting of Sarah, and Hannah, despite her surface enthusiasm, spent years resisting Bob and Sarah's relationship. (Years? Yes, Sarah stuck it out and is still sticking it out 12 years later.)

Hey, Be Cool!

Once you all get together, you may become aware of things you disapprove of, in the child's behavior, or in your true love's parenting. Remember that you have no say now. It is none of your business. Until you've made the decision—and the announcement—that you and this child's parent are a long-term item, you are merely an interested stranger, a polite observer, and a powerless friend.

I Kid You Not!

Whoops! A responsible adult! Sometimes people dating parents get drafted into the position of stepparent before a real partnership has been built. And sometimes, just for the sake of convenience, you might get drafted for a little child care. Watch out...unless you *want* the opportunity to try on a little child care for fun, you might end up feeling a bit resentful when that actually happens. Remember that it's your choice, and you may *not* be ready, willing, or able to take on the responsibility of caring for a child, or another's child along with your own.

"Oh Dad, Another One?"

Many times you won't be the first one, or even the fifth one, your darling has brought home to meet the kids. In that case, you may have to deal with jaded kids for whom you are merely "another one." Ask your sweetie to be honest with you. How have her kids reacted to her other dates? If the kids have been through a series of "new loves," they will not look at you with great joy and openness. Hey, why should they? They've been disappointed several times. They've opened up to a stranger only to have a friend taken away from them at a parent's whim.

If you're dealing with suspicious, wary, and angry kids, *go slow!* You may have the inclination to set the record straight and let them know how important you are in your honey's life. Resist this inclination. Be cool. Give it time. Be respectful of their distance. And if the relationship is "meant to be," they'll learn how much you mean to their parent through time and observation.

When the Kids Are Jealous

Kids are often jealous of their parent's friends, dates, and lovers. It's important for them to see that their parent has friends.

If a child is expressing jealousy, take a walk in his shoes. Is he only with his bioparent a limited amount of time? How old is the child? A child entering puberty and anticipating the fear and excitement of dating may have very strong reactions to seeing a parent being intimate with anyone, let alone someone he perceives as a stranger. This doesn't mean that you must always appear chaste and celibate, but keep the child's age in mind.

Let's talk about Tommy, who doesn't live with his dad, except for extended periods of time in the summer. Say you met his dad, Mike, in February. Life is cool; you and Mike hang out and have fun, and one day summer begins and it's…Custody Time! Be prepared for things to change. The child may resent you. Tommy came to see Daddy Mike, not you (and not your kids, if you have them), and Tommy's gonna fear the loss of dear old Dad. Here are some tips for jealousy:

Don't Be Wicked
The kids are expressing jealousy—is there a special reason? Are they being cut out of the loop? Is there too much hanky-panky going on?

➤ Don't be there the first night.

➤ Think before you flip out.

➤ Suggest a small, shared outing to begin. Keep it short, keep it light, make yourself a little bit scarce for a while so that parent and child can enjoy their reunion.

➤ If you're the bioparent, handle fear and resentment with directness: "It's not your fault that Mommy and I are divorced. I know you want us to get back together, but that is not going to happen. You cannot change that. Sue and I are good friends. She's not a replacement for your Mommy."

➤ Encourage the parent not to apologize for having friends.

Stepping Stones
Sometimes meeting away from kids is the best dating solution, especially in the beginning and during stressful times. It's easier on kids, easier on you, and easier on the parent, who doesn't have to deal with jealousy or resentment from either side.

➤ Encourage the parent to insist that the kids must treat friends (that's you!) with respect and courtesy.

➤ Be an adult. Look below the belligerence to see the wounded child.

➤ Encourage the parent to reassure his kids by letting them spend more time together (yes, and you butt out! Spend the free time with your children, use it to get a massage or do something equally decadent.) It's good for kids to see adults care for themselves.

➤ If things are very tense and stressful, suggest counseling for the child and parent.

Disasters and Demon Children

Okay, you listened to me (or you didn't), but either way, it was a disaster. You went home swearing to break it all off and never see your true love again. Of course, you should always be evaluating your relationship (especially when it is new), but a terrible first meeting does not—I repeat *not*—mean disaster for the rest of your life.

"I gave my stepmom hell while my dad was dating her," says Lianna, years later. "I laughed at her butt the first time I met her. I lied and told my dad she hit me. I told her she was uglier than my mom. I was disgusting. I don't know why she stuck it out after the first few dates."

If this happens to you, take a good look at your love's reaction. Is she egging on the little demon? Is she seriously trying to work with the child, to let her know that this kind of behavior is not respectful? You can learn a great deal about the kind of person your new love is by watching her parent her child. (If you don't perceive any support for you, you may want to reconsider the whole relationship!)

If you feel that the situation is being handled by the parent in a reasonable, responsible fashion, concentrate on getting through the date. The screaming *will* stop. You'll have other opportunities to work on the relationship. And try to *empathize* with the child.

Step Speak
Empathy means feeling what another person feels. (This is in contrast to *sympathy*, which means feeling for another person.)

When you're dealing with a demon child like Lianna, the key word is "child." The child is not being bad; she's hurt, she's mourning, and she's trying to deal with major changes in her life. Whether she realizes it or not, you represent a major threat in her psyche. Try to walk a mile in her size-two shoes. Maybe you wouldn't like you either. (There may be some "divorce grief" going on here. Check out the section on dealing with grief in Chapter 4, "Moving In Together.")

Warning: Love Makes You Obnoxious

Here's a little advice: At the beginning of the relationship, back off a bit on the *PDA* when the kids are around. No footsie under the table, cool the caresses, stop disappearing into the bedroom for a quick smooch session. Hey, I'm no prude, this is not for propriety's sake, but for the emotional health of the kids. These kids have already lost their family structure. And yes, they are in competition with you for their parent. Yes, they are protective. These are survival mechanisms. This is biological. Human children cannot care for themselves. They need parents to take care of them and to give them emotional nourishment. If Dad or Mom is off spooning and mooning with somebody new all the time, *yes* they are gonna feel threatened.

When can you resume public footsie? Oh, about the time you no longer feel the urge to do it.

Step-Speak
PDA stands for Public Display of Affection. When your stepkids are in high school, you may see or hear this phrase used as an on-campus no-no.

Prepping Your Kids to Meet Your Love's Kids

Before the kids—your kids and your new love's kids—meet each other, you'll need to prepare. Don't just throw them all in together and expect it to work; it might, but then again it might not, and this is too important to leave to random chance.

Here are some steps to take to make sure the meeting goes as smoothly as it possibly can:

➤ Do a pre-date survey with your Sweetie. Each of you should fill out The Parent Questionnaire (earlier in this chapter) and then sit down together to talk about the kids. Try to figure out what kind of meeting will work best for each.

➤ Assess each child's temperament and needs as honestly as you can. Fibbing here will do nobody any good.

➤ Talk to the kids about the meeting, but keep it cool. Don't suddenly announce that they are about to meet some other kids who may, some-day, be their new siblings.

➤ If you have teens or preteens meeting other teens or preteens, be aware of possible sexual energy and tension. (There's more on this in Chapter 21, "Stepfamilies in Crisis.")

➤ Plan an activity. Everybody staring at each other in a living room or restaurant may not be a lot of fun.

Don't Be Wicked
Don't freak out if your your child instantly hates your new Sweetie. Give it time, talk with both of them (alone), make sure any misunderstandings are cleared up, and then *stand back*. It's *their* relationship.

➤ If you're combining little kids and older kids, gear the activity toward the youngest common denominator, or toward the child who—temperamentally—has the most needs. A tantrum or meltdown will prevent anything else from working.

➤ The meeting place or activity should take place somewhere where there are opportunities for kids to retreat. Try a picnic in a park—some kids can be playing, some reading, and there is room enough to run around.

➤ Keep the activity to the length of a birthday party. That means no weekends away, at least until you all know each other *much* better!

Don't Leap to Conclusions

No matter how well or how poorly the first few encounters go, it's important to remember that while first impressions and first reactions are important, they are not necessarily true indicators of how all your relationships will change, grow, and develop over time. What you think and feel now is not necessarily what you all are going to think and feel later.

I Kid You Not!

Morgan had a 10-month-old adopted baby and was seven months pregnant—and on bedrest—when her 13-year-old stepson James was kicked out of his mother's house and moved across the country to live with Morgan and her husband Eric. What a time that was—it did not go well. Despite all the strains and her resentment at having a surprise child to take care of in the middle of her own problems, Morgan kept both her head and the awareness that it would take time to work things out.

Relationships are a process. First meetings are important: They can help smooth the way, but they are not the only determining factors in the relationship. As you'll learn, things will both ease up *and* get harder. Try to look at the big picture.

Winning the Little Heart Over

Who should you be when you are around your date's children? Besides the obvious answer ("You should be yourself"), there are some other things to consider, and to strive for:

➤ Don't scold the child. That is not your role.

➤ Don't ignore the child. Nobody likes to be ignored, and ignoring children doesn't work anyway. They just get more insistent and whiny.

➤ Don't judge them.

➤ Don't assume intimacy.

➤ Consider the child's feelings, wishes, and plans. Have the parent ask permission to invite a friend (you!) over for dinner. It's the kid's house too, you know, and you are asking to spend time with the kid's parent.

➤ Hold back. Let the child come to you. There's lots of time for intimacy.

➤ Realize that any bad reaction may not be to *you*. The child may need some asserting that he will be loved and cared for just as he was before the divorce. Go slow.

➤ Treat the child like a friend—a young friend, but a friend.

➤ Remember that dating relationships can provide good role models. You are not evil for being there. If you believe it, you're on the road to having the kid believe it, too.

➤ Concentrate on your love relationship, not your relationship with the whole family. The love and respect you are building forms the foundation of your relationship and, if you choose to take it further, of the family.

➤ Hope and wait for the kids to realize that they can't and won't scare you away, that you are not trying to replace their parent, that you are not trying to steal their parent, and that you are respectful of them. Over time and with the right treatment, the kids will see the joy you bring to their parent.

➤ And in case the adult love of your life isn't reading this book, too, and you've got little loves of your life at home, make sure you share the above words of wisdom with him. After all, you want your children's hearts to be won as well, yes?

Stepping Stones
As you think about your role as a stepparent, remember to turn the tables, and consider your own kids' needs and your partner's relationship with them.

Breaking Up

What happens if your love relationship breaks up (and I'm not talking about what happens to you here; I'm talking about the kids). You won't be there for her kids (duh), but you can hope that it will be a lesson to them that although disappointments happen, they aren't always as devastating as a divorce. Kids can learn that it is okay—it is *good*—to take emotional risks. (Of course, all this presumes that the parent doesn't show

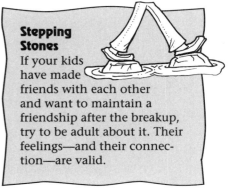

Stepping Stones
If your kids have made friends with each other and want to maintain a friendship after the breakup, try to be adult about it. Their feelings—and their connection—are valid.

the heartbreak.) It's up to all of you whether you feel that you can maintain your friendship with the child after your love with his parent ends.

The Least You Need to Know

➤ Any children that you and/or your sweetheart have are going to be part of both your lives, like it or not.

➤ It really helps to prepare before meeting the kids.

➤ Don't judge a child by her first reactions to you. It's not personal.

➤ The outcome of the first meeting does not predict the course of your entire relationship with the children.

➤ It's easy—and normal—to feel jealous of your date's kids. Communicate!

➤ Your own kids may need some extra care and attention before, during, and after meeting your new Sweetie and your new Sweetie's kids.

Chapter 4

Moving In Together

In This Chapter

➤ Tools for building a strong living-style agreement

➤ Communication exercises for enhancing stepfamily strength

➤ Tips for surviving societal judgments

➤ Advice on custody, paternity, and more

Ready to *cohabitate*? Whether or not you're considering getting married somewhere down the line, there are a few things to think about before you start living together. If you think that the official stepparent relationship is muddy and undefined, try the living-with-a-partner-who-has-kids relationship. It's completely vague! (And if both of you have children, then living with two sets of kids is…well, you can imagine.) Yet this arrangement is very common. This chapter deals with issues specific to people living in step without marriage. There are also a couple of exercises helpful for *all* couples living in step situations. (Gay stepparenting issues are covered specifically in Chapter 20, "Gay Stepparenting.")

Step-Speak

Cohabitation is a legal term that refers to two people of the opposite sex living together and having a sexual relationship. While cohabitation is extremely common—in some states, it is still against the law.

Stepping Stones

You never really know somebody until you live with them. That is certainly true for stepfamilies!

Confusing Transitions

People have lots of reasons to live together without being married: To save on rent. As a next step along the line to commitment. To share a life yet not give up alimony. To enjoy love but avoid ever, ever, *ever* going through a divorce again. Because (say, in the case of gay couples) marriage is not a legal option. To stave off the tax man. While the divorce is being finalized.

Perhaps the primary—and most important—reason people live together without marriage is to have the opportunity to find out what it's like to live together as a stepfamily, and to make adjustments accordingly.

Moving in together is the beginning of your life as a stepparent, and it is a critical and important time. If this is a trial run, here's when you start imagining yourself in this role on a permanent basis.

Basic Family Living Styles

When you move in with a parent, you are taking on the role (in at least *some* ways) of a stepparent. It's vital that you start defining what that role and your idea of family life mean to you. I go into depth about this in Chapter 7, "Instant Parent."

Here is an exercise for you to do as a couple so that you can begin establishing a meeting of the minds on family life issues. Sometime, preferably *before* you move in together, sit alone or together and try thinking about and completing the following statements and questions. (This exercise is adapted from Ruth-Ann Clurman's book, *Parenting the Other Chick's Eggs*). Write your thoughts down.

The most important part of raising a family is….

The worst thing about my Ex was….

The best thing about being a parent is….

The worst thing about being a parent is….

The best thing about my upbringing was….

The worst thing about my upbringing was….

It is important to me to celebrate birthdays by….

It is important to me to celebrate holidays by….

The manners I feel it's important for kids to have are....

My approach to discipline is....

My feelings about the importance of religion in my life and my family's life are....

My four most important moral values are....

I believe in handling conflict by....

What I want most from my family life is....

The things that I want to change in our family dynamics are....

The things that I want to keep the same in our family dynamics are....

After you've both completed these statements, spend some time together comparing notes. You are working toward the design of a new home life together. What kinds of things are you discovering about yourselves? About each other? (To help you with this, jump ahead a bit to the beginning of Chapter 6, "Building a Viable Stepfamily," and read Step 1: "Understanding Your Situation.")

Now work together to finish the statements below. This may take some time. Don't be impatient—I'm talking about the very basic parts of life. And don't feel discouraged if you don't have complete agreement right away. That doesn't mean you are incompatible, you hate each other, or that your love is wilting on the vine like unwatered tomatoes in the heat of summer. The important thing is to keep talking, and keep working on it. It's better to understand *where* you disagree than to pretend that you don't.

Our family's four most important moral values are....

What we want most from my family life is....

We will celebrate birthdays by....

We will celebrate holidays by....

The manners important to our family are....

Our approach to discipline is....

Religion in our family is....

We will handle conflict by....

Look at you! You've just created a family manifesto, of sorts. As Winnie the Pooh says, "The more you know (tiddly pom), the more you grow (tiddly pom)."

I Kid You Not!

Larry L. Bumpass of the University of Wisconsin found in a 1994 study that about half of the 60 million children under the age of 13 in the United States are currently living with one biological parent and that parent's current partner.

The Unmarried, Living-Together Stepcouple

Whether you're in total agreement or not (hey, I bet not, but that's what makes life interesting, huh?), you're together now. Welcome (or welcome again) to family life! The unmarried, living-together stepcouple has some *issues* to face.

How the Kids React to You

It was one thing while you were dating, but now you're sharing towels! There's only one thing you can rely on when you move in to a step situation: Things change when things get serious. They may change for the better, or they may change for the worse, but they will be different. Be alert!

"This Is...Uh...."

You're *sort of* a stepparent, but when you live together you have no official role, and therefore no official title. How will you be introduced? Too often, this question is not really addressed and you begin to be known to the community as "Uh," as in, "This is... Uh...."

It's up to you to get this straightened out, and it will help if you can do it ahead of time. When we all moved in together, I told Aaron and Rachel, "You can introduce me as Ericka, or you can introduce me as Ericka, my dad's girlfriend. But I want you to use my name." Tell the kids what you'd like. Find out what they think. Choose a title that feels comfortable to all of you.

Are You a Family?

Well, this is a question nobody else can answer for you. If you don't answer it, though, others will ("paramour, gigolo, loose woman"). People are strange, judgmental, and mean. People also are really nice but just may not understand how to deal with you. Here are two rules:

➤ You don't have to identify yourself as a family.

➤ Family is a state of mind as well as a legal designation. You are a family if you say you are.

Living In Step Forever

For some, marriage is not an option or a desire, so living together is *not* a trial run. Nevertheless, you most certainly are considering yourself a family. If this is true for you, make it clear to yourselves—and the kids—that you consider this stepfamily a permanent relationship.

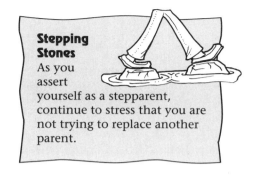

Stepping Stones
As you assert yourself as a stepparent, continue to stress that you are not trying to replace another parent.

When living in step, you are making a conscious choice to become a member of the children's family and to play an active role in supporting them.

Stepfamily Development

Forming a stepfamily is a process. It takes a while. For many people, living together is the next step after meeting, dating, and dating seriously. Like anything involved with stepparenting, living together has its own issues. (Can *nothing* be easy here? Not much.)

An Outsider in the Family

Stepparents often complain about feeling like outsiders, and this feeling may be reinforced both from inside the family and from society at large. Inside the family, you may feel outnumbered. The family may have their own ways of doing things. You may find yourself thinking, "After all, I'm not really related to these people. What can I do?" What *can* you do? You could get married. It won't fix things. Newlyweds in step situations often have the same feelings of dislocation. The primary solution is patience, communication, togetherness, and time.

Just an Outsider

Then there are the pressures from outside the immediate family. When Bill and I were living together before we tied the knot, a cousin of mine got married and Bill and I went to the wedding. When it came to be family portrait time, we stepped up to the plate. A relative pulled me aside and said, "I don't think it's appropriate that Bill be in the picture. After all, you guys are not married." *I* knew I had a firm commitment to the relationship, but what could I say? I bowed to family pressure. Here's the kicker: That marriage broke up in a mere two or three years, and nobody looks at the wedding pictures anymore. But Bill and I are still going strong 10 years later.

No matter how strong you and your partner believe your commitment to be, you do not have the full societal stamp of approval.

If You Do Eventually Get Married

Let's say somewhere down the line you get married after living together for a while. You may feel surprised when your relationship with your partner and with his kids changes. The changes may be subtle, but they're usually based on a change in expectations (there are those expectations again!). Here's what's up:

➤ His kids are really part of your family now, and you may react differently to them, no matter how hard you try.

➤ The kids will suffer the loss of their fantasy about their parents' reconciliation (there's more on this topic in the next chapter).

➤ The world will view your relationship differently. You're gonna be legitimate.

Step-Speak
Active listening means listening to and trying to understand the child's thoughts and feelings by listening silently and then paraphrasing—saying back again as closely as possible *without interpretation*—what has been said.

Communication? I'm Listening!

Soon after you move in, you may face your first *big* experience with stepfamily conflict. You may feel resentful or shut out, the kids may feel rejected and furious, and your Sweetie may feel utterly and completely caught in the middle.

The active listening exercise below is an excellent tool for improving household communication. Take a few minutes and try this. It can't hurt matters (sounds like they're pretty miserable as is), and it *can* help. Are you afraid you'll hear some things you'd rather not know about? Hey, better now than later. Resentments and resistance do not just fade away.

Before You Begin, Why Bother?

➤ Active listening helps the child by raising her sense of self-worth and self-respect. Whether or not your own child or your stepchild-to-be expresses it to you, your thoughts and your opinions of her matter *terribly* to her. The fact that you are listening to her concerns will really help her feel better about herself and your relationship.

➤ Active listening is a tool for building empathy in you. Once you truly hear the child's concerns, you'll be able to feel a bit of what he is feeling.

➤ Using active listening will help you better understand what the kid means. None of us are completely clear, but kids (especially kids who are churning inside with emotions) can be totally muddy in what they're saying. Active listening can help you decode the meaning.

➤ Active listening gives the child the opportunity to correct you. In other words, you paraphrase, and he tells you you're out to lunch. That's *good!* That way you can fix up any misunderstandings (and in a step situation, there are often many).

➤ By using active listening, you can help the child explore her own thoughts and feelings on a deeper level. Things may be so complex that she may not know *how* she feels.

Here's How to Do It

You can actively listen anywhere, as long as you pay full attention and do it deliberately. You can say, "I want to hear what you think about blah blah blah and I'm not going to say anything until you're done. When you finish, I'll tell you what you said and what I heard." If that feels like it might really scare the kid, try a casual approach. Simply listen silently and then paraphrase *without* calling attention to what you're doing: "So you're saying blah blah blah blah. You feel blah blah blah. Did I get that right?" You'll get the hang of it.

Wait! Hold It! Watch Out!

Things *can* go wrong in active listening when you make these mistakes:

➤ When you hear only what you expect or want to hear. (This is a biggie!)

➤ When you allow your beliefs and attitudes to interfere with your listening. I know, you *know* her biomom is loony and has a bad attitude problem, but try to get past that to *listen* to the child's perceptions. You can process later that stuff about how you shouldn't be allowed to eat lunch in the same county that the ex was born in.

➤ When you allow your feelings about what's being said to affect how you are listening (same type of thing as above).

➤ When you pay attention only to *how* the information is being communicated, not *what* is actually being said. That means don't try to correct Angelique's posture while she is talking to you about serious stuff.

➤ When you are too literal. Kids have their own dialects or ways of speaking, and if you listen to the words too exactly, you're gonna get lost.

➤ When you listen only for the facts. How the child *feels* about what he's telling you may be just as important. When you paraphrase back what's been said, make sure to include how you think the child is feeling. Let him correct you if you are wrong.

Legal Details

Let's look briefly at the law. (This will be a brief look here—there's more legal material in Chapter 22, "Legal Stuff." It will also be a casual look. I'm not a lawyer, so I can't really advise you). The first and only truly important point here is to know the law! Lawyers *are* expensive, but they can protect you. Nolo Press publishes a book I highly recommend, called *The Living Together Kit: A Legal Guide for Unmarried Couples*, by Toni Ihara and Ralph Warner (see Appendix B).

Out with the "Old," in with the "New"

Moving in with a new love while there is a divorce going on (either one of yours) can be problematic, particularly when there are children involved. There is nothing like children to heat up the fires.

> **Step-Speak**
> A *no-fault divorce* is a divorce where the judge considers nobody at fault—for instance, that the marriage has broken up because of irreconcilable differences. A traditional, *fault divorce* is where one party states mistreatment (such as adultery, desertion, or mental cruelty) as the reason for marital breakdown.

In some cases, the fact that your Sweetie (or you) have left your spouse and are now living with somebody else *can* lead to legal problems, especially if you live in a state with *fault* grounds and if your spouse wants to file for a fault-based divorce.

The traditional advice to parents is to *not* live with a person of the opposite sex and to be discreet in your sexual activity, at least until the court makes a decision on custody. That advice goes for both fault and no-fault divorces because custody of the children is separate from the divorce itself. And that's up to the judge.

Traditions are changing in some states. The best advice I can give you is to be aware of the laws and precedents in your state and (once again) to get some good legal advice.

Dealing with a Fault Divorce

If you live in a state that still has the traditional fault divorce and your Ex, or your new mate's ex, is so inclined to use it, beware before you begin cohabiting in a step situation.

We're not just talking legal dangers here; we're talking emotional dangers as well. Ugly divorce and custody struggles can make an already inflamed situation even more inflamed, and the tensions within the household can feel truly unbearable. During these kinds of battles, it can be very useful and helpful to have some outside support for what you are going through. No, neither you nor your honey bunch are insane, and the kids are not horrible little maniacs. They are just upset, very, very upset, and they, too, may need to talk to somebody outside of the situation, somebody who is not a major player. Check out the details and resources in Chapter 21, "Stepfamilies in Crisis."

Child Support

Not all marriages with kids end in happily-ever-after. A great many end in child support. Though it's slightly possible that your (or your live-in love's) child support payments may be reduced once you're living together, it's not likely. But there are a couple of vital things to remember:

➤ If the bioparent who has custody begins living with somebody else, the other bioparent is still required by law to support the child. He may not like it, he may kick in the door, he may pound on his head, and he may refuse to look for work (in which case he is committing a crime).

➤ Refusing to support your kids while you live high on the horse is also a crime, a legal crime. You can get arrested, or even put in jail.

➤ You have no legal obligation to support the children of the person you are living with.

➤ If you help support the children of your partner, his child support may be reduced (the same goes for you, if your partner helps support your kids).

> **Don't Be Wicked**
> Some states will reduce or end alimony if you begin living with somebody else. Some states will even raise the amount of alimony you pay if you move in with somebody with a lot of money. Don't be caught by surprise. Call your lawyer, and know the law!

The Emotional Custody Crisis

How long did the custody wars rage? What about child support? Did the divorce take months of negotiating little details? Well guess what, when there's a new stepparent, all those discussions are likely to be opened up again. Many parenting agreements have gotten bogged down in protracted discussions about the what-ifs that might surface with a new love interest (translation: with you!).

In Chapter 21, I'll go into more details about the legal aspects of living together and custody situations. Love and romance and all that is wonderful, but the legal stuff can hit you *hard* right where it hurts—in the heart.

One of the hardest things to take is all the shared parenting going on, all these discussions about the best way to do things. They don't involve you, you say? Buck up a little. They sure do if your partner is living with you.

Medical Treatment

You're not related to anybody, so unless you have explicitly been assigned some legal status, you technically have no power to even give the child an aspirin. There is more information about medical permissions, living wills, power of attorney, and the like in Chapter 21.

Adoption as an Unmarried Couple

Adoption laws are changing even as we speak and vary widely from state to state. Traditionally, unmarried couples have not been allowed to adopt, whether it's an unmarried partner adopting the other partner's biological child, or the couple jointly adopting a child who's not the biological offspring of either one. Things are changing, and in several states (at this printing, at least New York, New Jersey, Vermont, and Massachusetts) do allow unmarried couples to adopt.

According to Ihara and Warner, in *The Living Together Kit,* "In 1995, the New York Court of Appeals recognized the right of one member of an unmarried couple (either heterosexual or homosexual, it makes no difference) to adopt the biological child of the other." You'll need to do research about the law in your state. For more on adoption, see Chapter 24, "In Addition, There's Adoption."

Having Another Child

Having another one? While Chapter 25, "His, Hers, OURS?" is all about adding a new shared baby to the blend, there are special considerations for the stepfamily living together. The primary importance is establishing *paternity*.

Step-Speak
Paternity means "the state of being a biological father."

If you're a living-together stepfamily and you have a child together, it is vital that the father sign a Paternity Statement as soon as possible to protect everybody's interests, including Dad, Mom, and Baby.

For Dad, signing a Paternity statement means reduced chances of lost rights should you ever split up. For Mom, it assures her that (should the dread split-up happen) her child will be taken care of. And for Baby, we're talking not only child support in case of split-up, but also about things like life insurance and medical and disability benefits.

Being named Big Poppa on a birth certificate doesn't prove it to the courts. If somebody names you as father on a birth certificate, you can still contest paternity (then there's all that DNA-testing stuff). But *not* signing a paternity statement doesn't mean you're off the hook if that baby is yours. The courts don't care how and why babies are born—they just know that if it was your sperm, you are responsible to support the child.

The Least You Need to Know

➤ Establishing a basic lifestyle agreement is key to stepfamily success.

➤ Living together is more accepted than it used to be, but your relationship may not be taken seriously by everyone.

➤ As you build your relationship, communication is key.

➤ When it comes to divorce, custody, alimony, and the like, you've gotta know the law!

Chapter 5

The Wedding

In This Chapter

➤ Breaking the happy news to the kids

➤ Planning the big event

➤ How to incorporate the children

➤ Keeping chaos from the ceremony

This chapter is about weddings. The journey from bended knee to honeymoon can be a toughie for the new stepfamily. In this chapter, I'll tell you about the inevitable complications of stepfamily weddings and how to get to the reception without derailing your relationship—and your relationship with the kids, grandparents, and dear, bitter Aunt Abigail who sits shaking her head sadly in the last row. Grab your antacids, and let's go.

Surviving the Psychodrama

Here's a typical nightmare wedding: The room is stuffed with people. Little Tommy isn't there; he's home with his sobbing, screaming mother, the groom's ex-wife. Here comes the bride…followed by her three kids and her dad, who's giving her away yet again. She's joined at the alter by her groom. It's a crowd up there, too. The officiating party is squeezed up against the wall. He speaks, "Do you, Martha, and do you, Martha's children Pico, Alonza, and Sammy, take George (and Tommy, who is with us in spirit) for your lawful wedded husband, stepfather, stepchild, and stepsiblings? The kids and Martha chime in. "I do!" "I do." "Yeah, okay." "Uh…guess so." In the back of the room, two old friends of Martha's family shake their head over George: "Well, I can tell this one is a rebound."

Need I go on? All this and more *can* happen. All this and more *does* happen. Let's try to avoid this happening to *you.*

I Kid You Not!

A first marriage traditionally celebrates leaving the family behind to join with a spouse. A second marriage celebrates not leaving, but joining a family.

So are you totally stressed? Now you understand why so many people keep second weddings *way* small, or elope. Seductive as the idea of "just getting it over with" may be, don't cheat yourself out of a ceremony marking your love and commitment. Getting married is a public commitment to your relationship. It's a life ceremony, and it is an important symbolic celebration. Forget the statistics on whether it's gonna work out or not—it doesn't matter that it's a second marriage. As Miss Manners says, "Traditional ceremonies, whether civil or religious, express hopes and ideals; they do not make realistic predictions."

But let's start at the beginning.

Telling the Kids

Somebody has knelt and presented a sparkling ring; the other has said "Yes!" Or what-ever. However you, the couple, have come to the decision, it's been made. It's time to make the commitment public. That means telling the children. A number of contrasting approaches are offered here. Read, think, take the individual children in consideration, and decide together.

➤ **Tell them together.** This establishes your unity as a couple. This unity will be essential for the rest of your lives. Telling the kids together works best when you have established a strong relationship with the kids already. This method also keeps the step-to-be involved; having the bioparent spring the happy news can make the other person feel left out or unconsidered.

➤ **Have the bioparent tell them.** On the other hand, there's a lot to be said for assign-ing the task to the bioparent. This helps the kids to process their emotions—when they're alone with Mom or Dad, they can scream and cry over how much they hate the idea. If you are the bioparent, telling them alone could let the kids know that you are still their parent, that you will still be there for them, that they are still number one, and that the bond will not go away even when you are married.

➤ **Tell each child separately.** If there's more than one child, have the courtesy to tell each one individually so they can react as they need to without all that *sibling* stuff going on.

➤ **Tell them slowly.** John and Barbara decided to marry a couple of years before they actually tied the knot. In the meantime, they lived together, and John's three kids came for regular visits and for summer vacations. John started mentioning the possibility that he and Barbara might get married months before he officially made the announcement. This method of opening a dialogue and discussing the issues— and letting each of the kids express their opinions—meant it wasn't such a shock to the system when he finally told them that they had set the date.

➤ **Be clear that getting married is your decision.** No matter how the kids react (or how you think they will react) the decision to get married is *not* up to them.

➤ **Tell them before you do it.** Even if you tie the knot in a hurry—say you're off for a weekend in Vegas and you suddenly get the urge—I *don't* suggest you tell the kids afterward. They will feel like something has been put over them, that you are shoving them out of your lives. Your marriage will affect and directly impact the kids' lives, whether they live with you or not. Do them—and yourself—a favor. Call collect from Ye Olde Wedding Chapel if you need to, but tell them before the dastardly deed's been done.

Don't Be Wicked
A wedding is a beginning, but beginnings don't negate the past—his or hers. Know the difference between history and ghosts.

How Come the Kids Aren't Beaming?

No matter how you tell them, the kids are probably *not* going to be thrilled. Even if they seem excited or, at the least, accepting, they probably feel a mix of emotions, some positive and some very negative. Understanding what is going on inside them will help you and your sweetheart deal with the emotions to come.

Ending Their Fantasies of Reconciliation

Even if the former marriage was nightmarish, deep inside 99 percent of all the children of divorce, a hopeful little voice murmurs, "I wish Mom and Dad would get back together again." Remarriage kills that hope. Kids often feel a resurgence of the grief they felt at the divorce, sort of like a bad flashback. Many children will feel protective about their other parent—the one who *isn't* in the process of planning the big march down the aisle. All these feelings may show themselves as concern, or resentment and intense hostility.

Dealing with Concerns

If the kids are expressing distress, depression, resistance, and rebellion, listen! They need to have their feelings acknowledged. Sometimes when they see that you are listening to their feelings, they feel able to listen a bit to yours. (Hey, don't count on it, but wouldn't it be lovely?) Try some active listening (discussed in Chapter 4, "Moving In Together"). It can help.

Fear of Their Other Parent's Reaction

Sometimes the child may be concerned about how the other parent will react to your happy news. His or her concerns may be valid—divorce makes people desperately upset, and kids who are veterans of the divorce wars often have seen their parents tremendously distressed. To help the child, consider these tactics:

➤ If you're the step-to-be, assure the child that you will not try to take his parent's place.

➤ Remind sweet sulky Sarah that this marriage is not her choice or decision. This may actually relieve her mind—she may be trying to take responsibility, she may be trying so hard to be loyal to her other parent that she's trying to throw off the wedding.

➤ The child's bioparent should reassure the child not to worry about telling his other parent—the kid might be imagining a kind of "shoot the messenger" scenario where he tells the "happy news," the parent flips, and the kid gets the brunt of it. It *is* the responsibility of the bioparent to inform his or her ex. The child should not have to do it; it's unfair, and it's not the child's responsibility.

Will My Parent Still Love Me?

You're becoming the most important player in your spouse's life (and she in yours), and it's no wonder the kids are freaking out. They're afraid that they're losing a parent as they gain a stepparent. Each child needs a lot of reassurance. The child does *not* need, "Oh, stop being such a baby. Of *course* I'll still love you."

How "Your" Kids Will React

With Mom or Dad goo-goo in love and planning a wedding, it's common for your kids to feel like they are no longer the focus of your attention. They may feel the loss of you, especially if you've been a single parent for a while. It's true though, isn't it? Aren't you a little distracted? Once again, real reassurance is in order, as is a lot of attention. How long has it been since the two of you went somewhere just to hang out and have fun?

Be prepared for your kid's reaction after the wedding as you shift your focus from them to your new spouse. Here's an example: Many single parents of very small children allow the kids to sleep with them. As you're contemplating honeymoon activity, take into consideration that your new spouse will literally be displacing small Angie or Arnold from your bed. Angie or Arnold is not going to like that. Begin the "weaning" process before the wedding. Treat the little one with great tenderness, and be aware that you may have some rough nights before it works.

Stepping Stones

If you have young children who are used to crawling into bed with you in the middle of the night, discuss how you're going to handle this with your spouse-to-be.

But She's a Jerk!

It's possible you're making a big mistake—as I've told you, love is blind, deaf, and more than a little dumb. If the kids (yours or your spouse-to-be's) have strong, serious objections (particularly if similar objections come from more than one child), try to open your eyes and ears. Take the objections seriously—they may be correct!

If Possible, Take Your Time

Give the kids as much time as possible to get used to the idea of love, marriage, and so on. Since love has blinded you to reality, the more time you take, the better, for you as well.

I Kid You Not!

Famous stepparents in history: Marcia Williams, comedian Robin Williams' wife, is stepmother to Robin's eldest child. She began as the nanny in his life before they fell in love.

Planning the Wedding

Larry and Naomi had the kids—two of his, one of hers—stand up with them for part of the ceremony. Alphonzo and Abby got married by a justice of the peace, alone, because they didn't want to deal with all the relatives and angry ex-spouses. Joanne and Jeff had a private ceremony, without his two kids. There are many possible ways to get married. Here's a chance for you to get creative!

Arghh! Invitations!

Even in the simplest of weddings, the invitations are a bear. This is a time to be gracious. Do as is always done—decide on the number to be invited, split that in half so that each family gets 50 percent, and discuss in advance if anybody gets veto power. I've heard it said, "If you can get married, you can stay married," and the invitation process certainly points to the truth of that.

Stepping Stones
When the planning and etiquette of it all seem too much, check out Margorie Engel's book, *Weddings, a Family Affair: The New Etiquette for Second Marriages and Couples with Divorced Parents*.

Where's It Gonna Be?

A church, temple, rehearsal hall, courthouse, while skydiving, riding in a carriage through Central Park—where you actually do the "I do" doesn't so much matter. Locale is totally up to you (and the kids, the grandparents, and especially the people who are footing the bill). But sometimes it's hard to remember that a wedding is not a social event or a party so much as it is a public commitment to each other—and to the family. Remember that.

The Vows

Choose or write your vows carefully. Do you want to incorporate the kids? "But I'm not marrying the kids! I'm marrying Ellen, and this is *our* big day!" Think again. When you make the commitment to a parent, you are committing to help that person with life's responsibilities. That includes the kids. They may live elsewhere with the other parent, but they will have a financial and emotional impact on your life.

This marriage will also deeply affect the kids. No matter where they live, "home" will also be with their parents. You will now be a part of that home. I believe that it's important to acknowledge that importance as you make your vows.

The Child's Role

As you plan the ceremony, consider giving the kids some input and responsibility in the planning (even if it is small: "Sahkti, what color napkins should we have at the buffet?"). You are marrying into a family—in a way, this is their wedding, too.

I Kid You Not!

Kids, especially little kids who may have lived with the stepparent for years, may be delighted by the ceremony and feel very much included.

Also discuss well in advance what role the child will play in the ceremony itself. Some? None? Traditional roles include flower girl, usher, and ring bearer. In my nontraditional wedding, Aaron stood at Bill's side, along with Bill's two best friends, and Rachel stood beside me, along with my two best friends. The kids didn't want to speak, but I mentioned them in my vows.

What If the Kids Don't Want In?

Participating in your wedding may feel too painful for the kids. Yes, it's your joyous day, but they may not feel like celebrating. Some kids may not even want to be there. Remember, your marriage may be hurting their other parent and killing their reconciliation dreams. It may hurt not to have them there with you, but allow the child to make that choice. Discuss it, listen to their reasons, and then show them some respect by acknowledging their right to decide.

You may choose to mention the kids in the ceremony even if they aren't there—they will hear about it, trust me. And whether they are present or not, or participating or not, your commitment to them should be the same.

Alternative Rituals for You and the Kids

When you marry a parent, you pledge yourself to the children, too, as their stepparent. While some people like to acknowledge the kids during the ceremony, others prefer to have a private, alternative ritual. Here's an idea: Have a private "wedding" with each child, individually, where you pledge your commitment to being the child's friend and ally. Some possibilities include these:

➤ Make it a special toast after dinner.

➤ Give the child a special "wedding" gift.

➤ Take a walk, the two of you, and talk about how you see your relationship growing. (The older child might be too embarrassed or conflicted to let this happen.)

Hey Stepmom, What's Your Last Name?

Along with the ceremony, some other matters require thought. Are you going to take the last name of your new spouse? Perhaps he'll take your last name? If you're having any questions in your mind, maybe the following questions will help you clarify your feelings:

➤ Are you planning on having children? Is it important to you that you all have the same last name?

➤ Is his ex keeping her name? How do you feel about that?

➤ If you have kids, you might consider keeping the same name as theirs. If he'll be adopting your kids (more on this in Chapter 24, "In Addition, There's Adoption"), will they be taking his name?

➤ How do you feel about choosing a name unrelated to your Ex (if there is one), your maiden name, or your new husband? You have the opportunity to find a name that is just *you*.

In my case, I kept my name and barely questioned whether I should take my husband's. I liked my name (it's not beautiful, but it has been mine since birth). Besides, Bill's last name was too hard to spell, I had a fairly strong political commitment to keeping my own identity intact, and since Bill's first wife was keeping the last name, I was *not* going to be the second Mrs. Anything!

For other women, changing their name is a strong, symbolic way to become a legitimate member of the family and to acknowledge the importance of the stepparenting role (I didn't think this way when I was getting married; I was still denying that it *was* a new role.) A family that all has the same name says to the world, "We have one shared identity. We belong together."

Don't Be Wicked
Some people have a dream vision of their perfect wedding long before they choose the lucky partner. If that's true for you, it's time to redefine your fantasies, Love.

Legally, by the way, you have the right to call yourself by whatever name you want, as long as you are not infringing on somebody else's rights or doing it for purposes of fraud. "Hello, Ms. Peanut Butter!"

When Conflict Arises

Even in so-called simple marriages, people flip out before the wedding. It's a grand tradition! Tensions run very high around weddings, and because there are more than two people (and more than two families) involved, the flip outs may come from more angles.

These Are Not Tears of Joy

Divorce and death create discord. In the middle of all the hoopla of invitations and flower arranging, a sullen, miserable child sits like a little black cloud, spoiling all the fun. "Hey!" you might be thinking impatiently, "This is *my* wedding." Perhaps you're feeling sorry for yourself or you're actively ignoring the kid's feelings. Okay, let's be honest. Your wedding plans and ceremony may be muddied by ugly emotions. Some people might not be happy. They may be angry, furious, hurt, mean, spiteful, cynical…. They could be in the audience, and they could be the kids, sulking their way down the aisle.

Let them be. Be prepared for the worst, and concentrate on enjoying your wedding. Joy is infectious, and sometimes strife should just be ignored. (This is a good time to meditate, if you do.) Your wedding provides the perfect chance to show your belief in the future. Your attitude is what transmits itself to family and friends. No matter what they think, this *is* a joyous day!

Sabotage! The Ex-Spouse Strikes

An angry or resentful Ex can do a great deal of damage. In some cases, he or she may be able to keep the kid from coming to the wedding. Often, the Ex is so miserable that the loyal kid is in misery, too. This *is* hard. Support the child in whatever way you can, and take care of yourself, too.

Pay and Pay Again

Marriages are family affairs. Traditionally in first marriages, the bride's family plans and pays for everything. Typically (if *anything* can be considered typical in stepfamilies), the bride and groom pay, with maybe some help from their family (as in *my* backyard wedding!)

There is no right way and no wrong way—except when it comes to the kids. The ex-spouse should not have to pay a penny. You, the new couple, should pay for bus fare, plane fare, train fare, or bridge tolls and gas. You should buy the child's wedding clothes and shoes. You should pay for the haircut. No matter what kind of expense is associated with the wedding, you should pay it. It's your responsibility. This is your event, and it's only fair.

Stepping Stones
A wedding is a public event that joins families together in a legal and community bond. Many people—not just you—have needs that must be met. If you feel too compromised, plan an additional private ceremony so just the two of you can pledge your forever-love. Maybe a walk on the beach?

Remarriage, the Final Divorce

It's not just the kids who may have harbored secret fantasies of reconciliation. You or your partner may, too. I know, you *want* to get married, but grief takes a long time, and the unconscious is a powerful force. If you or your partner is showing signs of grief, follow these steps:

➤ Don't ignore; acknowledge it.

➤ Don't be angry, and try to reduce your jealousy. This is old stuff, and it *really* has nothing to do with you!

Reducing Stress in a Stressful Situation

Here are some areas to work on when everybody (including you) is just losing their heads:

➤ Try to keep things in perspective.

➤ Simplify, simplify, simplify. Organizing the logistics of a big wedding may be enough to send all of you over the top.

➤ Pace yourself. Try not to exhaust yourself.

➤ Take time for you. Make your partner take some private time, too.

➤ Call a "wedding-free" evening and have a special date. Don't talk about the wedding. Enjoy each other. You may not remember it, but that's what all this mess is about!

Honeymoon? Yes, If You Possibly Can

Work, money, exhaustion, the kids—it's tempting to skip the honeymoon and, after all the disruptions, just get back to the daily grind. I suggest, if at all possible, that you forget about this grim pull. Honeymoons are important—how I wish we had taken one.

➤ A honeymoon gives you a vacation, which you're going to need after doing *this* wedding.

➤ A honeymoon is a breathing space between the past and the future.

➤ A honeymoon lets you replenish your strength—you're gonna need it.

➤ A honeymoon sets the precedent that "the couple" is important.

➤ Celebrating life and celebrating joy are vital parts of a couple's strength. Take the time together; you deserve it.

Doing the Right Thing

A remarriage involves a great deal of emotional strain. Look at it as an opportunity to rise above the petty hurts and be gracious. Profoundly thank your Ex for allowing your children to come to the wedding. Bite your tongue (harder now!) and say nothing evil about your new spouse's ex (well, not where the kids and friends can hear you, anyway. Yes, you can vent at your therapy session—that's what shrinks are for). Teach the kids to treat their new stepsiblings graciously, in the interest of family peace. As etiquette master Letitia Baldrige says (speaking directly about stepfamily weddings in *Letitia Baldrige's Complete Guide to the New Manners for the '90s*), "If ever strong character and self-sacrifice were needed, it is now....The one who gives the most ultimately gains the most." In this case, I say "Right on, Sister!"

The Least You Need to Know

➤ Yes, it will probably be stressful. Take care of yourself.

➤ It's important to keep the kids "in the loop," but plan carefully how you're going to tell them that you're getting married. Be careful; many have mixed feelings (or worse!).

➤ Take a honeymoon if you possibly can; you'll need it!

➤ Your joy will carry the day.

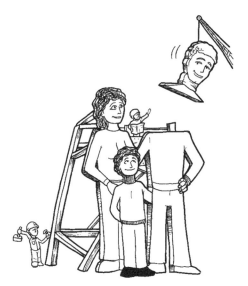

Building a Viable Stepfamily

What a journey you've taken already! You've met the kids, and you've moved in or married. And it's all just begun. As you now know, becoming a stepparent—and building a stepfamily—is a process. It doesn't happen overnight, and it doesn't happen without effort. I know you're ready, you're committed, and you're in love. You can't wait to grab hands and leap into your new life together! Everybody should share your joy!

Congratulations on your wonderful happiness. I am truly glad for you. Excuse me for a moment, though, while I throw just a sprinkle of water on your flames. You've stepped into a very tricky situation here. The odds are against it working: Sixty percent of second marriages fail.

So here you are: You're lying in bed or sitting at a desk or lounging on the beach (don't you *wish*) reading this book, and you're thinking, "That's okay, *we'll* make it." Good! Yes!

You *should* be thinking that. I only tell you the nasty, gnarly facts to wake you up, shake you up, and tell you not to be blinded so much by the light of love that you forget it's gonna take some work and effort. In fact, the *only* way it's gonna work is if you work at it. You'll save yourself a lot of stress if you think and plan a little. That's what this chapter is about: doing it right. In this chapter, we'll talk about tools to help you avoid the classic problems before they begin. If you're deep in the thick of it and having a hard time, this chapter will help you begin making positive changes.

Ready to dive in? Brace yourself—the water's a little cold, but it's pretty refreshing once you get used to it.

I Kid You Not!

Step success *is* possible, especially when you take a positive, active approach. The very things that can make a stepfamily so challenging are the things that will improve each member's ability to get along in the world. I'm talking about problem-solving, cooperation, and connection.

The Nine Steps to Step Success

I have identified nine steps or issues to think about with your partner (preferably *before* the blood pressure rises to unbearable limits):

1. Understand your situation.
2. Establish your relationship priorities.
3. Resolve old feelings.
4. Plan ahead financially and logistically.
5. Understand your vulnerabilities and blind spots.
6. Improve your communication skills.
7. Be flexible.
8. Look toward the future.
9. Take care of yourself.

Step 1: Understand Your Situation

What's the reality here? I don't mean the "we love each other and want to build a life together" reality. I mean the other realities, the financial and logistical ones. It's vital to have a clear picture of both partner's lives before you link your wagons together—and to the stars.

Step 1 entails learning the history, history, history of your partner's life. That means all the ugliness and all the glory. It means knowing the financial figures—you have a right to full disclosure (more details in Chapter 23, "Money Madness"). It means understanding where the kids are coming from (emotionally and developmentally) and, unfortunately, as much as you can about the divorce(s) or death of the previous spouse(s). You don't want any little surprises down the road, do you? (Actually, I hope you took my advice in Chapter 4, "Moving In Together," and read ahead to this Step 1 when you decided to make a commitment to each other.)

Sound overwhelming? Sound glum, grim, grimy, and gross? Worried that some of this might make for some pretty uncomfortable conversations? Don't stress: As we continue along, we'll talk a lot about ways to improve your communication skills, and ways to feel easier about communication in general. (You've already started—remember the exercises in Chapter 4?)

"Stepping in" is a big step, and another important part of Step 1 is understanding the depth of the commitment you've made. You've agreed to more than a relationship with your new love; you're beginning a relationship with a family. It's one thing to get together with somebody and hang with them, and then if it doesn't work out, well, that's that. But living together or getting married is another matter. Now that there are other people involved in this relationship (namely the kids), you shouldn't have such a casual attitude. Being a stepparent is *way* heavier than going steady. And because the odds are against it working out, you'll have to work harder to see that it does.

Step 2: Establish Your Relationship Priorities

Now you've got to look at and establish your relationship's priorities. Who comes first, the chicken or the egg? The oak or the acorn? The couple or the kids? Many people say that the way you achieve unity is by putting the *couple* first. To me, that doesn't sound very family-friendly, and it sounds as though the interests of the couple come *instead* of the interests of the kids. Others say that the interests of the children absolutely take precedence. Then what about the couple? No, no, no. This is all wrong.

Let's look at it slightly differently. This is not a race with winners and losers. Nobody should be first, nobody should be last, and nobody should be in the middle.

So, what does that mean? Well, in interviews and studies, stepfamily after stepfamily asserts that *unity* is what is most vital. Everybody (and each combination of people) in a stepfamily has needs that must be met, and the immediate priorities change depending upon the situation. The family cannot be united if anybody's needs come before everybody else's.

> **Stepping Stones**
> The foundation of the stepfamily is the couple. If the couple falls apart, the family falls apart. The couple must have a commitment to the couple *and* to the family.

Yet it's also pretty clear that the couple *is* the foundation of the stepfamily. You guys chose each other, right? Without you, no stepfamily. You're also the adults and therefore the leaders.

The couple's unity is what allows the stepfamily to function, but that unity cannot come at the expense of the children involved.

The Family's Needs

Jeanne Elium and Don Elium, authors of *Raising a Family: Living On Planet Parenthood*, have developed a fascinating and very helpful concept called *FamilyMind*. FamilyMind is a way of thinking about the family that puts the family's needs first, not the couple, not the individual, not the kids. Everybody is important in FamilyMind. You can generate FamilyMind by asking yourself, "What does this family need now, including me?" Hey, note the "including me" part. That's really important. Putting the needs of the family first does *not* include leaving yourself out.

Step-Speak
FamilyMind is a concept developed by Jeanne Elium and Don Elium that puts the needs of the family—all members—before the needs of any one individual.

Sound like group-think? Not really. Try it—it's an approach that helps conflict. In any troubling situation, you'll find it very helpful to stop a moment, close your eyes, and ask yourself, "What does this family need now, including me?"

As you form a stepfamily, remember that all people within the family should have their needs considered. Sometimes it's especially hard for the partner who didn't bring children into the stepfamily to remember to take time for her own needs. You aren't just punishing yourself, Honey. In order for the family to work, everyone's needs must be considered—including yours. To put the family first, you need to put each of you, both alone and together, first. For every situation, strive for a solution that satisfies everybody.

Don't Forget the Couple

That said, you—as the couple—are the adults. It is necessary and appropriate that you take leadership roles in the family. You are in charge. How is your household going to be run? You are going to be co-parenting. What kind of parenting style do you each have? With all the leading, your coupledom will need nourishment, so you must find time alone for romance as well.

Keeping Time for Romance and Sex

Children, work, school, home maintenance, more work, faxes, email, phone calls, beepers, traffic jams, children, yet more work—you don't have time for yourself. You don't have time for anything. You don't have time for romance. WRONG!!!

You have *got* to make time for romance. This is not optional, especially in a stepfamily. A stepfamily is filled with stress points and stretch marks. It is usually *not* calm living. The only way you, as a stepfamily (and you as a stepparent and perhaps a parent), are going to survive is by paying close attention to your relationship with your lover or spouse.

That means time alone together. It means time spent doing whatever things you, the couple, like to do and find romantic, whether that means attending cat shows or the opera, or walking on the beach at dawn, or simply spending time together making love. If you give too much energy to the family and foster too much guilt around stepkid issues (and we'll get into guilt in a big way later on), your sex life will suffer. Sex is not *all* there is to romance, but hey, it's important.

The Household

As partners and co-parents, you need to decide how the household should be run: like a ship-shape ship, a laid-back lair, or something in between. Who's gonna do the actual work? Household organization is an area where the couple makes the major decisions and the kids follow along. Before you decide how you are going to run things, you need to know what each of you needs and likes. In Chapter 10, "Your House, My House, New House," we'll look at the "household" issues in depth.

Parenting Styles

No two people have exactly the same parenting style, and your styles do not need to be an exact match. Some people tend to be laid back and casual, some more strict. Some believe in organizing the stephousehold with operating procedures, guidelines, rules, and regulations. (I tend to lean more toward the groovy side and say, hey, it's a family, not a business.)

Discuss your approach with your mate. You are the partner of your partner, and together you should decide on a parenting style and an approach to running a household. Whatever your style, make sure you respect the child, honor her autonomy, and nurture her needs. In their book *Growing Up Again*, Jean Illsley Clark and Connie Dawson discuss the continuum of parenting styles, from abusive on one end to neglectful on the other. Aim for the middle of the spectrum, acting as an assertive and supportive parent.

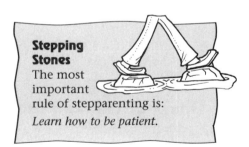

Stepping Stones
The most important rule of stepparenting is: *Learn how to be patient.*

Step 3: Resolve Old Feelings

A stepfamily has a history, or more aptly put, histories. Nobody comes to it as a blank slate. Even if you are coming in as a childless stepparent, you have expectations. It is truly important to try to face and resolve your old lingering feelings of guilt, blame, jealousy, and grief—the four uglies that usually accompany all stepfamily mergers.

Guilt

There are so many flavors of guilt that it's hard to know where to begin. Fathers might feel guilty that they left. Mothers might feel guilty that they broke up the family. Step-mothers might feel guilty that they feel resentful. Stepfathers might feel guilty that they don't love their stepkids. The kids might feel guilty that they like the stepparent. Yuck, yuck, ick.

You will not be able to dispense with guilt easily; it's a stubborn little bugger. But I'll tell you one way to start shrinking guilt: If you stare at it long and hard, it will start to shrivel.

Blame

Blame is guilt's hideous cousin. It has giant hands perfect for lots of finger-pointing. Like guilt, it is persistent and doesn't easily go away. Like its cousin, though, a good, hard stare at it will start the process of making it leave your house.

Jealousy

Jealousy is like an uninvited guest who comes early and stays late. Each member of the stepfamily will become familiar with this ugly feeling. Jealousy is best discouraged by smothering it (or, rather, the family member who is suffering from it) with affection.

Post-Divorce Grief

In divorce, everybody suffers, and—whether it has been two months or 10 years—dating, "getting serious," and remarrying all reopen the old wounds for the kids and for the divorced parent. As the new person on the scene, it's important that you remember that there is some pain here. Tread lightly, don't expect them to just "get over it," and know that your presence may be stirring up some pretty strong emotions.

That said, it's also important to remember that you are not the cause of the pain of divorce. If fact, you can—and may be—a strong healing factor. Don't let them pin the blame on you.

Grieving Your Own Life

If you've suffered a divorce yourself, you'll have your own mourning process to go through. If you are joining the family as a stepparent, you'll need to process the end of your own fantasy life. Very few of us grow up thinking, "Wow, I want to be a stepparent when I grow up!"

Grieving and grief resolution is a process that is rarely over when you think it is. I always picture those arcade games where you've got a large padded mallet and your task is to smash down the plastic animal heads as they pop up out of holes. The faster you smash, the faster other ones come up. (Perhaps the secret is not to smash them down at all but to confront them squarely, eye to eye.)

Step 4: Plan Ahead

Now you've got to look toward the future and plan your lives together. (Chapter 23 has more details about all that money stuff.) It's worth a "visioning" meeting with your love to figure out where you each want to be in five or ten years.

Visioning the Future Exercise

You'll need two pads of paper and two pens. Choose a quiet place and time to sit alone or next to your love. Take a moment to think about where you would like to find yourself in five years.

Think about each of the following questions (you can read each one aloud) before spending a few minutes writing down your thoughts, feelings, wishes, and dreams. These are to share. You can choose to share your answers after each statement or wait until you are all done.

Step-Speak
Visioning is the process of seeing the future with your mind's eye. It's not about magic or prediction; it is, rather, a way of expressing your own hopes and expectations.

In five years:

> Where would you like to see yourself living?

> How would you like things to be different financially from the way they are now? How do you see your role with the children?

> What would you like to be happening career-wise for you? For your spouse?

> What else do you envision happening in the next five years?

> What image comes to mind when you think of yourself in five years?

Getting to Really Know You

Sharing your answers is an important step in beginning to build your lives together. It also helps build real intimacy with your partner. How well do you *really* know your partner? As you begin your life together, are your values and desires synchronized?

To know what you want out of life, you have to know what you *don't* want. People creating a stepfamily have an advantage here over those young, innocent babes-in-the-woods with no history or experience. Remember, at least one of you is wise to what doesn't work for them in a relationship and from family life. Here's where you get to *use* that wisdom! In Chapter 4, the exercise "Basic Living Styles" can help you figure out what each of you do and don't want. If you haven't done it yet, now's as good a time as any!

Step 5: Understanding Your Vulnerabilities and Blind Spots

Is your head on straight? Your relationship, and you, are *especially* vulnerable at the beginning, when everything is new.

Admitting how you feel in the stepparenting situation is key. If you are gritting your teeth and smiling through your resentment, you're just going to ultimately make things worse. Look in the mirror. Be honest with what you see. Are you happy? What needs to be changed?

Know that you've made a choice to become part of a stepfamily and be a stepparent. It's a conscious choice.

Step 6: Improve Your Communication Skills

Perhaps this should be Step 1! Communication is a never-ending process. I live with a communication expert, yet we're constantly working on improving our own communication. I know, a lot of books tell you to communicate with your family. Communication involves learning to listen more effectively (as you learned in Chapter 4) as well as talk.

I Kid You Not!

Famous stepparent in history: The Great Communicator himself, Ronald Reagan, was a stepfather to Patty Davis before he adopted her.

Life in a Modified Democracy

Stepfamilies can be very complex, and decision making can become a major part of daily life. It helps to think and make some decisions about your family's decision-making style.

Back in the early 1980s, I was involved in some organizations that decided everything by *consensus*. In consensus decision making, everybody must agree, and any one person has the capability of "blocking" a decision. The advantage of consensus is that everybody involved in the decision-making process must truly agree, and everybody is invested in the decision that is made. One drawback is that consensus takes a very long time and a tremendous amount of energy. Oh, the hours of negotiations over relatively small decisions! Another drawback is that children, especially young children, are sometimes not equipped with the knowledge and savvy to truly make wise decisions.

The opposite of a consensus-run household is a *dictatorship* (hopefully a benevolent one). In a dictatorship, the dictators (in this case, the couple) rule. They make the decisions, and everybody follows suit. On the surface, this seems simple, and it sure cuts down on argument. But of course, family dictatorships do not work. For one thing, they are usually based on fear. What's more, kids need to have some responsibility over their lives, and they need to learn how to make decisions.

Then there is a *democracy*, where each member of the family has a vote. Depending upon how many kids there are, democracy *might* work for you (think about it, though—have they got you outnumbered?).

I believe that life in the stepfamily works best as a modified democracy, a blenderized concoction of democracy flavored with a large splash of consensus and the occasional light sprinkling of dictatorship. In a modified family democracy, the kids get to voice their opinions and be seriously heard. They don't get an equal vote. The adults are in charge of safety and morality; the kids get some input on everything else.

The best forum for discussing family issues and making decisions is the family meeting. We'll go over how to hold family meetings in Chapter 13, "Family Talk."

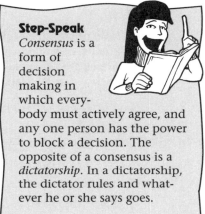

Step-Speak
Consensus is a form of decision making in which everybody must actively agree, and any one person has the power to block a decision. The opposite of a consensus is a *dictatorship*. In a dictatorship, the dictator rules and whatever he or she says goes.

Step 7: Be Flexible

Life and parenting are never predictable. Just when you think you have things figured out, they change. Hey, that's a *good* thing! Flexibility is one of the greatest strengths you can build in yourself and help build in your stepfamily. Here's the rule: When the family is in flux, you must flex.

Stepping Stones
Flexibility is the primary tool each member of a stepfamily must work toward. Rigidity breaks.

Step 8: Look Toward the Future

Patience is hard, especially when you're in the middle of day-to-day family crises. One thing I can promise you: Things change. Sometimes change requires a lot of work, and sometimes profound change comes when you least expect it.

The only thing certain is that things later will be different from how things are now. Change takes time. Your new baby stepfamily is going to grow, change, and develop, but you must have the patience to allow that to happen.

As you look toward your stepfamily's future, think about the areas you would like to change. Think about your dreams. Take some time alone to think about and complete the following statement: In five years I'd like to see this stepfamily....

There is no right answer, but writing down your hopes can help you move toward a plan.

Step 9: Take Care of Yourself

Stepping in as a stepparent is emotionally risky and draining. It is very easy for you to start taking care of everybody else's needs and ignore or set aside your own. You are no good to anybody if you do that.

Take care of yourself. Take time to check in daily and see how you are feeling. Sometimes that means asserting yourself to make sure you are being shown respect. In her book *The Assertive Option*, Patricia Jakubowski says that parents (in this case, stepparents) have some very basic rights. I've adapted them here. As a stepparent, you have the right to:

1. Act in ways that promote your dignity and self-respect, as long as others' rights are not violated.
2. Be treated with respect.
3. Say no without feeling guilty.
4. Experience and express your feelings.
5. Take time to slow down and think.
6. Change your mind.
7. Ask for what you want.
8. Do less than you are humanly capable of doing.
9. Ask for information.
10. Make mistakes.
11. Feel good about yourself.

Stepping Stones

Don't stepparent for duty. Don't stepparent for thanks—you don't get points. Do it because you love, need, and want your partner, and the kids are part of the package. Do it well because it's always better to do something well than poorly.

After the Steps

Take a deep breath and look toward the future. While you're being patient, there are a number of things you can do to speed up the process of building a successful stepfamily.

Take a Long-Range Perspective

Building a strong, viable stepfamily takes time, some say from three to seven years. (My friend Ernesta says wryly, "Yeah, I'm stepmother to an 11-year-old. In seven years, she'll be out of the house anyway.") Try to be patient.

Develop New Roles and New Rules

When remarriage or re-partnering happens and children are involved, there is terrific upheaval in everybody's life. Pain, confusion, and loyalty conflicts can abound. It's clear that society's mythologies about stepparenting and stepfamilies are largely negative or unachievable. Yet people in step relationships desperately need a sense of direction. It's time for new roles, for everybody in the family.

Do an Internal Balancing Act

As a stepparent, you've taken on a difficult task, and it's important to keep your head and nurture yourself. This means treating *yourself* nicely.

Be Giving and Forgiving

Stepparenting is your opportunity to be the best person you can be. There are lots of possibilities for failure, which means if you succeed, how sweet the taste of victory!

Use Humor

In families of all kinds, family situations can get sticky, and stepfamilies are more prone to awkward moments than most. When things get complicated, sometimes the only—and the best—way to deal with them is to laugh. Laughter is physically good for you, and it helps diffuse family tensions. Develop your sense of humor. Try to see it all as the plot line of a particularly bad *Brady Bunch* episode (*that* will make you laugh!).

The Least You Need to Know

➤ Getting married or moving in together is just the beginning of the relationship.

➤ Put the family unit first by using the concept of FamilyMind.

➤ Building a strong, viable stepfamily takes time; three to seven years is not unreasonable.

➤ To build relationships that last, look back to all your histories and forward to all your expectations, communicating each step of the way.

Part 2
The Stepfamily in Daily Life

"Stepparent" is both a noun and a verb. It's a description of who you are, *and it's a description of* what you do.

This part of the book discusses the daily ins-and-outs of the stepfamily in action. It's about answering the question, "Should I move in with you, or you with me?" It's getting used to what your new family looks like and answering, "Who is who to whom?" before you turn into an owl (who who).

There's information about the kids, little ones and big ones. There's also advice about holding your marriage together—and close to your heart—as you move through the hassles of life.

Chapter 7

Instant Parent

In This Chapter

➤ The top tips every parent needs to know

➤ Figuring out your role as stepparent

➤ The naming game—what are they gonna call you?

➤ Joining a new family and saving your own self

➤ Strategies for bonding with your stepchild

Hello, Stepparent! If you've never been a parent before, you're in for some surprises—it's not going to be what you expected. If you're already a parent, you're in for some surprises, too: Each kid is different (and parenting is different for each kid), you're watching your new partner and your kids form a relationship, and the family dynamics are completely different than anything you've ever been used to.

This chapter is a quick rundown of things every stepparent should keep in mind.

Learning to Parent in a Hurry

Here are a few quick tips for successful stepparenting. Keep in mind that

➤ You are the adult, and you are the parent; you are not a peer.

➤ You *can* set limits, also known as discipline. Kids don't hate a parent for giving them boundaries or making rules. As I stress in another book I wrote, *Mom's Guide to Disciplining Your Child* (with co-author Vicki Poretta), children need consistency, limits, and consequences. How you set these limits is important—go slow! Before you try *anything*, read Chapter 14, "Defying the Discipline Demons."

➤ Active parenting involves paying attention to the job, and this entails showing up every day—and I don't just mean being there physically.

➤ It's not a popularity contest.

Don't Be Wicked
Certain rituals should be reserved for the biological mom. Theresa bought her stepdaughter Sara her first bra, much to the dismay and hurt of Sara's mother Ann. In Ann's family, "the buying of the first bra" was a rite of passage—Ann's mother had done it for Ann, and Ann was looking forward to doing it for Sara.

➤ Remember the concept of FamilyMind (I explained this in Chapter 6, "Building a Viable Stepfamily"), and work in the best interests of the family as a whole.

➤ Try to keep the children out of the middle. Try to keep the bioparent out of the middle. Try to keep yourself out of the middle.

➤ Never confuse your role as stepparent with that of the biological parent (see the following section).

➤ Honor the rites, expectations, and roles of the other bioparent. You can provide a difference of opinion and experience, but don't undermine the other bioparent's beliefs or authority.

➤ Keep your animosity against your partner's ex away from kids' ears.

➤ Take care of yourself.

Defining Your Role

You are now a parent, but how much of one? It's confusing. Are you a *real* parent, or should you try to just be a friend? Talk to some experts and they'll tell you to always take a secondary role to the bioparent. Others will insist that you should take a stronger position. I say that *you* need to decide what role to take. (I also say you *need* to decide. Note the change in stress.) I also say that the hard part—and the key—is knowing when to parent, and when to step out. This depends a lot on the age of the child and the level of the other bioparent's involvement.

Parent/Not-a-Parent

You are in a parenting role (a responsible adult, the mate of the parent), but you are not a replacement parent. You are an additional parent. And despite the cries of kids who say, "Whoa, having two parents is more than enough," you are going to *add* something. It's important that you believe that you can be a positive force—this will help keep you from getting trapped in the "old" wicked roles. As you learned in Chapter 1, "Stepparenting Myths and Realities," most of those old roles are extremely negative anyway.

You'll do best if you create a whole new title and role for yourself. Be creative with this: Discuss your role with your mate. Ask the kids what role they want you to play in their lives. Following are a range of roles to explore, like trying on wigs, to see what you look like and to consider before you invent your own. Keep in mind that no role is perfect, and some are less perfect than others.

Stepping Stones
With children, adults often overlook everything they know about beginning a friendship.

"The Roomie"

In "the Roomie" scenario, the stepparent has little say about the parenting of the children. All decisions are made by the bioparent, and the "Roomie" simply is another adult in the house—one who may sleep in the parent's bed, but that's it. This scenario brings little commitment to sharing a life together. This arrangement *can* work; by sliding into it, the non-bioparent figure and the kids get an opportunity to know each other slowly.

These kinds of hands-off relationships might be good at first, but if they don't develop into something deeper, there may be conflict. Ramona's mom is on her fifth marriage, which means Ramona and her siblings have step relationships up the wazoo. "It's important that the stepparent relationship be defined," she says. "The hardest one was with John, because he was just sort of living with us." You couldn't go to him for advice, you couldn't go to him for permission, and you couldn't go to him for money. I think it was really hard on my mom, having to do everything and mediate between us all, too."

Hands-off relationships are ultimately not very satisfying for partners who want to deepen their commitment. The bioparent feels harassed—he or she is doing double duty. The nonparent often feels unconsidered or overruled, the kids often feel jealous of the time both adults spend together, and they're at sea and off-balance because the relationship has not been clearly defined.

"Who Are You?"

The "Who are *you*?" stepparent actively acts on his resentments at having the little rug rats around. It's his house, after all, and those kids sure are noisy (and expensive).

He's pretty wicked. Let's not talk about him, except to remind you that *everybody* deserves consideration, and that includes the kids, even if they *are* cramping your lifestyle. After all, the kids see *you* as cramping *their* lifestyle in this situation.

The Teacher

The "Teacher" is an authoritarian figure who believes in running a tidy, quiet classroom of diligent students. The teacher carries a yardstick good for pounding on desks; says, "Now class, what do we learn from this disaster?"; and sends the bad kids to the principal's office. Stepfathers tend to jump into this disciplinarian's role. Hey, some people run households like this with their biokids, and at least the role is clearly defined—enough of this frustrating vagueness! The Teacher role does have some problems: It doesn't show the kids much respect, it doesn't let the kids see the stepparent as a real person, and it establishes the family as a hierarchy, with the Teacher at the top.

Step Speak
Super Stepparent Syndrome (S.S.S.) is a condition of many overachieving new stepparents who knock themselves out trying to be the best possible parent (or at least, better than the ex-spouse).

Super Step

The "Super Step" is an overachiever on the family front, suffering from S.S.S.—Super Stepparent Syndrome. These stepparents want to parent better than anybody ever parented before. They aspire to be the kind of parent the poor neglected child never had, and by golly, they'll do everything they can to show that "evil" ex what a *real* parent can do. We're talking bake sales, homemade Halloween costumes, hours listening to confidences, chauffeur duty…sounds pretty good, huh? The problem is that, in their attempt to be a Super Step, these stepparents tend to put their own needs second and ignore family tensions. Eventually, resentments on all sides can build to a boiling point.

"Auntie" and "Uncle"

I was lucky growing up. I had, along with two parents and a sister, a large extended family that included four aunts. These four women played (and still play) an essential role in my life—they were advisers, ears, and role-models. I listened when they spoke because they were important people in my life. They cared about me but they were not my parents; they had no responsibility for me.

This is not to knock bioparents. My mother's advice, ear, and modeling were vital to me, but the other input was vital to me as well. When I was first struggling with my role as Aaron and Rachel's stepmother, I used my aunts as models.

The problem with the Auntie/Uncle role is that there *is* no authority for the stepparent. He can end up feeling as though his thoughts and opinions carry no weight. To survive the Auntie/Uncle role, you'll need support from your mate and agreement that your opinions *do* matter, that you are a decision-maker and that the two of you will discuss major decisions. Think of yourself as the power behind the throne (yes, hissing in the bedroom is allowed).

Additional Parent

For some people, this is the best role—you're a parent, you have all the responsibilities and rights of a parent, yet you take a secondary role to the bioparent. Aim for "detached warmth." It's sort of a seniority thing: Final decisions are up to the bioparent. Even with your detachment, you can and do play a powerful and significant role in the child's development.

The Active Ally

In Chapter 3, "Getting to Know You," I defined an "ally" as somebody you trust to be there for you, somebody who is on your side. No matter what stepparenting role you decide to adopt as your own, you'll need to learn how to be an active ally to the kids.

> **Don't Be Wicked**
> Avoid Super Step Syndrome at all costs. You will only fail; coming on too strong will just breed resentment.

Names and Titles

So what are they going to call you? What are you going to call them? For some people, names don't really matter, but for some they are a source of heartbreak.

"Call Me Idiot"

"Call me Idiot, as long as you call me with kindness," says Marianna. Her two teenage stepdaughters have different titles for her: She's Ma to one, Marianna to another. But Marianna has been stepparenting a long time, since the girls were both under three, and their natural mom has always insisted on being called "Mother."

In my case, I opted clearly and decisively to have my stepkids call me "Ericka." (That is, after all, my name and it took me a long time before I even admitted I was a stepmother; the idea of it sounded so foreign and unlike me.) You may be different from how I was and hanker to be called Daddy or Mom.

Be careful when you take a title that by rights belongs to somebody else. Sonia decided that Teddy should call her "Mom;" after all, he was only 18 months when she "got" him, and his biomother was not in the picture. But when Teddy was four, his biomom returned. She insisted on being called Mom, too. It was only after a great deal of stress and agony—much of it suffered by Teddy—that they resolved the problem. Now Sonia is Mom, and Teddy's natural mother is Momma Ann.

As you decide on your name, keep these considerations in mind:

➤ Your name should be a conscious choice. Discuss the topic with the kids (if they are old enough) and with your mate.

➤ If you avoid talking about it, you may become a grunt, as in, "Uh…I'm going to take a shower now," or "Uh…can I get some money to go to the movies?"

➤ Titles that identify your role *can* work, but they can also hurt. "Dad's wife" is a term often spoken with a slightly demeaning tone, or with the word "just" in front of it, as in, "Oh, that's just Dad's wife."

➤ Identifying yourself as a parent with "Dad," "Father," "Momma," or "Mother" may work, depending upon the circumstances. Is there or has there ever been another Daddy or Mom in the children's lives? Then it isn't fair. Be "Big D" or "Maw," but don't force the kids to replace their loved ones with you.

➤ Discuss it, provide options, and let the kids have the final decision.

Introducing the Kids

Now how are you going to introduce *them*? If you don't think about it ahead of time, it can get awkward. Much depends on how they and you feel about the relationship at that point in time. Much also depends on the child's age: Teenagers are notoriously embarrassed by their parents, whether bio or step. Here's a place to rise above petty stresses and be the kids' ally by being conscious and sensitive to their sensitivities.

➤ "This is Adam and this is Elsie." By introducing them by who they are, you leave the problems of figuring out the family structure to the person you are introducing the kids to. They may very well assume you are the natural parent. The "pro" of this: So what? Why is it anybody's business? The "con" of this: The kids may not want people to make this assumption. That's their right.

➤ "My boyfriend's children" is a term that, when spoken in a detached manner, relinquishes all responsibility. The kids will not feel threatened by you, but they also may not believe that you really care. If spoken with warmth when the relationship between you and the kids is on an even keel, it merely describes the configuration.

➤ "This is Annie's big sister, Rachel." Once my own daughter Annie was born, I began sometimes identifying Aaron and Rachel in terms of their relationship to Annie. This established clearly who they were to me and included them as family members.

Joining an Existing Family

When you become a stepparent, you are joining a built-in family. (If you are combining two sets of kids, you are *still* joining a built-in family, though they are in the same boat because they are joining one, too—yours.)

Built-in families already have years of established ways of doing things. They've had years of the kinds of experiences that build closeness, including the end of another family. You're the new kid on the block. It's common to feel overwhelmed. You'd be very odd—or very stupid—not to feel a little out of your depth.

When They've Got You Outnumbered

When I moved in with my soon-to-be husband, Bill, he shared custody with his ex-wife. In this fairly new relationship, we weren't just two lovebirds, feeling our way cautiously to a lifestyle and living patterns. Besides me, there were three Sonnenscheins who, as a family, had certain traditions such as staying up late at night, watching *Star Trek: The Next Generation*, cooking and eating dinner together every night, lounging around on Saturdays, and salivating over every crumb of chocolate that came across their paths.

I could tolerate some of these practices, I admired a lot of these practices (particularly the cooking, eating, and chocolate part), but I still felt outnumbered. Besides, coming from a free-wheeling lifestyle of a young art student on the loose, the immensity of so much *family* was a shock to the system.

It's hard to hold your own when you have two, three, or more people in a family who have different ways of doing things, as well as "in" jokes and patterns of living that are familiar to them but foreign to you. How, then, can you arrange things so you don't *feel* outnumbered, even if you are? Here are the three basics:

➤ Choose your battles.

➤ Don't try to move mountains.

➤ Respect your own boundaries, and ask that they be respected, too.

Enlisting Your Partner as a Partner

Ellen and Joe got married and moved into a house with Joe's three boys. Joe, who had a very busy work life (and who'd been slacking off *far* too long after his ex-wife ran off to Central America with a dashing young guerrilla fighter named Comandante Pancho), basically dumped the responsibilities for raising the kids on Ellen.

Ellen was overwhelmed. Not only had she never parented before and didn't even know what questions to ask, but she felt abandoned by Joe. She was suddenly expected to take the kids to and from school and lessons and play dates, buy them clothes, do their laundry, pack their lunches, make sure that they bathed, help them with their homework, discipline them when they misbehaved, and so on and so forth.

Step-Speak
A *parenting partner* is anybody with whom you share parenting responsibilities on a full- or part-time basis (so that means that evil ex, too).

Joe, who hadn't been a very hands-on parent to begin with, didn't *mean* to consign Ellen to a life of servitude. But whether he meant to or not, she certainly began to feel resentful.

Joe and Ellen needed to enlist each other as *parenting partners*. They needed to realize that neither one of them had much of a clue, and they needed work out *together* issues of family maintenance, involvement, and discipline.

Your Kids, Your Spouse's Kids

Hey, "instant" parent, if you are combining two families into one blend, your issues are doubled (or perhaps squared). It's unrealistic to think that the two groups of kids will magically meld into one gorgeous whole. Chapter 9, "New Family Structures," has a whole lot more on combined families. No, don't turn the pages now to find it—we'll get there soon enough!

Bonding with Your Stepchild

Stepping Stones
A step helps get a person from one level to another.

When people get overwhelmed (and stepparenting can certainly be an overwhelming situation), they tend to withdraw and get resentful. I used to hide in the bathroom or bedroom for long periods of time feeling all churned up inside—who *were* these strangers in my house? *Was* it my house? Part of making the transition and commitment to stepparenting involves making a firm attempt to know each of your stepkids individually, and apart from your mate. It will take time, work, and respect for the child.

Solo Outings

Here's an approach: Try the solo outing. Go out on a date with the child, just the two of you. Does that idea clench your stomach? The prospect fills many a stepparent with fear and horror, but it's not a bad idea. Getting to know the child one-on-one is an important part of building a real relationship. Here are a few tips for your solo "date":

➤ Make it an activity with some, but not all, the focus on each other. This is not an encounter session, it's an outing.

➤ Don't push for too much intimacy. Respect the child's privacy. Make yourself emotionally available, and let *him* come to you.

➤ Do something that will be fun for both of you, but don't expect your stepkid to gush over it. A child may act sullen throughout the day, and then you'll overhear her on the phone to a friend raving about the fabulous time she had.

➤ Don't believe everything you hear. If the child is having trouble with the set-up, she may still try to sabotage things.

➤ No bribes—expensive gifts or lots of candy will backfire on you. You'll get no gratitude, and you're setting yourself up as Sugar Daddy instead of the reasonable stepparent you want to be.

➤ *Don't* do the "How's school?" thing. Forget your parental role, and just hang out.

➤ Work on feeling comfortable with silence. You may *not* have anything to say to each other. Concentrate on relaxing.

➤ Make it a regular thing; a one-time outing doesn't work. So what if you don't have instant chemistry together. A relationship requires work, time, and more time.

When Solo Outings Are Too Much

Many stepparents steer away from the idea of solo outings (hey, you may be feeling so resentful that you don't even want to be in the same *room* with the beast, let alone go out just the two of you). Often stepkids will feel so uncomfortable that they refuse as well.

In terms of your resistance, remind yourself that things will probably be better when it's just the two of you, and that sometimes the only way out of a problem is through it. If the problem is that you don't really know each other, then you have to get to know each other, painful as that process might sound.

About the child's negative reaction to the idea: Don't flip out. Try not to feel rejected (I know, you have just *been* rejected.) Fight the bitterness. Here's the time to practice your long-term perspective.

Stepping Stones
Relationships are built through shared experiences, and solo outings are a good way to begin putting in the time.

➤ Invite the child again. And again.

➤ Practice "special time" at home, such as impromptu popcorn when he's up doing homework, but he has to eat it in the kitchen with you.

Cramming for the "Big Test"

Kids test limits. That is part of their job of being children. Once the honeymoon's over and the novelty wears off, and once the kids get comfortable around you (this might be after you move in with their parent, or it might be after you're married), the testing will increase. Now's the time for you to gather your patience, understand the testing for what it is, and gently assert yourself and your opinions.

Try not to take testing personally. Children push as hard as they can, but they're not doing it to be cruel. It's an instinct—they need to know how much they can rely on you.

Loyalty Clash!

Your stepkids may also be suffering from a conflict of loyalties. Deep in their psyche, they fear that caring for you and liking you (on some level, even acknowledging your existence) is a disloyalty to their other parent and to the memory of their previous family structure.

How are you going to feel about this? The human reaction to rejection is to feel hurt. "After all I've done…" or "What's so bad about me?" You may feel like a second-place, second-class member of the household. You may feel jealous. You probably will feel angry.

It's hard to wade through all those emotions alone. In Chapter 21, "Stepfamilies in Crisis," we'll discuss ways to get the support you need. In Appendix B you'll also find some wonderful parenting resource books. It helps to know you aren't alone.

Give It Time

You've stepped into a parental role, and it can be utterly daunting, especially if you've never been a parent before. Treat it a bit like a new job. When you get a new job, you aren't expected to know how to do everything right away; you've been hired for your potential, as much as for your specific skills. Your employer is in charge of training you.

If the child is old enough to understand, approach her as a reasonable individual who can work to help the two of you solve your problems. Tell her that you are in your training period. You might even say, "Look, I've never been a stepparent before, and I've never been *your* stepparent before. I'm learning how to do it. I need your help." By actively seeking a solution to your problems with her you are opening a dialogue, diffusing both of your resentments, modeling how you like to be dealt with in the world, and gaining information on what you can do or change in the relationship.

Stepping Stones
All kids "train" all parents how to parent them. It's on-going. You're in training. Let the kids teach you what they need. (Note that I say "need," not "want.")

The biggest challenge of stepparenting is knowing when to parent, and when to step out. This knowledge is something you have to learn by trial, error, and communication. Growing a stepfamily takes time. Shared experiences, love, loss, fun, adventure, and daily life all add up, and slowly you'll start having those moments when you *feel* like a family. Give it time.

The Least You Need to Know

➤ Establish what kind of parenting role you will play, and stick to it. Get your partner to support you in it.

➤ Joining an existing family is challenging—open communication is key.

➤ Family is built through time and shared experience.

➤ Patience, my friend, patience.

Chapter 8

Your Marriage

In This Chapter

➤ Understanding your marriage dynamic

➤ Coping with the many forms of "Parent-itus"

➤ Your privacy and your sex life

➤ Competing with a dead ex-spouse

Say it's been one of those days with your stepkids: tears, fears, recriminations. You lock yourself in the bathroom to get away from it all for a couple of minutes. Staring into the mirror at your frazzled expression, you wonder, "How and why did I get into this stepfamily? What ever possessed me to make my life this complicated, this *stressful?*"

Splash some cool water on your face. Dry it off. Okay, now listen. You got here because you fell in love. You fell hard, you fell fast, and the kids were merely part of the package deal. Your stepfamily is contingent upon your relationship. There would *be* no stepfamily without the relationship, and your stepfamily is only as strong as your marriage.

This chapter is about your marriage (or your long-term relationship, if you are not married). It's about keeping the bond strong. And it's about the dynamics and issues a couple faces when the couple is part of a stepfamily. Be vigilant! Inside the couple is where the stepfamily is made or broken.

I Kid You Not!

The first year of "stepping" is the hardest. Non-steps get a one-year honeymoon; you get a trial by fire. (Well, that's not necessarily true. While life is certainly not as complicated in first marriages, year one is often the hardest in *every* marriage.)

Remarriage Dynamics

A relationship with "steps" involved is different from a plain vanilla "Just John and Jane" relationship. Chapter 1: "Stepparenting Myths and Realities," looked at the difference between "natural" families and stepfamilies. This chapter looks specifically at remarriage. Here are some of the realities and peculiarities:

➤ In your new relationship, one or both of you has been married before (look below for the exception).

➤ One or more of you has been divorced or widowed. (Unless you're talking bigamy— if so, get a different book!)

➤ Children are involved.

➤ The remarried parent (or parents) feels the strong responsibility of keeping the fledgling family together: "Damned if I'm gonna let a divorce happen again!"

➤ All this additional responsibility happens while you're getting to *really* know each other.

➤ There's at least one former spouse in the picture, even if he or she is dead (more on this later in the chapter).

You Are Old, Father William

Most people marry for the first time when they are in their 20s. The average age of second marriages is the early 30s. Your increasing decrepitude often feels like a negative, particularly with all your responsibilities now: your own aging parents, your mortgage or rent, and job stress, job stress, job stress. You are no dewy-eyed couple frolicking in the tulips before the first little bundle wails its way into the world. No, it's all at once for you: mid-life crisis, thinning hair, career pressure, thickening hips, and kids, kids, kids. Nothing is simple.

But wait! Your maturity can also be a plus: Think of the wisdom and sense of perspective you bring to it all. You are wise and patient enough *now* to handle the stresses of stepfamily life. Could you have done this 10 years ago? Yes, but it would have been harder.

Remarriage Bonuses

A remarriage has some distinct advantages:

➤ Hey, trial and error! Now you know more of what you want in a relationship.

➤ A person who has had the experience of being in a close relationship has the know-how to form another close relationship—yours.

➤ People who have been through a failure tend to really care about making the next one work.

➤ Second marriages are usually more closely based on shared values than first marriages.

➤ The kids provide the "family" feeling. They can help bring you together in a shared cause, shared activities, and shared challenges. If you've never been in a family before in a parenting role, you may find that the kids add a lot to the marriage. If you've struggled as a single parent, you now have an ally, and lots of little ones.

➤ People who have been through divorce have had to do a lot of soul searching. They've faced the demon "self" and won. All this agony has a good aspect to it; they may be more skilled at intimacy.

Marrying the Single, Never-Married Parent

Okay, it's not always a *re*-marriage. Perhaps neither or only one of you has been married before. You may find that parents who have always been single or who have been single for a long time tend to be very set in their ways. Think about it: The parent who has never had anybody to rely on before may be grateful for your help, yet she may also have a hard time giving up authority. She may feel some sorrow and a sense of loss; her job is being taken away from her, and she's not the only one in charge anymore.

If your love has been a single parent for a long time or always, take some extra time. Sit down with your love and spend some time defining your roles in the family. Don't march in immediately with grand reforms—you'll only meet resistance. (And then there are the kids, who may feel strongly proprietary. Their parent is *theirs*, not yours. Beware! You are moving in on their property. Go slow, and be respectful.)

Married to a Parent?

Some say that parents are different from nonparents, and in some ways it's true. For the never-before-parent who is in a relationship with a parent, here are some insights into that strange beast you've married or have committed to, your reactions to the beast, and the beast's beastly little offspring.

They're a Nuisance!

Even though you *want* to include the children, you may feel that, in reality, the kids are getting in the way of your relationship. Your spouse may not see it that way at all.

Say that 9-year-old Nancy has a nightmare and wants to crawl into bed with you in the middle of the night. You're more likely to get annoyed at being woken up, while your Sweetie concentrates on hearing about the evil monster dream. You're also less tolerant about what you call "bratty" or "spoiled" behavior and what your Sweetie calls "cute" or "age-appropriate rebellion."

The truth is often in the middle. You'd be wise to read about ages and stages of childhood development (hit the Parenting section of your local bookstore or library—there's loads of literature out there), and your Sweetie would be wise to bend a little toward your need for privacy. (Read on, there's more about privacy to follow.)

When Your Spouse Pulls Rank

Sometimes bioparents pull rank on non-bioparents—they get that patronizing look on their face and say, "You're not a parent, so you don't understand." This kind of "pulling rank" can be very hard, especially for the stepparent who wants to have a baby of her own. It's hard enough when people act like you don't know anything; nobody likes to feel stupid. But nothing gets a person's back up more than to be reminded that she doesn't have something that she desperately wants. Gently point out to the love of your life that this is not fair.

If you both are parents, be careful that you don't start competing for "Best Parent" award. This kind of competition and judgment will only lead to both of you feeling bad. I'm sure you each have your strengths (and weaknesses) as parents. Learn from each other—don't pull rank!

Parent Guilt

Don't Be Wicked
Your child should *not* play the role of your therapist or your best friend! When a parent relies on a child for emotional support, the child may have a difficult time establishing independence.

Parents often feel guilty for not spending as much time with the children as they did when they were single. Parents feel guilty for being happy, especially if their kids have been left behind in a nasty situation. Children are scarred by divorce, and remarried parents often feel guilty that they are no longer sharing their child's misery.

Parent Guilt is also common if a parent has been relying on the child for emotional support. The parent may feel guilty for not needing the child in the same ways as before.

For the parent who has relied on a child for advice, guilt may strike when he realizes that, in the important decision of taking a new mate, his child's opinion wasn't sought. He needs to overcome his guilt and make it clear that his choice of mate is his alone. If kids think they have some say in the matter, they will make the life of the stepparent tough. Kids do not have the right to determine the adult's choice of mate. It is an unfair responsibility, and it's not setting the boundaries that the child needs.

Parent Guilt can manifest itself in a million ways. What can you do about it? There's no easy cure. The first step is for you to recognize the guilt within yourself; otherwise you may start to downplay your own newfound happiness and solidity, which is exactly the wrong thing to do!

Step-Speak
Parent Guilt is an insidious disease characterized by feelings that you are not giving your child enough love, support, money, sympathy, time, you name it. While not uncommon in married parents, it runs rampant among divorced parents and remarried parents!

The Bioparent—Monkey in the Middle

Especially at first, the bioparent is going to feel stuck in the middle between his new spouse and his kids. Feeling torn like this is not going to help the health of your marriage, or your family. If you've also got kids, you, too, may feel torn between your new partner's wants and needs, and those of your kids.

Usually the "in-the-middle" position is very uncomfortable. It also can be just part of figuring out how to live together as a stepfamily. In our house, for instance, my stepdaughter Rachel expected soft drinks in the refrigerator, and I was completely against keeping them in the house. Bill felt stuck in the middle, like a mediator, trying to make everybody happy with the situation. He didn't want soft drinks around either, but he wasn't comfortable changing what had been a family pattern.

Sometimes "being in the middle" becomes unbearable. James has felt terribly torn between his wife Clara and his daughter Janice. James and Clara have been married nine years, but Clara has never met Janice, who is now in her early 20s. Until last year, James hadn't seen Janice since the divorce from his first wife — it was an ugly divorce, sides were taken, and Janice cut James off.

Now James and Janice are reconciling their relationship, but Clara is resistant. She is resentful of the time James spends with Janice and angry that James is helping Janice pay for college. She feels jealous, as though Janice is seducing James away from her, and she also is angry with herself for feeling this way. James feels terribly torn. He wants to see his daughter and wants her in his life, but the woman he loves and lives with is completely antagonistic. Clara has put him in the middle, and James cannot win.

Being a "monkey" is part of being a bioparent in a stepfamily. As a step, you can help by listening to your spouse when she expresses her dismay, and you can do your best to problem-solve your way out of situations in which the bioparent is being split in two. (Chapter 13, "Family Talk," has tips on problem-solving.)

Privacy? What's That?

Your marriage is affected by the lack of privacy that's part of having kids in the house. Not only are they there physically, they also take up emotional space.

Stepkids and Your Sex Life

If you are the custodial parent, share custody, or have the kids visit often, you might feel like your sex life has been impeded. (If you have kids of your own, this probably won't be as much of an issue—you're already used to never sleeping and having it tough to find time for romance!)

Yes, romantic life with a parent is quite different. You can't chase each other naked through the house, you're gonna have to be quiet, and you run the risk of being interrupted.

As with all aspects of stepparenthood, the first year or so is the hardest on your sex life, when the honeymoon hormones are flying at the same time that you're doing all that *adjusting*. You can help yourselves out by establishing a couple of house rules:

➤ Everybody must knock on closed bedroom doors before entering (even little ones 2 years old can be taught this). Stress that just knocking is not enough — they have to wait for an answer!

➤ Assert your need for private time. This is a problem not just for stepfamilies; kids the world over seem to have "sibling prevention" wired into their genetic code.

Private time is not just about sex—you also need intimacy. Especially during a stressful visit or a hard time in family life, you have to be able to check in with each other. Sometimes this means making love, and sometimes this means just lying on the bed playing cards or giving each other back rubs.

There is no need to flaunt your sexuality, but it's also not healthy to deny it. Children who observe loving relationships with physical affection grow up to become loving, affectionate adults.

Time to Talk

It's vital to talk with each other, even if it's about almost nothing. The craziness of the era we live in, combined with the hullabaloo of children, can kill conversational opportunities. Don't let it! Talking is an essential part of intimacy. Schedule a check-in walk 'n' talk if you must.

I Kid You Not!

Famous stepparent in history: Dr. Benjamin Spock, the famed baby doctor, "got" his stepdaughter when she was 11. He was (as he admitted in a *Redbook* magazine article) *way* too critical of her at first. Yes, he lost his cool (being only human, too) and told her that she was the rudest person he had ever met!

As a stepparent, you may find yourself feeling competitive and jealous of the time your partner spends with the kids. I used to lie in bed waiting for Bill to come in to talk with me. After a long day, I just wanted to have some time alone with him. When he did come in, it was often just for a quick cuddle or game of cards. Then he'd leave, and I'd hear him hanging out and talking with his kids until late in the night. I could have gone out and talked with them, too, but I was "socialized out." I felt the lack of privacy, of not being able to walk around the house in my underwear or sit in the kitchen without talking to anybody. I lay in bed feeling jealous and forlorn.

(I learned years later that their perception was quite different. They thought I was being cold and that I was rejecting them, and that it was odd that I disappeared just when "family time" began.)

Going Out Without

One way to get privacy is to leave together, without the kids. Hiring a baby-sitter has its problems; some kids are too young or too old, and sitters are expensive. But dating is important. I'll say it again: You lose the relationship, you lose the stepfamily, so it's in the stepfamily's best interest to support your romantic time together. (The opposite is also true: If you lose the stepfamily, you *will* lose the relationship.)

Guilt Interferes with Privacy

Sometimes Parent Guilt makes bioparents feel guilty for wanting time alone with their Sweetie. Sometimes

Stepping Stones
Your marriage may be under fire from the kids! Children of divorce understand weakness in marriage firsthand and will be looking for it. You guys had better be a strong team. Be each other's allies. The kids really need the stability that comes from your solidity as a couple.

Don't Be Wicked
What are you really furious about? Are you picking a fight with your wife over dirty clothes strewn about the bedroom, or is it really because you're annoyed at your stepdaughter—*her* daughter—and can't voice it? Don't misplace your anger. Ask yourself: "Why am I so angry about this?"

Stepparent Guilt makes you feel guilty for depriving the poor dear child of her parent, perhaps her only good one. Kill that guilt! Stab it dead! Yes, you can go overboard and *never* spend time with the kids, but a little time alone as a couple is a requirement.

Living with a Partner Who Doesn't Have Custody?

When you live with a parent who doesn't live with her kids, be prepared for a whole lotta longing. It seems to make it worse if *your* kids *do* live with you. (If your kids live with you and hers don't, be prepared for *mega* Parent Guilt.). Your spouse may rack up huge phone bills, and at times it may seem as though she loves them more than she loves you. When the kids do visit, the world revolves around them.

It hurts to be separated from people you love, particularly children. Realize that your jealousy is misplaced. Your spouse is living with and loving *you* on a day-to-day basis, and there's room in your Sweetie's heart for you *and* the kids. Some empathy is required on your part.

Married to a Widow or Widower?

Competing with the dead is never easy. The dead are sometimes more present than the living, and if your Honey's ex has gone on to higher pastures, you've got a particular set of problems. She may never be there, but she's never *not* there either. You're fighting a ghost.

In general, an ex who has passed away is easier on the marriage than a living ex but harder on the relationship with the kids. Yes, she isn't screaming at you on the telephone because Angela arrived home with holes in her socks, but you've got to fight against her being bigger than life with the children.

If the ex has died, you may find yourself feeling involved in the children's deep grief. You also may try to save your mate from the grief. You may feel left out, especially if you never knew the deceased.

It's hard living with a saint's memory. I guess it's lucky for our reputations that people tend to remember the good things about us when we are gone. Yet all the good memories can lead to some sneaking doubts: Does your mate really love *you*, or are you just a security blanket, somebody warm in the night who will keep the grief away? Are you the ultimate rebound? If the ex had not died, would your mate even be interested in you?

If you feel that you or your relationship is stuck in these problems and that the dead ex is taking up too large of a presence in your life, you might consider counseling to help the grief process work faster and to help you feel more chosen and less the default or fallback plan.

The Least You Need to Know

➤ The couple is the engine that drives the stepfamily train. Keep it stoked with fuel.

➤ Be aware of Parent Guilt and Stepparent Guilt and their impact on your marriage.

➤ A dead ex is easier on the marriage but harder on your relationship with the kids.

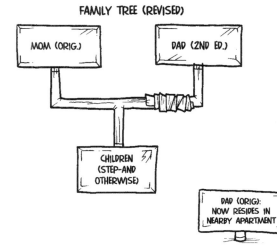

FAMILY TREE (REVISED)

MOM (ORIG.)

DAD (2ND ED.)

CHILDREN (STEP- AND OTHERWISE)

DAD (ORIG): NOW RESIDES IN NEARBY APARTMENT

Chapter 9

New Family Structures

In This Chapter

➤ The ups and downs of custodial stepparenting

➤ The back and forth of sharing children

➤ Surviving visits

➤ Avoiding getting "creamed" in the combined or semi-combined family

➤ Custody, all of a sudden!

What does the stepfamily look like and feel like from the inside? Are you custodial, half 'n' halfer, long-distance, or combined? Do you feel like a walking stereotype, or are you sure nobody's family structure has *ever* been as bizarre as yours? This chapter discusses a variety of different configurations and some of the complications each can entail. Do you recognize yourself anywhere here?

Custodial Stepparenting

Step-Speak
Having *custody* means being in charge of raising the child, making the decisions, and holding the responsibility. The buck stops here.

Don't Be Wicked
If you are planning an open home, make sure that you've worked out good communication strategies, both with the child and with the child's other bioparent. "It's eight o'clock. Do you know where your stepchild is?"

You're a custodial stepparent when you and your Sweetie have physical custody of the kids. They live with you. (Often it feels as though that statement is reversed—you live with *them!*)

Living with somebody else's kids is a hard adjustment to make, even if you have children of your own. Some people say that custodial stepparenting is easier than the constant adjustments of part-time stepparenting. "At least you have some authority," you'll hear. "At least you know where you stand." Well, that's not necessarily true; authority and a clear understanding of your position in the family are things you may need to work toward with your spouse, with yourself, and with the kids.

Gaining Authority

When you and a stepchild move in together, you may feel as though you are in a sink-or-swim situation as a parent figure. This is the time to sit down with your partner and figure out what role you'll play in the child's rearing. (Refer back to Chapter 7, "Instant Parent," for help.)

Dealing with Discipline

Who's in charge? Well, among others, you are. How each family deals with the issue of discipline is a highly personal thing. But remember that you are *living* with the child day in and day out, so you're gonna have to deal with the discipline issue and make some decisions. You can't just shuck off responsibility on the bioparent or on the family as a whole. Discipline is one of the scariest parts of stepparenting, but don't fret yet: You've got Chapter 14, "Defying the Discipline Demons," to help you!

Sharing the Sweeties

When there is shared or joint custody (you'll find out more about custody options in Chapter 22, "Legal Stuff"), you can divvy up the kids' time in a variety of ways. Sometimes you get the weekdays or the weekends. Sometimes it's divided one-third/two-thirds. Sometimes (and this usually works best when the kids are older and ready to dictate their own movements) there's open times between homes, and the kids come and go as they wish.

Half 'n' Halfer

Many times, divorcing parents have their children spend equal time in each house. In some ways, this is the fairest and most reasonable approach, both for the parents and the kids. But in other ways, it's more stressful for the kids, especially if they are shifting houses every week or more than once a week. When kids have two houses all the time, they can begin to feel like nomads, never quite sure of where they are or where they belong: "If this is Thursday, this must be Mom's house." On the other hand, some kids *love* the flexibility of always having another place to call home, especially if they get into trouble in the first place!

Here's something to be especially aware of: If a child is totally in charge of when he goes where, he may use this freedom as a threat, or weapon against you. Say John wants to stay up late at your house, and you want him to go to bed. John may say, "If you don't let me stay up late tonight, I'll stay at my dad's all the time—he lets me stay up as late as I want!" Open houses only work when there is good communication between the two bioparents (and there is more on this in Chapter 16, "The Ex: That *Other* Birth Parent").

Isolina Ricci, author of *Mom's House, Dad's House*, describes the various types of time splits, and says that half-and-half arrangements work best when they're balanced:

➤ Overnights. Kids should have overnights with each parent and get the reassurance of waking up in a place they feel they belong.

➤ Outside activity time. It's important to spend time together doing sports, music, dance, and/or community activities.

➤ Holidays, special days, entertainment, and recreation. Have special occasions together, whether planned, high-budget, low-budget, or impromptu.

➤ Time away and time together. Lots of most kid's time is spent away from both parents, at school, daycare, or work. Be careful that there *is* together time with your child in your life. Your stepchild (as well as your own child, if you're a parent) needs it, and so does your family.

Stepping Stones
Little children and infants need a primary residence, a predictable and comforting routine, and as much time as possible with each bioparent—daily, if possible.

Half 'n' Half and You

As a stepparent, you have some real advantages in having the kids half—and only half—the time. You get the pleasures and relief of both private time and family time. On the other hand, it's easy to start feeling schizophrenic, especially if you are having a hard time with the stepkids. Here you are, relaxed, on top of it, and lovey dovey with your partner. The stepchildren arrive, and suddenly you're snarling inside. It's Dr. Jekyll and Mr. Hyde time!

Because the stepchildren are with you half the time, you are definitely a part of their lives as a parental figure. Talk with your partner about the role you most feel comfortable taking (go back and review Chapter 7). Work together on discipline issues, too (check out Chapter 14).

Regular Visitation

Let's say your partner doesn't have primary physical custody, but the kids show up on the weekends. Once a week, or once every other week, your life changes.

Even if their main home is elsewhere, it's vital that the stepchildren feel that they are residents (albeit short-term ones) rather than guests. Reassure them that this is still their home. This is not only for the children's well-being, though that's important too. It's essential for yours. You can't be on host or hostess duty whenever the stepkids are there. Even young children can take on some responsibility. Having small jobs to do (such as clearing the table or hanging up their wet towels) will keep you out of the role of "hotel staff" and will make them feel they belong.

Even kids who are rarely around need a private spot to call their own, such as a shelf, a drawer, or a whole room (more on this in Chapter 11, "It's the Children!").

"I Didn't Expect This!"

Often people marry parents without knowing ahead of time how much the children will be visiting. Pete and Sarah fell wildly in love and married after a four-month romance. "I thought Chuck had custody and that Sarah only had visitation rights, but I didn't realize we'd spend every weekend of our lives with her kids," says Pete. "I work all week, and I want to see my wife alone once in a while."

Often the kids don't visit as much while the parent is dating, but once the parent is settled down again, they become a big part of their parent's life once more. Unless the extent of the parent's involvement with his or her children is discussed ahead of time, it can lead to deep resentment, like Pete's. Partners need to talk about visitation and its attendant problems at the first signs of strain. There's more on visiting in Chapter 15, "Surviving Visitation."

Vacation Stepparent

If, like many steps, you "get" the stepchildren for the occasional weekend or holiday and then for big blocks of time (like summer), be prepared for a very different experience. There will be more strain than if you are regularly in each others' lives (see also Chapter 19, "Holiday Conflicts and Vacations"). But you'll also be getting a closer look at the kid who goes to the park with your spouse once a week during the school year. The glow will be gone. The romance will be over. You'll all get *real*. And what you may find is a kid you really like.

Nasty Gnarly Transitions and Comparisons

Whenever *any* kind of transition is made within a child's environment, there will be some equal (if not opposite) reaction time. Be prepared for some nasty comparisons, often voiced by a child beginning a sentence with something like, "At home we…" or "But Dad *used* to let us.…" Here's a strong suggestion for dealing with the comparison game (and my advice goes for the full-time stepparent as well):

Don't play! Simply say in a neutral voice that leaves no room for debate, "Well in this house we *all* clear our own dishes to the sink." If there's still resistance, add, "We have different rules for different houses."

Time for Yourself

When the going gets tough, the tough need some recreation. This is a good time to spend doing something special with your own child, if you have one. (After all, you *both* might be feeling stressed and appreciate the time together away from the others!) Or schedule in time for yourself to do whatever *you* do to relax. Have a massage, a bubble bath, a chocolate binge, a long chat on the phone with a friend. Organize a golf game. You'll be at your best as a stepparent when you're at your best personally.

> **Don't Be Wicked**
> It's important to take care of yourself when your stepkids are there, but it's also important that you don't do it at the expense of your mate or your family. Consult with your mate. Is it convenient for you to play poker with the guys that night? Or did she have a big family dinner in mind?

Long-Distance Stepparenting

Say your partner has kids, but they live far, far away. Perhaps you've never met them. At the least, they're not in *your* life. You don't have much of a relationship, and you may not want to! Sometimes you chat with them on the phone, but since you don't know them, it feels awkward. Here are some things about long-distance stepparenting:

➤ Be prepared for them to demonize or romanticize you—or sometimes both! You're not with them, so it's impossible for them to really know you.

➤ That's true vice versa: You may feel more than geographically distant from your stepkids. How can you not?

➤ You may not want a relationship with the kids. (It's probably a good idea to have *some* relationship with them, though; they'll probably appear in your life at some point.)

➤ You may feel nonexistent. You pick up the phone only to hear, "Hi, is my mom there?"

➤ Getting to know your long-distance stepchild is up to you. You can write letters or email, send small gifts, or become active in the child's life in other ways.

➤ Don't expect kids to write back!

The Combined Family

You know the story (well, the myth) of the Brady Bunch: He's got a pack o' boys, she's got a pack o' girls, and together they have a big, fun, wacky family of love.

Give it up, and give it up now.' You're being arrested for Brady Bunch-itis, illegal in all states, plus Canada. It's amazing to me how many people have internalized the *Brady Bunch* TV show and somehow think that their combined family is going to be like that.

Even with a lot of work, your family will *never* be the Brady Bunch (no, not even if your last name happens to be Brady). Okay, admit it, you're breathing a sigh of relief right now. I am, too.

Stepping Stones
If you are combining families, make sure you all get together a few times before the moving vans fight for parking in front of Home Sweet Home. Try casual activities. Break some bread together.

Don't Be Wicked
Choosing to parent your own set of kids—and let your partner parent his own kids—is setting up a house divided. If you correct or interact only with your own, how are you gonna develop family unity?

Here's the reality: When you all live together, you have more opportunities to work out the kinks, and a whole lot more opportunities to rub each other the wrong way.

Salad Dressing

Delicious salad dressing is made with oil and vinegar, but unless they're combined in exactly the right way, the ingredients will not emulsify. A combined family can feel the same way.

Beating the Crowd

Unless you have a lot of financial resources, the combined family tends to be crowded. Life in the combined family is characterized by less room; more people; and different ages, genders, and living styles (loud or soft, early or late). Everybody requires more attention, and it's on *you,* the adults, to make sure that all the kids are adjusting as well as they can.

Learning Patience

In a combined family, you are both parent and stepparent. You're going to be stretching a lot in your dual role. Hey, growth and change are *good* things. Be patient with yourself. Be aware of your limits. Getting the combination right in a combined family is a tough balancing act. It won't always be easy, and it won't ever be what you expect, but it *will* be its own thing. Go slow, but go.

When the kids see you and your darling united in your desires for a smooth and respectful family, the kids will relax and say (at least subconsciously), "Okay, we'll give it a chance. Why not?"

The Semi-Combined Family

In this corner, it's the Residents! And in this corner, their fearsome opponents, the Intruders! Some of the most complex stepfamily configurations fall into the semi-combined family category. You've got a semi-combined family when your kids live there most of the time and your partner's kids visit occasionally, or the other way around.

Step-Speak
A *semi-combined* family is a combined stepfamily where at least one set of kids lives only part-time in the household.

Changing of the Guard

Semi-combined family life is hard for many adults because, with all the comings and the goings, there's little time to relax, to be adults alone. Semi-combined family life is hard on the kids, too, because with uneven amounts of time spent in the family bosom, power balances often occur.

Moira's two kids live with her and Andrew during the week. They spend every weekend with their dad. Andrew's daughter lives with her mom during the week and comes to visit during the weekend. This means that Moira and Andrew never have down time. When Andrew's daughter comes, she stays in Moira's daughter's room, a fact nobody's happy about. Moira's daughter feels imposed upon, and she constantly complains about messes and stuff being moved. Andrew's daughter feels she's imposing on someone else's space and feels unwanted because she doesn't have a place to call her own. Friday night dinners, when they happen, are the only time they are all together, the only time the kids have an opportunity to talk and work it out themselves.

Be on Fairness Alert

Andrew and Moira's situation is typical. The full-time children (or the ones who spend the most time in the household) often feel territorial. They may consider the "intruders" to be spoiled: "How come Elizabeth *never* has to clean up her dirty dishes. You're so happy to see her that you let her get away with murder!" Watch for fairness. Try to make sure that nobody gets "guest" treatment, and do your best to create a special private place for each child, even if it is just a drawer. Having their own bedding and towels can also help establish their space when they visit.

I Kid You Not!

Guilt is the middle name of the bioparent in the semi-combined family. This guilt might make it tough for you to get close to your partner's kids (who live with you) if your own kids live somewhere else.

Surprise Custody!

It can happen. You marry your Sweetie aware that there are children in the picture but way in the distance, perhaps a little blur on the horizon. Though you know your partner has kids, you've downplayed their importance. After all, they aren't going to live with you. Maybe they live far away, and maybe there are regular, short visits. But basically, your house is your own.

Then suddenly, boom! For whatever reason (death in the family, Junior not doing well in school, bioparent flips out, or bioparent moves and kid wants to stay in neighborhood), Junior is moving in! I know, you're feeling panicked, and guilty for feeling panicked. You should be thrilled, right?

Your biggest struggle may be the fight to remain gracious. The child may be very upset, and you won't help move things into a rosy future if she overhears you yelling at your spouse in the kitchen about how you don't want to be living with her daughter.

I Kid You Not!

Surprise custody often happens at adolescence when suddenly cute little Johnny towers and booms over his mother, or Janey is busting out of her brassiere—and her room at night. The overwhelmed parent, throwing up his or her hands, sends the overgrown child to live with the other bioparent. The rebellious child, who may have been romanticizing the idea of life with the noncustodial parent, is often all too ready to go.

Tea and Sympathy

When a child is uprooted, not by their doing, they need sympathy and concern, and so do you. You have to adjust at the same time you are helping the child adjust. Your life has suddenly been turned topsy turvey, and no, it doesn't matter if there are other children in the household. It's a different mix now.

The bioparent should play a big role in the adjustment, reassuring the child that she is wanted and welcomed, and being actively involved in her life. No ducking out now!

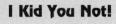

I Kid You Not!

Kids are smart; they can pick up on when they aren't wanted. If this is the case, talk with the child. Assure him that though this is a circumstance nobody asked for, you're a family and families stick together. Problems get solved by talking about them and working on them. You are all in this project together.

Chill with the Guilt

You feel guilty that you feel resentful. Who wouldn't? Your life is being disrupted. You are being called upon to handle more responsibilities. It's normal to feel betrayed, like, "Whoa, this isn't what I signed up for!" Be aware that you are in an adjustment period, and it may take you and the child some time. As the emergency stepparent, take care to nurture yourself; chill out, honey. Take lots of walks and rack up a big phone bill calling your friends out of state.

The Least You Need to Know

➤ The stepparent with full-time custody must work to gain authority.

➤ Creating small household responsibilities and some private place of their own (no matter how small) will make weekend stepkids feel more at home.

➤ The child who is suddenly uprooted needs tremendous reassurance—and so do you!

➤ When the going gets rough, be kind to yourself: Keep the guilt on a short leash, and find yourself some private time.

Your House, My House, New House

At the heart of family life is the home, and for stepfamilies, the issue of houses and homes stands large. Especially at the beginning of the relationship, questions about where to live and how to organize the household loom over the young stepfamily like Godzilla over Tokyo. This chapter deals with home-based issues and delves into some of the challenges of stepsibling relationships (which are also biggies, especially in the areas of sharing bathrooms, telephones, and toys).

Whose House, Honey?

You've got a brand new family configuration, and you're starting a brand new life. Almost everybody says, and I agree, that it's best if you can start all this freshness in a new, neutral place. When you all move to a new place, you'll have these advantages:

➤ You all have the excitement of creating a new life together.

➤ You can look for a home with the correct physical requirements for your larger family.

Disadvantages of Simply Combining

Moving somewhere new isn't always possible, or perhaps one person has a dream house with enough room for everybody. It seems so easy that all the new step has to do is pack the bags and come on over.

Watch out! A lot of people have tried just this, and a lot have found it to be disastrous. Inevitably, the newcomer feels like an intruder, a visitor, as though he's trying to fill another person's shoes.

When one family joins another family in its old homestead, the issues are different for each set of kids, both the movers, and the moved-in-ons. The ones who are moving in (the movers) have a whole new environment to get used to. They may feel "new-kid-on-the-block-itus," that horrible sense that they know less and matter less than the kids who have seniority.

Many of these issues can be avoided by having everybody move, finding a new house or apartment that fits everybody's needs.

Don't Be Wicked

Don't just write off a child's distress at moving. The loss of a home can feel devastating. Consider the child's temperament and developmental situation (there's more in Chapter 11, It's the Children"). Listening to children's real needs is *not* just "catering to their whims."

Uneven Finances

When stepfamilies begin discussing living situations, money issues often come up, especially when couples who have uneven financial situations come together as a family. Perhaps she's been used to a middle-class house in the suburbs with a pool and a large mortgage, and he's fresh from a small urban rent-controlled apartment downtown. How much rent or mortgage can they afford? How much do they *want* to afford?

This couple could try to find a place where they each can afford half of the housing costs, or they could approach it differently. Each could figure out how much they can contribute individually, pool the money, and decide what they can afford for that amount. As long as everybody is happy, it doesn't need to be 50/50. Keep the lines of communication open to prevent resentments from building up.

When Not to Move

There are times in each child's life where a big change, such as moving to another community, can be devastating. Sometimes it's a little child who needs the security of a familiar home and school. It might be a teenager who wants to finish high school with friends. You may want to reconsider your plans. Perhaps when you really think about it, the child and his parent should stay put, and the stepparent (given she's got no kids) should move in. Hey, you can always try it for a while. Moving vans are for rent any day of the week.

I Kid You Not!

As strange as it may seem at first, perhaps your best option is to have the child stay in his house and have the adults move in and out. Jimmy keeps his house, room, neighborhood, and school. Mom lives with Jimmy for a month, and then she moves out and Dad moves in for a month. Yes, it's more complicated when it's Mom and her Love, and Dad and his Honey—and it probably won't work if Love or Honey has kids, too. But it's something to consider, especially if the child is having a hard time adjusting to changes.

Post-Move Letdown Syndrome

A new place won't fix everything. Moving is traumatic and expensive, and when everybody has to move, everybody is traumatized. Yes, the new house has fresh clean paint, but you are the same old, cracked people. After the movers are gone, you may find yourselves standing around and looking at each other thinking, "Now what?" Post-Move Letdown Syndrome (PMSL) is common. Hang in there and try to enjoy setting up your new household. This stage, too, shall pass.

When You Move In with Them

When you (and your kids, if you have them) move into an already established household, you come in as an interloper. Never mind that you were invited or are there by mutual consent; you'll still have to deal with this issue of claiming the home as your own without appearing to be an alien invader.

Claiming Your Space

You're the new doggy on the block, so it's time to mark your territory (in proper style, of course). Claiming space is touchy, especially if you or your brood is literally displacing somebody. Go slow. Wildly redecorating the entire house will feel like an emotional challenge to the stepkids, and possibly to your mate. You might want to shift bedrooms around, or at least reorganize the furniture, especially if this is a home where the ex used to live when the first family was all together. You'll feel more comfortable if you're not making love in the same spot—or same bed—where little Joey was conceived.

Defeating Ghosts

If the ex is deceased, the family might take your reorganizing and redecorating very personally. Be prepared for the kids to react. "But it looked better before! What did you do with our dad's shaving gear?" You do not have to live with the objects of a deceased ex's life. Tell your mate that you need support on this issue. Enlist the kids to help you pack the stuff. If they aren't ready to sort and dispose of the "effects," invest in a small storage rental unit until they are (and this may take a few years).

When They Move In with You

Perhaps you're the one with the dream house and everybody is joining you. If you don't have kids of your own, be prepared for an adjustment period as you get used to living with young ones.

Are you prepared for fingerprints on the white drapes, cracked dishes, and piles of damp towels on the bathroom floor? Loud, rambunctious kids can cramp the quiet, elegant style you've spent years cultivating. And why are they so *messy*?

You've gotta let go. Get Zen about your possessions, or put them in storage. Put the really good china way high on the shelf and invest in playful plastic tumblers. It's time to put the *fun* back in *fun*ctional.

Stepping Stones
Enhance the past with the present. Incorporate the "old" furniture into a new look. Mix 'n' match! You cannot erase the past, so combine it with the present and move on into the future.

Stepping Stones
Create an "off-limits" area—a room, a corner of a room, a desk, or a bookshelf—where you can keep the stuff that you don't want tampered with and that you don't want to put into deep freeze. And be prepared to have it be a very tempting spot for kids. If it's *really* valuable or fragile, it shouldn't be accessible.

Their "Ugly" Furniture, Your "Cozy" Chair

What is tradition, comfort, and esthetic taste to some is putrid, worn-out crud to others. Yes, you may love each other, but you may hate each other's choice in home decorations. Wars have been fought and relationships have broken up—all over furniture.

Furniture and other furnishings reflect who all of you are, survivors of your lives so far, bringing your history and past with you. My friend, Allison, 'fesses up: She hated Anton's possessions. He'd given his ex-wife the house and most of what was in it and had taken the broken-down extras that had been in the storage shed in the backyard. The sets of things—dishware, utensils, pots and pans—were half sets, and none of them suited Allison's taste. The items she didn't object to esthetically she hated for another reason—they had been "hers."

Not that Allison brought much. She was just finishing up years as a starving student, and only two years before she'd prided herself on being able to move with a single car load, except for the separate trip for her bike and plants. The couple didn't have enough money for all new everything. (Hey what do you think weddings are for?!)

Allison slowly carried on a campaign of ridding him—and them—of the most "offensive" stuff. But she had to go slow, because for the kids, those gross, shoddy pieces of decrepit furniture represented home. The kids each reacted differently to other changes Allison made: Cherie didn't care much about decorating, but Hannah, with her artistic eye and sense of beauty, did.

Allison and Hannah warred because their esthetic was quite different. It took months before everybody felt comfortable in the apartment they shared.

> **Don't Be Wicked**
> Sometimes hostility toward items is really misplaced hostility toward people. Do you *really* hate your stepson's macramé plant hanger, or are you flinging it wildly into the trash because you resent how he's been ignoring you?

Establishing Family Style

Part of becoming a family is forming your own family style. At first, it's going to feel like a combination of two broken sets, but slowly you'll add new things, perhaps in a totally new style.

Hey, matching is boring! Live eccentrically!

Including the Kids in Decorating Decisions

It's the kids' house too, you know. Including a child in decorating decisions will help your relationship (he'll feel valued) and give you another way to get to know him. Listen to the child's needs and tastes. It also provides opportunities for two important activities:

➤ Education. You may know that this is a Louis XV chair, but for the stepchild it's just some old spindly furniture—until you teach her the distinguishing signs.

➤ Shared activities. Shop together at flea markets, auctions, or estate sales for old furniture. Refinish or repaint that old bureau—the stepchild will feel more a part of the process and enjoy using something that he worked on.

Don't Take It Personally

Stepping Stones
Be very careful about disposing of people's possessions. It might *not* be junk! Always consult with the owner!

Teenagers tend toward klutziness, and when Bill, Aaron, Rachel, and I all first moved in together, the number of spills and crashes in the household drove me crazy. When my blue glass pitcher that I'd nursed back from Mexico on the train was accidentally broken, I was crushed! I thought it was symbolic of how I wasn't really cared for in the family, how my special things were discounted and treated roughly. Before long, I'd been dubbed "Little Miss Perfect," a nickname that was *not* affectionate. In time I realized that I was out of line, that accidents happen with kids, and that my stuff wasn't really under attack—and therefore, neither was I.

Space for Everybody

Everybody needs to have a private place. Even in the tiniest of houses with gobs of kids, you can create a private space for each child, even the visiting ones. If you are really short on space, take a tip from family home daycare centers, and provide each child with a cubby-hole that's P-R-I-V-A-T-E. For the visiting child, provide special towels or soap, and leave the child's toothbrush in the family holder, all year round.

"But It Used to be My Room!"

When families are combined, kids often go from having their own rooms to having to share a bedroom. If you all are moving into a new place, giving up privacy will be hard for the kids, but at least they'll all be in the same boat. It's harder when one family moves in with another and the "original" kids must give up their privacy. Try to help each child through the transition:

➤ Talk with them. Stress that it's hard, but they're not being singled out; everybody is starting fresh.

➤ Allow each child to choose something about the new situation ("Do you want the top bunk or the bottom?").

➤ Reward them somehow (so their loss of privacy doesn't feel like a total loss).

➤ Praise them in public for it, and frame their generous deeds in a positive way, even if they act ungracious.

Sharing Dynamics

At certain ages or times in their lives, kids may look forward to sharing rooms. But even if they basically enjoy the company, all kids will suffer the loss of privacy. While it is important for the adults to be aware of the struggles and help the kids through if they get very upset, the process of working out their own conflicts and learning to live with each other can bring the kids together into the family.

Facilitate the sharing process. Allow them to divide the room in half with masking tape down the middle of the floor. Make accommodations with ear phones and tiny directional lights for those who like to blare their music and those who like to read late.

Think of alternative "private" spaces. Is there an unused cranny that can be turned into a reading nook? How hard would it be to fix up a portion of the basement so Sandra can do her oil painting without gassing Emma out with her fumes?

If there are enough bedrooms for each kid to have his or her own, there may *still* be some unfair comparisons going on ("Daddy, Margaret's room is *huge* compared to mine!"). If room sizes are uneven, rotate. Switch rooms around every six months. This will be a hassle, but at least all rooms will get *cleaned* every six months!

A Smooth-Sailing Household

How will your new household be run? Many experts suggest establishing guidelines for important family behaviors, especially divisions of labor and difficult areas such as telephone courtesy and mealtimes.

Jeanette Lofas, President and Founder of the Stepfamily Foundation, Inc., suggests assigning specific job descriptions: "We need to be as detailed as we are in business." Other people resist the idea of too much regimentation: "I'm living in a house, not an army camp." I suggest holding family meetings to discuss these issues, whether or not you want to write down the Family Rules and pin up a calendar of responsibilities. (You'll get to family meetings in Chapter 13, "Family Talk.")

Telephone, Internet, Big Black Box

In the electronic realm, you'll find there's lots to discuss and decide upon! Many families find that the telephone becomes a source of contention: too much time spent talking, one person tying up the line, messages being lost or not taken, styles of answering the phone. If phone usage becomes an issue, consider more restrictions—or be prepared to pay for more phone lines.

Another phone line issue involves when and how often people use the Internet. You might want to discuss restrictions on site access, too.

Television use varies from kid to kid, from family to family. I hate television, but I'll not preach to you here. TV usage is another area where the entire family should discuss and agree on policy.

Making Allowances

Ah, money issues. Allowance for chores? Allowance at all? Money for the asking? Whatever you decide to do about money, make sure that you're being even and fair with all kids involved and that you and your partner are consistent.

Chores, What a Bore

Go ahead and have family meetings (see Chapter 12, "Stepteens: the Brutal Years"), if for no other reason than to discuss and divvy up chores. Fighting about whose job is what is one of the biggest sources of stepfamily tension between the adults, between the kids, and between the adults and the kids. Having clearly defined expectations can really help. If you've got a semi-combined family, it's important to discuss how the responsibilities of visiting stepchildren will differ from those of the kids who live in the house all the time. On the one hand, all the kids are family members—if some have chores, all should have chores. On the other hand, if a child visits only one weekend in a blue moon, it's not fair (or fun) to ask him to spend his entire time cleaning the house. Perhaps *all* kids should be exempt that weekend. Whatever you decide, be fair and as equal as possible.

Cooking Chaos

When it comes to food and meals, anything can become a battleground. Food is touchy. People feel that their family food is part of their identity. You may find yourself making a dynamite meal and then facing a child who stares at the plate, looks utterly betrayed, and asserts with finality, "That's not how *we* make it."

I Kid You Not!

Our family used to argue over how to make tuna fish (I like it with lemon, celery, and a bit of mayo; they like it with relish and gobs o' mayo). We solved our tuna problems by opening two cans and mixing up two different styles. With bagels, we argue about the right way to eat one: toasted or warmed. When Annie was old enough for bagels, Bill and I each (mostly jokingly) tried to recruit her to our own style. Alas, she's like her dad and half-siblings; it's got to be warmed.

Sit-down meals, or grab-'em-on-the-run? You may have run your previous family's mealtimes in utterly different ways, but you're starting over now. Shared mealtimes are a valuable, essential part of healthy family life, an opportunity to cool out and catch up together at the end of the day.

The Least You Need to Know

➤ Moving in together on "neutral" ground works best for most people.

➤ That ugly furniture and those awful knickknacks represent the past—be careful before you replace them!

➤ Include the kids in your decorating decisions.

➤ Establish a special, private space for everybody, including visiting children.

➤ Establish guidelines for running the household, and enforce them in a consistent manner.

Chapter 11

It's the Children!

In This Chapter

➤ Dealing with resistance and guilt trips

➤ Becoming a friend and ally to your stepchild

➤ Young stepchildren and what they need

➤ How temperaments affect relationships

➤ Sorting out stepsibling relationships

Face it: It wouldn't be a stepfamily without stepchildren. Here we are at the core of the matter—you and the kids. In this chapter, we'll take a good look at the kids, their reactions to you, and your reactions to them. Ready to walk the gangplank? All aboard the Relation Ship!

Once Burnt, Twice Shy

It's a challenge to build a close relationship with children who have been emotionally injured because their parents split up—yes, even if it *was* a long time ago. People are reactive; they learn from experience. As a stepparent, you've walked into a relationship with kids who are leery about trusting, both trusting you individually and trusting a new adult relationship.

It's common for kids to withhold their affection from a stepparent, no matter how nice you are, no matter how carefully and kindly you treat them, and no matter how strong your relationship with your Honey is. Be prepared for a cool reception. And be prepared for that cool reception to last a long time. *You* are going to have to take the risks.

I Kid You Not!

One of the measures of intelligence in the scientific sense (I don't mean "brainy," I mean as in "able to think") is the quality of being able to learn from experience. This is one of the criteria imposed by computer scientists as they seek artificial intelligence in computers. Can a computer learn from what happened in the past and adjust? By being suspicious of a new adult relationship after his own parents' relationship ended in divorce or death, your stepchild is only being intelligent. Suspicion is the *appropriate* response. Don't judge him for it!

You're In Charge

Ignoring the evil eye and calming the baleful stares will take time, unconditional respect, care, and courtesy. You are the adult here; act like one. Your job is to *not* withhold approval and affection, and to look behind the negative behavior to see what is driving it. It could be many things: fear of being hurt, loyalty issues to the bioparent, the need for independence, and so on. Being the adult means trying to understand what is going on with the child and to deal with her *as you would like to be treated,* even if she's treating you like scum. I'm not talking dishrag, floor rug, weak-kneed wimpiness. I'm talking about modeling appropriate behavior. Part of *your* appropriate behavior may be getting angry about being treated like scum and requesting better treatment.

How do you do this? It isn't always easy. One way is to try to look for the *positive intent* behind the nasty actions.

Positive Intent, Negative Behavior

Jeanne Elium and Don Elium, authors of *"Raising a Family,"* say, "There is always an underlying meaning—a positive intent—to our words and actions." Looking for positive intent enables you to stop taking a child's behavior personally, to help you see it as a problem the child is having, and to ease your own frustration level.

"You're not my mother, and you can't tell me what to do!" Henry snarls as he tosses his filthy clothes on the floor and storms out of the room. What's Henry's positive intent? It could be one of several things: Henry is feeling concerned that you are trying to step in and take over his mother's role. He's feeling loyal to his mother. Henry could also be feeling the need to take on more responsibility, and he doesn't want to be told what to do by anybody.

Seeking to understand Henry's positive intent doesn't mean that you have to put up with his dirty towels or his snarling. But beginning to understand *why* he is so surly is the first step to solving the problem. In Chapter 13, "Family Talk," you'll read more about communication strategies with snarling, surly kids.

Step-Speak
Positive intent is the underlying positive meaning behind any action.

Demonstrate Your Relationship's Strength

All kids test; it is part of their job description. Testing limits and boundaries is healthy (even when it is uncomfortable for the parents). Kids test more than their physical environment and their parent's patience; they also test the strength of their stepfamily. It can be unbearable, but hang in there. Kids are not looking for weakness; they are looking for strength.

Stepping Stones
You may notice that your stepkids flip out when there's conflict in the house. Kids who have witnessed a divorce firsthand tend not to be able to tolerate fighting because they witnessed so much of it in the past.

Ignoring Behavior

One of the most aggravating stepparenting situations can arise when your stepkids ignore you. Don't take it too personally. "Ignoring" behavior is common, especially at first. By ignoring you—your words, deeds, and physical presence—your stepchild is saying, "I'm not ready to accept this situation."

It's terrible not to exist, especially when you're trying *so* hard to be accepted, to make the family work, and to make your partner happy. Here's another time when you are going to have to rise to the occasion and be the serene, calm, Zen-like adult who, above it all, is accepting and patient. Little or big, kids aren't thinking about you or your feelings. They are simply coping as best they can.

You have to think for both of you, to be sensitive while not being a doormat. At least you have to make the kid *think* you are feeling calm, accepting, and patient. Challenging? You bet.

"Why Should I Bother?"

Why should you bend over backward like this? Why *should* you bother? Listen, you are not acting like a saint out of altruism. You are "being the adult" because it will work, because your goal is to ride out the storms and gain a peaceful, mutually respectful household. You're also doing it because this is an opportunity to teach your stepchild appropriate ways to "be" in the world.

Stepping Stones

Equity does not mean "same," especially when you're talking about kids, both your own and your steps. Treating everybody the same diminishes the importance and individual needs of each child.

Guilt, Again

"You're not fair!" Especially in combined families, kids—both step and bio (if you have any)—tend to blindside with guilt. Your task is to avoid being manipulated by cries of favoritism. Here's a specific area where partners need to back each other up.

While your love for each child is different (of *course* you're going to love your own kid more), your parenting style and approach should be the same. This doesn't mean treating all the kids exactly alike. Treat every kid as an individual, and strive for equity.

The Selfish Beast!

Here's a parenting rule that goes double for stepkids: They will never, ever, ever, ask you about yourself. This doesn't mean they don't care about you—they just may not have the social skills to do so yet. When I was young, I was particularly guilty of this. I remember being aware that when I was talking to adults we always talked about me. I was interested in them, but I never knew what to ask. On top of this, like many young people, I assumed people were more interested than they really were.

I've observed this not only in my stepkids, but also in my young cousins. Because they don't have a frame of reference to put *me* in, they ignore me and assume that what they are doing is the most fascinating thing on the planet. It still drives me up the wall when my stepkids do this, but I understand what's happening and have some sympathy.

Dealing with Little Ones

In many ways, the younger the stepchild, the easier the adjustment to smooth stepparenting. Little ones have little memory of "the good old, bad old days" and more rapidly accept the step situation as normal. Nevertheless, avoid these pitfalls:

➤ Be open about the situation. Don't ever pretend you're not a stepfamily, or it will come back to haunt you. As the kids get older, they will come to resent it and to resent you, if they feel you've not been truthful.

➤ Don't take over as a parent. Encourage the children's relationship with their bioparent.

➤ Don't ever make children choose between the households.

➤ Little ones require more hands-on care than big ones. Take an active role in parenting, and share duties with your partner, the bioparent.

Dealing with Teenagers

If parenting *any* teenager is a bear, stepparenting a teenager is a large, angry, blood-thirsty dragon. Having a relationship with teenagers in a step situation can sometimes be very tricky. Toughen your skin, dust off your library card, and go get some good books on teenage development. Also work on increasing your tolerance level!

Teens and their foibles are too big of an issue to cover in just a few paragraphs here. Turn to Chapter 12, "Stepteens: The Brutal Years," for much more detail.

Stepping Stones
Joseph Cerquone, author of *You're a Stepparent…Now What?*, strongly urges stepparents of teens and preteens to "Keep expectations low, patience high."

Dealing with Adult Stepkids

If the "kids" are adults, many of the immediate day-to-day issues of stepparenting won't feel as pressing. However, if you are a stepparent to kids your own age (or older), some other issues may apply. It is up to the bioparent to assert that you are his or her equal partner and mate.

Anna married Larry when she was in her early 20s and Larry was in his late 40s. Larry had two sons, one five years older than Anna and one two years younger. His daughter Carla was exactly Anna's age. The sons welcomed Anna, and in time she grew very close to them. "Carla was the hardest," Anna says, "maybe because we were the same sex and age, so it was like I should have been one of her friends, not her dad's wife."

Carla was suspicious of Anna's motives, and suspicious that the relationship would not last. She began calling her father every morning—something she'd never done before—as if to reassert her presence in his life. At family parties, she subtly skewered Anna with hostile words disguised as jokes. It wasn't until Carla had children and Anna took on an active grandmothering role that Carla began to accept Anna's role in her father's life.

As the stepparent of an adult "kid" who is your age or older, keep these things in mind:

➤ You may have a problem being taken seriously as a person and as the bioparent's mate.

➤ Your motives may be looked on with suspicion.

➤ If you've moved into the family house, you may have difficulty asserting yourself as an " adult."

➤ The "kid" may stereotype the relationship and you: "She's looking for a father figure." "He's a gold-digging little gigolo."

➤ Your partner's son or daughter may feel threatened that his or her territory is usurped by the relationship.

➤ You may have to deal with increased sexual tension between you and the "kid."

➤ You may run into generation gap issues. Where do you belong?

➤ Legal issues—wills, powers-of-attorney, and so on—may become more of an issue.

➤ You have the potential for a very rewarding friendship.

Consider Temperament

Some kids are just easier than others. Some combinations of adults and kids mesh better than other combinations, and it doesn't always have to do with genetic bloodlines.

Steve, a high-energy, quick-to-anger type, has a hard time dealing with his bioson Martin, a quiet, thoughtful type. On the other hand, his stepdaughter Suzy (who drives her own biomom nuts with her emotional sensitivity) is a young woman he can understand. Steve and Suzy have similar temperaments, or ways of approaching the world.

Every child is born with her own temperament (so were you!). Ask any parent who's been with a child since he was an infant. "Oh yes," they'll reassure you, "Toby came out that way. He's slow to warm up but very easy-going once he knows you."

Looking at a child's temperamental approach to the world (and how it meshes with your own) can be a big help in understanding your stepchild's behavior. Is Betty being stubborn and bullheaded, or does she just have a hard time dealing with change? Is Jimmy capable of sitting up "straight, young man, and don't kick the table!"?

Try to think of your stepchild's temperamental traits objectively (the exercise to follow will help). Even though everybody is born with a certain temperamental slant, you can help direct "challenging" traits into more positive ones. It also helps to reframe the traits in a more positive way: "Tara isn't slow and lazy; she's thoughtful, and when she does a project, it may take her a while, but it's done thoroughly, with great creativity." Or, "Mariah's high energy helps her achieve great things on the basketball court."

Temper, Temper!

Your stepchild and you may be as different as fire and water, and seemingly equally incompatible. First, stop blaming him, and stop blaming yourself! He is not a jerk, and you are not wicked. You're just very different. There are many different styles of being human. Much of your stepchild's behavior is a function of his temperament, his approach to things. By looking at his approach and by really understanding why he reacts in certain ways, you'll gain more patience. *Your* way is not the *only* way.

Temperament Contrast Exercise

Check out these traits. For each one, write down in the middle column which ones apply to you. In the last column, write which ones apply to your stepchild. Compare and contrast. You'll see some areas of agreement and some where the two of you don't speak the same emotional language at all! Understanding a problem is the hardest part of solving it.

Temperamental Trait	You	Your Stepchild
What's your general **Mood**? Up or down? Smiley faces or frowns? Pollyanna or Eeyore? Glass half-full, or glass half-empty?		
What's your general **Intensity**? High or low? How strong are emotional reactions? Are you a screamer or a cold fish?		
How important is **Regularity**? Same breakfast every day for 10 years or catch-as-catch-can? How regular are your sleep, bathroom, and flossing patterns?		
How **Physically Sensitive** are you? How's your tolerance for scratchy clothes, loud noises, fingernails on blackboards, runny eggs?		
How **Environmentally Sensitive** are you? Can you spot a tree frog on a tree from 50 paces? Do you do like Dr. Dolittle and talk with the animals? Or is the smell of your bathroom freshener your idea of "natural"?		
What's your **Activity Level**? Are you go, go, go, or ease with the breeze? Today!!! or mañana?		
What's your **First Reaction**? Do you jump right in the pool, or dabble your toesies?		
How **Adaptable** are you? Do you like surprise parties? Are you thrown off by a change in the routine?		
What's your **Persistence** level? Once started on an activity, how easy is it for you to stop? Can you take "no" for an answer?		
How **Perceptive** are you? Do you notice when the furniture has been moved an inch, or do you walk into walls 'cause you just don't see 'em? Do you stay focused on a job, or are you easily distracted?		

Stepsibling Rivalry

Stepsibling rivalry manifests itself in a myriad of ways. Encourage, but don't coerce the kids to get along. Give it time.

Here are some tips for setting up stepsibling relationships that work:

➤ Before you-all step into the blender and flip the switch to "on," each adult should talk with each of his or her own children and encourage them to give it a chance. Talk about *how* they can help make it work (see Chapter 12). Talk about the benefits of making it work.

➤ Tell them it's okay not to like the situation and not to like the stepsiblings. Assure them it is okay to get angry. Encourage the kids to talk with each other about conflicts before arguing.

➤ Kids may worry about shifts in age order. She used to be the youngest, but now there are two little ones below her. Or he was the "man in the family" but now he's got two older sisters telling him what to do. Assure the child that everybody will be treated as they were before: privileges, restrictions, and all. Everyone's roles change when a stepfamily is formed—remind the child of this (you may want to refer back to Chapter 6, "Building a Viable Stepfamily").

➤ Stress to the kid losing age status that this is her big chance to show her maturity. Point out to the child gaining age status that this is his opportunity to be a big kid. Paint a positive picture.

➤ Treat each child as the individual he or she is.

➤ Encourage interaction rather than competition, and involve the kids in activities that encourage them to open up to each other.

➤ Watch for "sibling" rivalry that is more intense or angry than it would be if the kids were biologically related or raised together.

When the Kids Don't Like Each Other

Stepping Stones
Often it's the bio-siblings who are the *least* similar in the family, or who fight the most.

Kids will not always like each other. That's fine. Assure them that liking or loving is optional but that everybody must be treated with respect. Hey, it can always become a lesson in appreciating and tolerating differences.

Help! They're Attracted!

Incest—or the dark shadow of it—is always a risk in stepfamilies. Don't ignore the possibility. There's more in Chapter 21, "Stepfamilies in Crisis," about sexual energy between stepkids.

"You're Not My Brother!"

As part of your general "what's my name" discussions (if you don't remember them, look back to Chapter 4, "Moving In Together," and Chapter 7, "Instant Parent"), don't leave out the kids. How will they refer to each other? You should take the lead here in resolving this question. Whatever they decide ("this is my idiot stepsister"), it's best to have explicit agreement. And it's an opening to communication.

Getting It Even

Families have different styles when it comes to how much responsibility and independence is granted each child. When two families with children merge, these differences in style may leap out as big issues. As the couple, you need to decide how you'll deal with them. Equality and fairness is not a destination, it's a process. It's too hard for a protected child to be suddenly given total freedom, or for Independent Izzy to suddenly find himself under lock and key. Begin where you are, and move toward a style everybody can live with.

Kids with a Deceased Parent

When your predecessor has died, the kids may struggle with heavy-duty loyalty issues and worry that you are trying to replace dear old Dad or Mom. Don't try to be a replacement; you can't replace a saint. But you can reassure the kids that you are *not ever* going to be their parent. Do assure the children that you are making a commitment to them and the family, however.

A family that has gone through a death rather than a divorce is still mourning. Grief takes time. Let it be; the kids need their grief. You can help move the family forward by representing the future. Don't dwell on the past, and don't romanticize it. (That doesn't mean ignore the past—just use the information you gather to move the family into the future).

It's a challenge if you've moved into the house where the deceased parent used to live. You read this in Chapter 10, "Your House, My House, New House," but it bears repeating here: Be cautious about making wholesale physical changes to the house without actively consulting with the kids. If the ex has "passed on" and you've moved in, yes, you *can* make the house your own, but don't toss anything without asking for the kids' permission and involvement. The possessions are theirs, not yours. Problems in this area ("You moved Mom's chair!") may show you that the kids have not finished processing their grief. Counseling may help all of you move forward into the future.

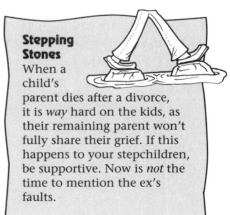

Stepping Stones
When a child's parent dies after a divorce, it is *way* hard on the kids, as their remaining parent won't fully share their grief. If this happens to your stepchildren, be supportive. Now is *not* the time to mention the ex's faults.

Love-Hate Relationships

You won't always even like your stepkids, and they might not always like you. Step-parenting is hard because you don't usually have the long-term bond that a parent-child relationship has had years to establish, and you don't have the biological bond that happens at birth or when a very little child is adopted.

Here are some tips for defusing trouble areas:

➤ If accused, don't deny that you love your own kids more. Say you are trying to be the best you can be to them all.

➤ Never dis the child's other parent within hearing range.

➤ Sometimes you will *lose* it. It can be humiliating when it happens in front of people to whom you want to appear very much in control (meaning your stepfamily). It's human.

Stepping Stones
Forget *love*, and go for *loving*.

➤ Be open with your stepkids and kids, but don't use them as confidantes. Distinguish between sharing feelings and dumping on them.

Even if there is no love lost between you all, you share something important: You both love the person who brought you together, the bioparent/partner. Although this isn't always enough for the long term, it's enough for a good beginning.

The Least You Need to Know

➤ Look for the positive intent in negative actions.

➤ Young stepchildren need a lot of reassurance and physical affection.

➤ If your stepkids are adults, be prepared for your motives to be challenged.

➤ Looking at a child's temperamental approach to the world and to you can help you understand his behavior.

➤ Allow stepsiblings to resolve their smaller battles themselves.

➤ The child whose other bioparent is deceased may feel that liking you is disloyal to that parent's memory.

Chapter 12

Stepteens: The Brutal Years

In This Chapter

➤ The truth about teenagers

➤ The many faces of a stepteen

➤ Dealing with what's dished out

➤ The stepteen, the new baby, and you

Here's an interesting bit of trivia: Most marriages with children break up either when the kids are very young or when they're teenagers. Let's follow the figures. Most remarriages happen within a few years of a marital breakup. That means that there are a lot of teenagers who are newly "in step." It also means that you may find yourself stepparent to that dread species, The Teenager!

Hold it! Stop right there! It ain't that bad! Teens get a bad rap in this society. Adolescence combines the best and the worst of life experiences, and for many parents and stepparents, adolescence is the most interesting, moving, and gratifying part of parenting.

This chapter is all about adolescents—which parts of their odd behavior are normal in any situation, and which are specific to stepfamilies.

Misconceptions and Corrections

Here's what you may think:

➤ Teens are awful, thoughtless, and impossible.

➤ Teens from "broken" families get messed up with sex, drugs, and criminal elements.

➤ The stress of a stepfamily added to the normal stresses of adolescence lead to depression, eating disorders, and suicide.

Stepping Stones
A little knowledge goes a long way. Understanding what teens are normally like will help you understand when your stepteen is having problems.

Here are the realities:

➤ Adolescence is a time of stress, and, yes, your stepteen may be awful and cruel at times. A new stepfamily doesn't make it easier (but may not make it harder, either).

➤ Adolescents can be charming, warm, caring, and interesting to be around. It's a joy to watch kids come into their own.

➤ Teenagers don't want an adversarial relationship any more than stepparents do.

➤ Rebellion is part of any teen's job, and your stepteen is not necessarily going to be more messed up than other teenagers.

➤ What matters is not the structure of the family, but the quality of it.

Adolescence 101 for Stepparents

Teenagers are beautiful, angry, sexual, sassy, messy, moody, and often lethargic. Think of them as lions: big, gorgeous cats with huge feet who lie around all day in the sun but spring into action without notice to rip the steaks off an innocent grazing zebra.

I was 25 when I got my stepkids. Aaron was 15 and Rachel was 12. Luckily, neither kid realized what a small difference in age there was between us (and I didn't tell them!). There was one advantage of being so close in age: I was still fairly tuned in to the teenage psyche. I still remembered clearly what being a teenager was like.

If you're older than I was, time has probably taken its toll and you may not have a clue about whether your teenage stepkid is "normal" or not. Talk to other parents. Read some books. Educate yourself. In the following sections, I've included a few details about what to expect. But I feel I gotta add this major disclaimer: Because all human beings go through adolescence, and because human beings vary widely, I'm generalizing. Take what applies and move on. I'm only suggesting possibilities here.

When Does It All Begin?

Adolescence is a combination of physical and social shifts that begins for different kids at different times and in different orders, depending upon the person. When my husband Bill was 13, he grew 12 inches, from 5 to 6 feet, in three months. His legs stretched like silly putty, and his point of view literally altered drastically. (While his body raised an octave, his larynx stayed behind in the same physical location, changing him from a soprano to a baritone.) My physical transformation from girl to woman seemed as sudden to me, from "Flatso" to "Va va va voom!" over the course of a summer.

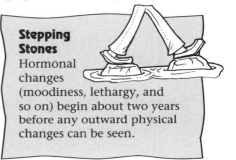

Stepping Stones
Hormonal changes (moodiness, lethargy, and so on) begin about two years before any outward physical changes can be seen.

It's not always that drastic (Bill and I share a flair for the dramatic, even in puberty), but for every adolescent, the shift from child's body to adult's body is profound, affecting mind, mood, and self-definition. "Who am I? What kind of person am I going to be?" the adolescent asks, and then tries to find out, in all sorts of ways.

Pushy and Rebellious

Teenagers (and preteens) are rebellious and reactive, and they do exactly the opposite of what they are told. This is a normal and essential part of growing up and becoming a free-thinking, self-reliant adult. It's their job to establish their own identity and to separate from their parents. It's not a pleasant job, but somebody's gotta do it. (Ironically, they sometimes act the least free-thinking and self-reliant just as they are asking most for more independence.)

While your stepteen strains against the reins of authority (that's you and your partner), your challenge is to remain calm. Understanding the teen's job description helps. When he pushes you away, he's not deliberately hurting your feelings. It also helps to understand what "normal" rebellion looks like so you can help prevent (or deal with) the more destructive and self-destructive forms. Some recommended readings are listed in Appendix A, and there's a public library in your neighborhood. Some high schools have parent education nights that can truly help.

Master of Disguises

One day she's a biker chick, the next a prissy cheerleader. A week later her hair is bleached and dyed green, she's got pierces in the oddest places, and she's asking permission to get branded (ouch!). Watch closely. If the identity changes are manifested on things that can change (like clothes and hair), you probably don't have to worry. It's a peer thing. (Now's the time to haul out your old high school yearbook and look at how bizarre and awful you and your chic friends truly looked.) The time to worry is when the style is irrevocable (branding and tattoos won't wash off when Junior wants to look like a young stockbroker), or when the disguise seems more than skin deep (a bubbly kid changing into a morose one, a quiet one becoming hyper-energetic, or wild fluctuations in weight or other odd behavior shifts).

I Kid You Not!

About 35 percent of all American teenagers have a stepfamily.

Social Butterfly, Lone Wolf, and Clinging Vine

All teens, step or not, would rather be with friends than with a parent figure. With custody issues and visitation battles, sometimes an essential is left out of the picture: the fact that teens often don't want to hang out with any family that much. Teenagers are social beasts. They want to be with their friends. They *need* to hang out with their friends—it's part of establishing their own identities.

Stepping Stones
Kids need to feel like part of a group. Young adolescents assert their independence and uniqueness by trying to look and act exactly the same as all the other kids. Don't worry about this sheeplike behavior. Most people grow out of it, and the older people get, the more individualistic they become.

Much of the distance you'll feel from a stepteen has little to do with whether he likes you. He wants to hang out with his buddies not because he has something against your very presence, but because, for many teens, too much time away from friends verges on physically painful. Peers matter. As stepparent to a teen, be sensitive to his social needs. Try not to push for too much family togetherness. And lay off the guilt trips about it—they won't help.

At the same time, stepfamily life may affect the teen's quest for independence. It's hard to rebel against your parents when you feel insecure about their love or worry about how much you matter to them (kids often feel as though they're in competition with their stepparents for their parent's attention). A teen may end up clinging to a parent as tightly as a limpet clings to a sea-swept rock.

The Hormone Years

Teenagers are very sexual beings. They think about sex and romance all the time. Freshly minted hormones course through their veins. Plus (and this is the annoying part), they tend to think that they invented sex, that you are an old fogy who did it a few times maybe and never do it anymore. Or they flirt with trouble—and you. Teenagers and preteens are a mass of roiling hormones, and it's common to find some of that hormonal energy directed at you. Your new, sexually supercharged relationship with your partner may be adding to the cause; the kids may just be more aware of sexual energy.

Teens often become sexually provocative. If you find your stepdaughter walking around the house in a tight bikini or landing in your lap for a neck massage, or if your teenage stepson lifts weights around you in a muscle shirt, you may find yourself reacting on a physical level. You are the adult here; you must resist this energy. It might help to make your partner aware of flirtatious behavior you're seeing. The child should not be reprimanded, but it is important for the lines of communication to remain open.

It's very common for a parent who is attracted to a stepchild to be overly strict. You may also find that you are uncomfortable being physically affectionate with a teen or preteen stepchild, or that the child is uncomfortable with you. If hugs and embraces are uncomfortable, you can instead be affectionate and loving with your words and your smiles.

I Kid You Not!

In Eugene O'Neill's *Desire Under the Elms*, a stepmother and her stepson have a passionate affair. She gets pregnant, the child is born, and she passes it off as her husband's. When the truth comes out, she murders the baby. It's hot, it's steamy, it's taboo, it's destructive, and it's great theater. But who needs that in real life?

Moody, Moody, Moody!

Respect the moods of a teen. Can you imagine it? Do you remember it? It's hard being a teenager. Not only is your body betraying you by sprouting all this hair and odd fleshy bumps, but there's school and work pressure, an increased understanding of the world and what terrible shape it's in, and all that pressure of what you're going to do with the rest of your life. If all teens have it bad (and all teens do), the stepteen has an added stress: a new stepfamily to get used to. A moody teenager needs room to simply exist, and he also needs you to offer to talk about it. Do some active listening, but don't push.

Teenagers need privacy: time alone, private space, and private thoughts. Respect this need and don't pry. Knock on a closed door (and wait for an answer) before entering. Don't ever read a kid's journal. You'll be sorry, and if you're found out, you will break the trust between the two of you forever and ever and ever.

Don't Be Wicked
Allowing privacy doesn't mean absolving yourself of responsibility. Maintain an active interest in your teen's life, but do it by creating the space for him to come to you. Just don't pry.

133

The "I Don't Care" Adolescent

Stepping Stones
If you have something to talk about with your stepteen, save it for an appropriate time. What makes the time appropriate? When the teen is ready. You can get a teen ready for a "big talk" by making an appointment first. And make the offer at least somewhat attractive. "Janine, can we have a chat after dinner? We'll talk over hot chocolate, okay?"

Teenagers define cool. The slouch, the poker face, and the lazy, slacking attitude. Do you think they really don't care? (You're wrong. They care desperately. It's an act.) The stepparent who is feeling insecure can easily take the nonchalance of the average teen as rejection of the highest degree.

Inconsiderate? You Bet

Your stepteen may not show much interest in getting to know you, the step. All kids tend to ignore grownups (you read about this in Chapter 11, "It's the Children!"), but you may simply not matter that much to your stepteen. Hey, it wasn't up to her that her parent found and fell in love with you. Friends come first, second, and third for the adolescent. A parent comes fourth. How does it feel to be in fifth place? Now think back to your own teen years. It's your friends you remember most, right?

Defender of Truth

Teenagers have built-in b.s. detectors and no tolerance for phoniness or hypocrisy. Don't try to be somebody you aren't. You'll be seen through and skewered with disdain. Teens are notorious for scoffing at adults who dress too "young," for example.

The Humiliation Factor

All parents, not just stepparents, are embarrassing. You're so uncool. Your clothes are so dorky. Need I continue? Try not to feel too insulted when your stepteen makes you drop her off around the corner from her rendezvous spot because you're driving a brown, functional Taurus instead of a totally cherry '63 Mustang.

Sweet, Thoughtful, Supportive

Really? Absolutely.

Teens *do* get a bad rap. These years are a time of great growth and exploration. You, as a stepparent, get a front row seat watching one of the greatest shows on earth—presto, change-o—the ugly ducking becomes a swan! It's an interactive show, too. You get to participate! You'll have fun, you'll have moments of great satisfaction, and you'll catch those looks of affection and gratitude.

Adolescent Child of Divorce

Divorce is traumatic for the whole family. How do teens, in particular, react? After it's over, after the re-partnering, now that you are in the picture, what's the best living situation for your stepteen?

"You're Getting a WHAT?"

Adolescents are egocentric, and their initial reactions to their parents' divorce is to feel that the divorce is something that's being done to them. Parents should expect an extreme response (on the other hand, a teenager's response to everything tends to be extreme!). A teen may experience and express anger, sadness, regression, denial, and he may act out (taking risks, coming home late). Experts suggest getting outside help when an intense reaction lasts more than two months or is extreme or dangerous, such as deep depression, running away, or displaying abusive behavior.

Step-Speak
Regression means reverting to childish, immature behavior, usually due to emotional distress of some sort.

"Where Am I Gonna Live?"

Friends matter. Stability matters, too, and adolescents tend to do best when their outside life is disturbed as little as possible. Look at it this way: A teenager's life is composed of family, school, social life, and activities. Disrupting the family is bad enough, but disrupting it all at once (moving to another home, community, and school) can be very hard on a teenager. Look, even her body is new right now.

Kids also differ in their needs. My stepson Aaron didn't mind doing the 60-mile bus journey twice a week between his mom's house and ours (he said it gave him time to think), but it was hell for 14-year-old Rachel, whose school and friends were near her mom's house, who hates buses, and whose idea of traveling light is one jumbo suitcase, plus a special pillow and a small backpack. (In later years, Rachel lived with us full-time while she finished college, so it all evened out.)

Here are a few suggestions:

➤ Try to keep a teen's exterior life as stable as possible during the times of breakup and re-partnering.

➤ Be objective, if you can, about which parent would be best for the teen to live with during this big time of change. Consider who is better able to give supervision, attention, and physical space to the teenager. Which parent's lifestyle is more appropriate?

➤ A teenager should definitely have input into where she'll live, but don't put her on the spot by making her choose between your households. Loyalty issues can tear a teen apart. If she expresses a preference, listen. (Yes, even if she wants to go live with that old goat of a dad instead of living in peace and prosperity with you and her biomom.)

➤ Try not to take it personally if the other household is "chosen." He's going to be your stepson for many years to come, and all relationships have different seasons. Think long-term. Perhaps your household's turn will come (and perhaps sooner than you think).

Moving In with the Other Bioparent

It's fairly common for a kid who has lived primarily with one parent for years to want to change households and live with the other parent. Part of this is the adolescent's quest for identity and trying on new roles and new lifestyles. Part of it may be that it's not always easy for a teen and a teen's parents to get along. Household shifting is especially common when a boy has been living with his mom and wants to be in closer contact with his dad, a male role model. As a stepparent, be prepared for a sudden change in your lifestyle. You may have a live-in stepkid with little notice, or all at once you may find yourself with far less child in your daily life.

Plunging into Stepparenting

Are you a new, previously childless stepparent? Then you're in for a bit of a shock. Besides getting used to the parental role, you've got some particular adjustments to make. The teen years are not the most serene years of life (they are rather intense), and teens don't suffer or enjoy in silence.

Stepparent = Scapegoat

Okay Stepparent, here's the bad news. Stepparenting an adolescent often means that you, not your partner, will get the brunt of the teen's anger and rebellion. Why? What did you do in this lifetime to deserve such a fate? Probably nothing. Adolescents are often cruel beasts who say and do mean things. No, the values of goodness, kindness, and compassion are not gone forever, but they're hiding for a few years.

"But why me?" you wail. Here are a few reasons why you, and not your partner, suddenly look so wicked, no matter what you do:

➤ Parents are the bane of all teenagers, and stepparents are just more parents to answer to. That's true even if you are utterly hands-off in terms of discipline (not a bad idea, by the way, as I'll explain a little later on).

➤ Your stepteen has already lost one family. Insecurities being what they are, she's frightened of expressing anger toward her bioparents, frightened that she might lose them, too. Anger at her parents is thereby displaced onto you. (Aren't you lucky!)

➤ Your stepteen fears that he's losing his bioparent to you, the new partner. He goes into attack mode to protect his "property."

➤ Challenging authority is an adolescent's job, and you're such an easy target. The standard-issue teenager is very wise. She's old enough to know you are insecure. She sniffs your fear and moves in for the kill.

I Kid You Not!

You don't necessarily love your teen stepchildren, and the reverse may also be true. That's okay. You're aiming for mutual respect. But teenagers are known for their lack of respect, and this makes life hard. How can you respect them when they are treating you so badly? Here's where looking for positive intent (think back to Chapter 11, "It's the Children!") comes in again. Here's also where you need to step out, buy some chocolate or sushi, have a massage, and take care of yourself.

Boys 'n' Girls

Which are more challenging: teen boys or girls?

According to some people who study such things, teen girls and stepmothers tend to have the hardest time of it. (Keep in mind that I'm dealing, once again, in gross generalities.) Other experts say that teen girls are particularly hard on their stepdads. There's the sexual thing (see previous section), there are issues of authority, and there's a fear that they're being replaced as Mom's confidante by the stepdad.

Teen boys have it less hard with stepmothers, but they often feel very ambivalent about stepfathers. At this age, a boy is concerned with identifying with his father, and the stepfather confuses matters. The boy doesn't always know how to react to him.

Scrutinized!!!

Living with teenagers is strange. They don't notice the wet towels they drop on the floor or the dishes they leave in the sink, but they're keenly aware of every phone call you make and how you organize your desk. You may think they don't see you, yet they are noticing every little twist of how you live.

Cyndi's teenage stepdaughter and stepson live with her half the time. She warns stepparents to give up any sense of privacy. "Believe me," she says, "they'll know what kind of birth control you use. They'll probably tell their mom, who's going to just eat it up. They'll never tell you anything about *her* life, though."

Dealing with Your Adolescent Stepchild

You can make life around your household easier if you try the following:

➤ Don't take it personally. Think of your stepteen as somebody who is hormonally impaired (he is!). Try to be tolerant, and give it time.

➤ Don't try to compare or compete with the other bioparent. Be more yourself than you've ever been in your life.

➤ Spend time alone with your stepteen doing activities that interest you both.

➤ Be neutral about your partner's ex. If provoked by the stepteen about him or her, take five deep breaths and take the high road. ("We're very different people. I'm glad you have both of our influences in your life.")

➤ Don't push for affection, attention, or response.

Encourage your partner to follow these steps:

➤ Reassure his kid that he'll never abandon her emotionally or physically, and that nobody (meaning you) will ever come between the two of them.

➤ Spend time alone with his kids doing things they used to do, such as talking together and playing games.

➤ Occasionally side with the kids against you (ouch) and, also occasionally, let you and your stepchild side with each other. (United fronts are important, but let it be a front, not a stone wall.)

Your partner should let you and your stepchild work out your own disagreements (boy, this can be hard). Both of you can help matters by following these pointers:

➤ Be nice. Your stepchild is sensitive in his new body and hormone-laden mind. Try not to nag. Work with him, perhaps at a Family Meeting (see Chapter 13, "Family Talk") to find ways to get information across. Write notes. Leave simple messages on the answering machine ("James, the garbage man comes on Wednesday, so please take out the trash."). In *How to Talk So Kids Will Listen and Listen So Kids Will Talk*, Adele Faber and Elaine Mazlish suggest using very short communications: "James, Garbage!"

➤ Let Go. You're looking for balance here, giving her more autonomy while remaining involved in her life. She needs room, but she also needs guidance and interest.

➤ Show you care. He'll treat you with nonchalance, but you show you care anyway. Don't be put off by his seeming indifference. "Kill 'em with kindness," is what I say!

➤ Be aware of transitional periods. The coming-and-going transitions can be worse with teenagers than with younger kids, simply because they tend to be moodier anyway. Give them time and space to adjust.

Discipline and the Stepteen

Adolescents thrive on the balance of caring and positive discipline, but things are complicated by this step business. It usually takes a long time for a teenager to respect a step's authority enough to do what you ask her to do.

➤ Go slow. Build rapport before asserting your authority. (Review the Steps to Authority in Chapter 9, "New Family Structures.")

➤ Talk about it. Verbal communication is the most important aspect of discipline. (Chapter 13, "Family Talk," is all about family communication.)

➤ Hands off! If it needs to be handled, let the bioparent do it. Do you really think any self-respecting stepteen will listen to *you*? Discipline should always be lighter for teenagers than for younger kids. Allow consequences to be as natural as possible; let them demonstrate what they've learned.

➤ No scolding. Voicing disapproval just doesn't work. Saying, "You're gonna flunk chemistry if you don't study" may be taken as a challenge. He's not dumb; he knows very well what will happen if he doesn't study. Don't make him prove it to you. Show him the respect of letting him make his own decisions, and live with the consequences (so long as nobody is in physical danger).

The World's Dangers

Kids are exposed to temptations of sex, drugs, and alcohol everywhere, at almost all ages. By the time your stepkid is 13, she's already making decisions about becoming involved with chemical substances. Sex rears its head early, too. If you're not used to teenagers, it may shock you what they are like, what they are into, and what they are exposed to. My primary two words of advice? Be knowledgeable. Be knowledgeable about the risks and dangers. Be knowledgeable about the "norms." Check Appendix A for some excellent books. In Chapter 21, "Stepfamilies in Crisis," we'll talk about what to do if things are really bad and you need some help for your stepteen, for your stepfamily, or for yourself.

"You're Having a What? Gross!"

For a teenager between the ages of 13 and 17, the idea of having a pregnant mother or stepmother is just about enough to make him curl up and die with embarrassment. Sex feels like his domain (even if he isn't doing it, he sure is thinking about it). Your stepchild doesn't want to know that you are having sex. The idea is repulsive, horrifying, humiliating, and oddly titillating (and that there is some titillation makes it feel even more uncomfortable!).

Unfortunately for your sensitive stepchild, remarriages are often more sexually charged than first marriages, especially at first. And sex is harder to ignore. In his book *You and Your Adolescent*, Laurence Steinberg says, "When parents stay married, adolescents tend to write off their expressions of physical intimacy as affection. When parents are single and dating, this self-deception is more difficult." When there's a pregnancy, this difficulty changes to impossibility.

There's more on general reactions to a parent or stepparent's pregnancy and to the new baby in Chapter 25, "His, Hers, OURS?," but here are some specific hints for teens:

Step-Speak
Stepsiblings are related to each other only by marriage. When parents of unrelated children marry, the children become stepsiblings. There's no biological relationship between stepsiblings. Half siblings share one biological parent, either a mother or a father.

➤ Look for the positive intent. When 14-year-old Ramona screams, "You're just as bad as a cow!" upon hearing of the upcoming little wonder, look beneath the cruel words to hear the fear of displacement and anxiety about sex. (It doesn't make it okay for her to behave like that, but it may make it easier for you to cope with her reaction.)

➤ Don't automatically limit your stepchild's involvement. Willa's 14-year-old stepson Barry attended childbirth classes with her and her husband Hank, paced with her up and down the hallways during her labor and, though at the last minute he felt too squeamish to watch the delivery, was one of the first people to hold baby Brianna.

➤ Encourage them to be involved in their baby brother or sister's life, but don't assume that they'll automatically baby-sit.

➤ A new baby in a parent's life when a teen is already struggling with separation issues may make her feel even more displaced. Think about holding a special ceremony to mark a stepchild's entry (or re-entry) into the world of being a sibling. A teenager may laugh when you bring it up, but it will matter to her. She'll feel cared for and thought of.

I Kid You Not!

When my daughter Annie was 3, her half sister Rachel was living with us. Every week, Annie and Rachel had a "sister night," an evening where Rachel cooked dinner for the two of them (while Bill and I played backgammon at a local café). Two years after Rachel moved out, Annie still misses their evenings together.

Stepteen Advantages

There can be some wonderful advantages to being the stepparent of a teenager. Teens desperately need adult allies who aren't their bioparents. If you play your cards right, you can be the confidante, the "other" grown-up, the understanding one when the bioparents don't have a clue. The same teenager who is so beastly to parents that they want to turn her in for a new model often shows her very real charm, enthusiasm, compassion, and fresh view of life to other adults. And that may very well be you.

The Least You Need to Know

➤ Teens get a bad rap.

➤ Your stepteen is not necessarily going to be more messed up than other teenagers.

➤ Sexual energy between teenagers and stepparents is common—and dangerous. Be aware!

➤ Teenagers may act uncaring, but that's rarely how they really feel.

➤ Understanding the sexual and substance abuse risks your stepteen faces is essential.

➤ Teens need adult allies. You can be one.

Family Talk

Communication defines who we are. Without it, relationships dissolve, cities fall (and so do bombs), and everything ends up as rubble.

The stepfamily is often filled with resistance, and sometimes it feels as though everybody resents everybody else. The cure? Time and communication. Time will take care of itself (we all know that there's no stopping it), but you must always work on communication. Here's the down and dirty, the nitty-gritty, the core of it all: Stepfamily life is *hard*, and without effective communication, you won't all make it through intact. Stepfamilies are built on the power of communication.

This chapter discusses communication strategies within the family: the way you communicate daily, ways to hold a family meeting to resolve larger issues, and how to problem-solve when things get really rough.

Communicating with Children

Stepkids! Talk to them wrong and they'll shut you off. How *do* you get it through their thick skulls? Effective communication involves talking *with* your stepkids, not *to* them. Easier said than done, huh? Here are a few tips:

Stepping Stones
Honest communication is the *only* policy when it comes to the stepfamily. Withdrawing in an attempt to be self-protective will backfire on you. The family will continue its biological bond, and you'll be left out in the cold.

Don't Be Wicked
Don't lecture! I guarantee that if you shake your finger at a child, they will *not* hear what you are saying. Kids are deaf to stories with a moral. Save your breath.

➤ **Lose the lectures**   Nobody wants advice. And don't nag! The minute you start getting "that tone" in your voice, you become inaudible. From a long distance way off in his head, your child sees your mouth moving, with nothing audible coming out.

➤ **Tell the truth**   Remember that childhood b.s. meter! Truth-telling with kids doesn't mean confessing all, but it does mean not lying.

➤ **Use active listening**   Remember that active listening means listening to and trying to understand the child's thoughts *and* feelings. Listen silently and then paraphrase, say back again as closely as possible *without interpretation* what has been said.

➤ **Don't let your disagreements escalate**   Try to keep to the specifics. Nothing turns a kid's brain off worse than "You always…" or "You never…." If accusations escalate, don't play. Try taking a five-minute break.

➤ **Cool it with the general criticism**   It doesn't help, and it can be very damaging.

➤ **Never set a kid up to be a liar**   Forget the rhetorical questions: "Did you break my umbrella?"

➤ **Use "I" statements**   Saying, "I feel…" is more effective than saying, "You make me feel…." (You'll read more about "I" statements in a moment.)

Daily Communication

A stepfamily's identity is built slowly, through effective communication and shared experiences. Communication can happen in family meetings (and we'll go into those later), but primarily it happens every day, each time family members interact with each other. As a stepparent, your daily communications with your stepkids should involve three points:

➤ Communicate respect

➤ Communicate affection

➤ Communicate your expectations and goals

Communicate Respect

It's simple: You gain your stepkids' respect by showing them respect. People respond to being treated well, and kids learn by imitation. When you *model* respectful behavior, they *learn* appropriate modes of behavior. You can communicate your respect for a child's body and personal space, temperament, privacy, needs, and opinions by listening to them, observing carefully, and taking them seriously.

Sometimes it's hard for stepparents to listen to a child. It takes energy, and if you are feeling resentful of the emotional space a stepchild takes up in your life, you may not want to consider his needs. But paying respect to your stepchild will *lessen* the energy drain you feel. When a child (or anybody, for that matter) feels respected, he returns your efforts twofold.

Respect is *not* a hands-off policy (the child still needs your guidance), nor does it mean agreeing with the child's every opinion, belief, or action. Respect is an acknowledgment that a child's feelings and beliefs are valid. Respect is a starting place.

Communicate Affection

Communication is not just what you say; it's also how you say it, and it involves your body language. Not all people are comfortable expressing their deepest thoughts and emotions with words. Even for those who are, words are not always enough. A kiss, a rumpled head, a smile across the room, a wink when things are rough—nonverbal affection is just as important as beginning every sentence with an "I" statement or writing your Family Values and posting them in the kitchen (both of these are covered later). Being affectionate with your stepkids shows in a very tactile way that you care about them.

Affection doesn't always involve touching. You may not be a naturally "touchy" person. Little kids have a biological *need* for physical affection, but physical affection doesn't always feel natural in a stepfamily, nor is it always appropriate. (Older kids need physical affection, too, but not necessarily from you.)

If your stepchildren are preteens or teenagers, hormonal issues may come up. Incest taboos are not as strong in stepfamilies, and without the biological bond or long-term experience of raising a particular child, sexual attraction may make hugs and back rubs inappropriate or even dangerous (see more about this in Chapter 21, "Stepfamilies in Crisis"). Yet affection and nonverbal communication are *not* necessarily tied to physical contact. So much is communicated by the way you look at a child (and by how you say things).

Stepping Stones
Family identity is built through shared experiences. Eating together every day, or almost every day, sets up an automatic forum for communicating as a family.

Whether your stepkids are little or big, it's important to have some kinds of nonverbal communication with them. Talk together about how much physical affection you all feel comfortable with.

Communicate Your Expectations and Goals

Preconceived expectations of what stepfamily life should be like are never helpful. Once the new stepfamily has formed, however, the kids need to know what they can expect in terms of family structure, and they need to know what kinds of behaviors are acceptable and expected of them. Kids need to understand these three points:

Stepping Stones
Organization and structure within a family make children feel more secure.

➤ **Family expectations**   These are moral- and value-based expectations about how people in the family should behave and treat each other.

➤ **Personal expectations**   These are achievement-based expectations that kids and adults have, such as goals and expectations for academic, athletic, and developmental growth.

➤ **Relationship expectations**   These are socially based expectations: "I expect you and your stepsister to cooperate when you are cleaning up your room."

Defining Family Expectations and Goals

Set your sights on successful goals, which should be specific rather than vague and general. If your goals are, "I want this family to get along, be happy, and work hard," you risk disappointing yourself and the rest of the family. These goals are *way* too vague. How can you measure your progress? How can you even begin? It all feels completely overwhelming!

Family goals also need to be realistic. Start small, and start with a specific goal you *know* you'll be able to reach, like, "Let's get through dinner without arguing, and all clean up together." Now you'll have a chance at success.

Keep your goals limited in number. Keep them explicit—these are things to discuss with the entire family. Also make sure that everybody shares an understanding of the family goals; try some active listening to make sure that you're all on the same page.

Defining the Family Values

Part of defining your expectations and goals, whether personal or for the family, is understanding your values. You probably have at least a vague sense of your values and how they fit into your image of ideal stepfamily life. But have you written them down? Have you clearly communicated them? Bet not. Here's how to do so:

Make a List of Values

Hey, you're not doing this alone: This is a family activity that works best when it includes everybody. Defining the Family Values is best done, or at least begun, during a family meeting (hold your horses, we're getting there!).

The Family Values aren't so much a set of specifics ("Put the toilet seat down when you are done") as they are a set of behavior guidelines that reflect the underlying values ("We listen to everybody's opinion"). The list of Family Values is sort of like a mission statement that states explicitly how you (the family) expect family members to behave.

Here are some questions (from *Mom's Guide to Disciplining Your Child*, by Vicki Poretta and Ericka Lutz) to talk about as you begin developing your own Family Values list:

➤ How do I like people to treat me?

➤ What's the best way to let somebody know how I feel?

➤ Is it okay to hit somebody when I'm angry?

➤ How do I like my things to be treated?

➤ What do I feel are important manners?

➤ When we have a fight, what kind of behavior is okay with me, and what kind of behavior don't I like?

As you chat, jot the answers down and begin forming your list. The values you write should be nonspecific enough to apply to *everybody*. Make sure there are not *too* many values. If you keep them basic, you'll do fine. When you're done, you can post the list on the refrigerator, or next to the toilet—somewhere where everybody will see them on a regular basis.

In her book, *Positive Parenting from A to Z*, Karen Renshaw Joslin recommends the following four values:

1. We use words to tell others how we feel. We do not name-call or use bad language.

2. We do not hurt others physically or emotionally.

3. We do not hurt each other's property or our own.

4. We work to get out of a problem, not stay in it.

Use "I" Statements

Stepfamily relationships are very delicate. When you're talking about serious stuff in a stepfamily, you have to be careful to strike the right tone, or you risk putting your stepchild (or your mate) on the defensive. There's a real danger in beginning your statements with the word "You." You'll appear to be blaming, and you'll give the impression that you think only *your* perceptions are correct.

You will get nowhere with your stepkids when you begin sounding accusatory. Blaming and self-righteousness (or the appearance of them) are not good places to begin a dialog. You also risk escalating negative feelings—if you start with a "You" statement and they come back with a "You" statement, then it's "You," "You," "You!" all the way to misery.

Step-Speak

An *"I" statement* is a statement about your feelings, views, needs, likes, or dislikes that begins with the word "I." "I" statements tell the listener that you're speaking from your own point of view.

On the other hand, when you begin a statement about your perceptions, feelings, or preferences with the word "I," your family *can* listen because you don't seem accusatory, and you're obviously speaking only from your own point of view. Using "I" statements is humble—it implies that you're willing to at least *hear* another opinion or perception. Using "I" statements will also help you to clarify your own perceptions, feelings, and preferences. The wonderful thing about "I" statements is that they don't call special attention to themselves. You don't have to announce that you are using a new communication technique—just try and watch the results.

Don't Judge

Here's a warning: Beware of that wolf in sheep's clothing—the lowly judgment parading as an "I" statement. "I" statements are designed to describe your feelings, not your opinions. If you can change the word "feel" to "think" in your "I" statement and have it make sense, you are *judging:* "When you ignore me when I ask you to set the table, I feel that you're a spoiled little brat." Whoa, Nellie! Try again: "When you don't respond to me when I ask you to set the table, I feel disregarded and angry."

Family Meetings

Daily communication is essential, but it's also helpful for a stepfamily to have a regular forum for discussing family issues. Enter the Family Meeting!

A family meeting is a time for the entire stepfamily to meet and chat about family matters. They work best when they happen on a regular basis, such as once a week or twice a month. (I know, scheduling is gonna be hard, but it only works if everybody is included.) Holding them frequently reduces some of the stress people might feel if these meetings only occurred in times of terrible crisis. Family meetings are not just for the heavy "issues" stuff. Use them to schedule chores and vacations, share jokes, applaud achievements, and play games. They aren't just important for families where the kids live in full-time; they can actually *help* visiting stepkids feel included, and they can help build family identity.

Family meetings should not be grim events with Junior sulking on the couch and the adults lecturing. Here's an opportunity for you to practice your active listening and "I" statements. Here's also an opportunity to resolve conflict through problem-solving activities (more on this later).

Keep family meetings short, no longer than an hour. Keeping them brief will assure that nobody loses focus and interest, and you might have a better chance of actually finding times to meet when everybody is around. Here are some suggestions:

➤ You can have a family meeting in a family as small as three and as many as…well, how many have ya got?

➤ Trade off as facilitator. Even an 8-year-old can cofacilitate to make sure the meeting goes smoothly, that all agenda items are covered, and that nobody is cut off as he or she speaks.

➤ Use a modified democracy or a consensus for decision making (refer back to Chapter 6, "Building a Viable Stepfamily," if you need a refresher).

➤ Plan the agenda in advance. Post a list in an easily accessible place (how about near the family values list?) so that everybody can write down their concerns and ideas ahead of time.

➤ Focus on the positive. Enjoy each other—how often do you all get to sit down in a room together? Because feelings in stepfamilies tend to run hot, family meetings run the risk of "going negative" and turning into mud-slinging, hot-headed scream sessions. Keep the "I" statements coming. Schedule in a time to discuss the wonderful elements of stepfamily life. Haul out the cards and play a few hands of gin or poker. Do the Hokey Pokey and turn yourself around…that's what it's all about!

Problem-Solving

Daily communication and family meetings are vital tools to keep your stepfamily running smoothly, but what do you do when there is…(cue the shark music)…conflict?!

Ah, conflict. As we all know, stepfamilies are full of it. In the following list, I'll lead you through a basic five-part approach to resolving interfamily struggles.

Before you begin your problem-solving, let's briefly explore a few general conflict-resolution approaches:

➤ The unilateral adult as Big Boss, "because I say so" approach. Many of us are guilty of at least occasionally falling into this trap. It might work for a moment, but the problem isn't really resolved—it's just been overruled. Beware of the ugly overrule! Those overruled issues are gonna come back when you least expect them, and they'll bring along their aunts, uncles, and Big Uncle Bubba.

➤ The "Anything you say, L'il Darlin'" approach, where the adults roll over and play dead while the kids run wild. If you let this happen, you're not exactly going to be filled with self-respect and happiness. ("Boys and girls, can you say *re-sent-ment?*")

➤ The "You give a little, I'll give a little, let's make a deal!" approach. This is otherwise known as *compromising*. 'It ain't bad, but it's sort of like nonfat sour cream: It doesn't *quite* hit the spot.

➤ The "win-win, come on, everybody, get happy" approach that involves collaboration and cooperation. When you problem-solve, you seek a solution that may not be initially obvious. Problem-solving has some real bonuses in terms of training people how to get along in the world. It teaches respect and empathy, it empowers a child by using her as a collaborator in solving her own problems, and it teaches her how to think through problems, apply logic, come up with solutions, and act respectfully and responsibly.

A Problem-Solving Approach

You can problem-solve in family meetings or one-on-one. Here's how to do it:

Step 1: Define the Problem

"Wassup?" (In this example, the stepchild is having a problem with you, the stepparent. If you're having the problem with Sarah, you can try to have her do active listening, or you can skip to Step 3.)

Stepping Stones
Kids are smart. If you listen hard enough, they may just give you the answers both you and they need.

Say the issue is Sarah's desire to hang out with her friends on weekends instead of coming to visit you. Use active listening. When you paraphrase what Sarah has said, state her feelings as well as her words. Give her room to correct you and amplify. Keep cool! Don't jump in with judgment ("I feel so rejected!"), criticism ("You teenagers are all alike!"), analysis ("This seems to be a case of misplaced hostility"), or advice ("You should…").

Step 2: Empathize

Let Sarah understand that you "get" her problem and know how she feels. This step isn't about you, though, so keep it short: "I used to hate having to go visit my grandma in the nursing home every weekend, especially when my friends had regular Sunday lunches at the pizza parlor."

Step 3: Say What You Think and Feel

Use "I" statements: "Sarah, when you don't come to visit us, I feel sad because I miss you, and I worry that our special time as a family is being compromised. I'm also concerned that you won't be participating in family responsibilities." Whatever you do, don't blame Sarah: "You're destroying our family!" If you express yourself in a clear, respectful way,

Sarah might begin to understand your perspective. As you begin to look for solutions, try not to compromise, give in, or exert your own mighty will.

Step 4: Brainstorm for Possible Solutions

Brainstorming is a way to produce lots of creative ideas in a short time. Your creative brainstorming session may very well provide a surprising—and pleasing—solution. Here are the brainstorming rules and procedures (these were inspired and adapted from William Sonnenschein's book, *Workforce Diversity*):

➤ Have one person write down all the ideas generated. This works best if it's on a chalkboard or a white board so that everybody can see what's been written down.

➤ You can start by taking turns, but don't stick to such formality for too long. Jump in! Get excited! Generate as *many* ideas as possible. Let the juices flow!

➤ Try to stay away from the words and phrases "should," "I would," "I think," and "If you ask me."

➤ No judgments or idea rejection is allowed. This is a free-for-all, sometimes silly time: "Sarah should be forced to come over, and be locked in her room!" "Sarah can use her allowance to hire a maid to do her chores!" "Let's have the whole crew of kids visit on weekends; they can sleep in my room, and I'll go to a motel!" "Sarah should drop out of school and visit on Tuesdays!" Often the silliest, most ridiculous, most unfeasible concept leads to brilliance.

➤ Let one idea generate another. ("Maybe she can go to school here and stay with her mother on weekends!" "Yeah, and then we don't have to share a room anymore!")

➤ Stop. Read what you've got. Now get real—cross out the ones that don't work, and combine the similar ideas.

➤ Here's the serious part: Evaluate, prioritize, and decide on the ideas you have left.

➤ After you evaluate the brainstorming ideas, agree on a trial solution. Say you've decided: "Sarah can skip every other weekend and arrive early on the next Friday, but she's gotta do her Sunday chores on the Sundays she's here and trade with Lucy on dishwashing duty on the Fridays she's here." *Write it down.*

You, the adults, may have arrived at the same conclusion or option without the brainstorming session, but including the whole family (or at least Sarah) assures that everybody understands the decision and is more likely to agree with it.

Step 5: Act On It

Once you've decided on a solution, put it into play. ("I'll call Sarah's mom to make sure this will work." Then follow up. Check back in after a while, perhaps at the next family meeting, to see how it's working. If it isn't, maybe you need to do the problem-solving process again.

The Least You Need to Know

➤ Stepfamily communication happens every day, each time you interact with each other.

➤ You'll gain your stepkids' respect and affection by showing them respect and affection.

➤ Explicitly define your family goals, expectations, and values.

➤ "I" statements are a nonthreatening way of getting your feelings heard.

➤ Family meetings are an essential communication tool for the stepfamily.

➤ When you problem-solve together, everybody wins.

Part 3
Special Stepparenting Challenges

It's true, stepparenting is not always easy. In fact, sometimes it feels nothing but hard. This section of the book is designed to hold your hand through the most challenging parts.

Here you'll find chapters on discipline, visitation, and dealing with your partner's horrible, despicable, crazy ex-partner (though many of them aren't that bad).

Other chapters focus on grandparents (what do you do when they ignore your biological kids?), understanding your stepkid's communication style if he's from another culture, and surviving holiday event planning. There's a chapter on gay stepparenting, and for every stepfamily who can use some help getting through the rocky parts, there's a chapter on what to do in times of crisis.

This part is designed to help you sleep better at night, to provide real tools and resources for your problems, and to free you from worry so you can enjoy stepparenting's satisfactions.

Chapter 14

Defying the Discipline Demons

In This Chapter

➤ Developing a positive, daily approach to discipline

➤ Establishing your family's rules

➤ How to set limits and decide on consequences

➤ Understanding your role

➤ Special stepfamily discipline issues

Discipline is one of the scariest, most confusing, and biggest challenges of stepparenting. If you go into it unprepared, you may face resistance and resentment from a stepchild, struggle with a partner over ideas of appropriate behavior, feel "evil," or let your own ideas and values be overwhelmed and undermined.

How do you—and how should you—discipline somebody else's child?

This chapter is all about defying the discipline demons. You'll find out what discipline is and see how to understand what values and behaviors you want to teach the kids. Once that's squared away, then (and only then) you can decide on disciplinary approaches for both of you, both stepparent and bioparent.

Discipline Means Education

What *is* discipline, anyway? Before you decide whether to set a curfew, take away a privilege, mope in your room while the bioparent gives Janey a good talking to, or haul out the belt (*don't* do that!), let's get on the same page.

Discipline comes from the word "disciple," which means "a pupil." Check out your dictionary and you'll find that the definition of discipline includes words such as "instruction," "teaching," "learning," and "to train or develop."

Saf Lerman, author of *Parent Awareness Training*, calls discipline "a process whereby children learn to make parental standards their own. It is a slow, gradual process that extends throughout childhood. The goal of discipline is the creation of a strong and reliable conscience in a child."

Effective, daily, positive discipline accomplishes these aims:

➤ It respects the children and yourselves.

➤ It prevents problems through understanding, communication, and modeling.

➤ It sets rules and limits.

➤ It encourages and rewards proper behavior.

➤ It understands the problems—what's behind the behavior?

➤ It provides related, respectful, and reasonable responses.

Step-Speak
Discipline is the educational process of instilling values. Discipline is most effective when it incorporates encouragement, praise, trust, and respect for children with firm, wise limits. It teaches kids how to make choices and understand the consequences of their choices. When necessary, it provides related, respectful, and reasonable responses to misbehavior.

Whether you realize it or not, you first read about discipline back in Chapter 1, "Stepparenting Myths and Realities," and then in Chapter 13, "Family Talk." Communication *is* discipline; talking and listening to the child and establishing family rules are your primary disciplinary tools.

That said, the stepfamily, as we all know, has complications, and discipline often *is* more of an issue. It's not always enough just to talk about things.

When a child is shown respect and trust, and is guided with gentle correction, she'll grow to be a respectful, trustworthy individual who likes, respects, and believes in herself—and in others.

Setting Your Family's Rules and Limits

When deciding on your family's approach to discipline, ask yourselves this question: "How do we want this family to function, and what should we do about it when things break down?" In Chapter 13, "Family Talk," you read about ways to establish family values. Rules and limits are more specific than values; they're how the family values, which are general, are expressed.

In any family, but especially in a stepfamily, kids need to understand specifically what is expected of them (the rules), and they need to understand their boundaries (the limits).

I Kid You Not!

What's the difference between family values, family rules, and limits? Family values are a general set of behavior guidelines that apply to everybody in the family: "We solve our problems with words." Family rules are more specific: "Homework must be finished before TV is allowed." Limits are specific behavior boundaries for each child: "Annie cannot cross the street without a grown-up," and "Sherry must have the car back by 9:00 each night."

The Family's Rules Discussion

Here's a tool for setting your family's specific rules of behavior.

Any disciplinary approach and action works best when it comes from joint decisions made by you and your partner. If you're not consistent, the kids are going to play you off, one against the other. They also need the security of seeing the two of you as a solid unit. The couple, as the keystone of the stepfamily, should provide a *unified front*, even if you are still struggling with each other about some family matters. When two families combine, providing consistency and a unified front become even more challenging. There's more on this later.

Sit down together with your partner (yes, just the two of you for this discussion) and go over the list. You may need to talk about it in several sessions. As you work on developing your family rules, write down what you come up with. You may want to use the table here to get you started. Discuss the questions on the left, and jot down your answers and thoughts on a separate piece of paper or right in the book.

Step-Speak
A *unified front* is an agreed-upon approach to an issue. In disciplinary matters, it's best to at least have the *appearance* of total agreement.

Setting Family Rules and Limits

Rule	Notes
What kinds of household responsibilities should family members take (chores, messes, breakage, and so on)?	
What specific activities are not allowed in our house?	
What kinds of participation in family functions do we expect from the kids?	
What food- and mealtime-related behaviors are important to us?	
Who takes responsibility for pet care?	
How does our family approach money issues (allowance, savings, and earnings)?	
Are visiting stepkids welcome at any time? Do they need to call first?	
What's our policy on guests? If kids are having friends over, should they ask first?	
What are our feelings of modesty or immodesty. (Whoa! Incest taboos!)	
In what ways do we respect each other's privacy?	
Do we impose limits on the TV, computer, car, VCR, phone?	
What are our rules about homework?	
Do we believe in curfew?	
Do we have feelings about when dating should begin?	
What other dating rules do we have in our family?	
What are our feelings about teenagers being sexually active?	

Rule	Notes
What kinds of religious practices does our family participate in, and how much involvement do we expect from the kids?	
What's our policy, beliefs, and feelings about drugs, drinking, and smoking?	

Family Limits

Before you decide on a limit, make sure it passes the "limit test." Review your family values and rules, and make sure that the limit fits within your value system and agreed-upon family rules. Make the limit explicit: The child should be informed exactly what the limit is.

I Kid You Not!

What happens when you don't agree? Keep working on your approaches to misbehavior. Figure out what issues you agree upon, and acknowledge those on which you differ. Discuss these matters in the bedroom. (This part is *not* a democracy, modified or otherwise; it's a relationship issue. Do it behind closed doors.) Agree to disagree, but show unity in front of the kids.

Positive Reinforcement for Proper Behavior

Teaching discipline involves far more than establishing rules and limits (and providing consequences when they are broken)—it means encouraging the kids when they do a good job. Reward and encourage the kids every single day. Providing positive reinforcement for what a kid does *right* is not just cheerleading; it's an active approach to improving behavior, and it helps kids see and understand the value of their own positive qualities and actions.

Take time to notice when you see a kid improving, showing kindness, or trying extra hard in an area that's giving him trouble. Be specific. Specific praise helps a child begin to recognize for himself when he is doing a good job: "I watched you clear the table today without having to be asked." Or, "You really worked hard on your Spanish homework today."

Be Understanding of Misbehavior

Stepping Stones Discipline *always* includes respect and affection; otherwise, it's just punishment, and the child learns nothing. A child needs to know that you care about him, *no matter* what mistakes he makes or how angry you are at him.

To find an appropriate response to a misbehavior, it helps to first understand *why* it happened. Understanding what happened and why doesn't preclude being angry about it—it just gives you another tool to use when selecting the appropriate consequences. Use active listening to talk with a child. Look for the positive intent.

Select Appropriate Consequences

Consequences are not punishment. They are simply the result of an action. Consequences can be "natural" (if you throw your TV against the wall, it will break) or "logical" (if you consistently tell lies, soon nobody will believe you).

When you select a consequence for misbehavior, think about your goal. What do you want the child to learn? How will this particular consequence teach that? Keep consequences consistent, reasonable, related to the misbehavior, and explicit! If you can define your consequences ahead of time, you'll be in better shape to respond correctly when a misbehavior happens.

Stepping Stones Consistency isn't just for matters of limits and consequences—it's a general parenting tool. If you promise ice cream for dessert, or one extra chore for each one not done, then do it. Keep your promises, pleasant or unpleasant.

Consistent Consequences

Consequences should be applied consistently. Kids *need* consistency, especially in a stepfamily. Children who have been through a family break-up need to be able to rely on the solidity of the couple, and that includes being consistent in your responses to misbehavior and in setting limits. Unless you're going to be able to stick to the enforcement of a limit or rule, don't set one.

Reasonable and Related Consequences

Stepping Stones Consequences aren't just for misbehavior. If you do your homework and study hard, the logical consequence will be a good grade.

When a child misbehaves, the consequence assigned should be related to the misbehavior, and it needs to be reasonable: "Joanne, you're late from school; you can't take gymnastics for a year!" is a completely unreasonable and unrelated response. What does it teach? A better consequence might be, "Joanne, you're late from school again, which means you don't have time to do your homework *and* clean up your room as you promised. You may not go to gymnastics this week—you'll stay home and clean your room instead."

Explicit Consequences

When applying consequences, always state the what and the why so the child understands. It's best if you can do this in advance: "Annie, if you throw your food on the floor, I'll have a bigger mess to clean up. That's not considerate of you. If you choose to throw it on the floor, you'll clean it up, and you won't get any dessert. Dessert is a privilege, and you are abusing your privileges by giving me more work to do."

Disciplining as a Stepparent

Now that you've determined an approach to discipline and made a few decisions, the main question comes up again: What about discipline and the stepparent? What part is done by you, and what part does the bioparent handle?

As a stepparent, your approach to discipline will depend on where you are in the process. A new stepparent has a different role than a stepparent who has been part of the family for years. James K. Keshet, author of *Love and Power in the Stepfamily*, has developed a five-stage approach he calls the Stages to Stepparent Authority. I like them a lot, and with a number of changes, I've adapted them here.

Keep in mind that each family will move through these stages at a different rate. Some may happen concurrently.

1. Be an adviser.
2. Protect your rights.
3. Enforce established rules.
4. Join with your partner to set new guidelines.
5. Make spontaneous choices.

Stepparents can move through these five steps swiftly and concurrently—or (more often) it can take years to get through them.

Step 1: Be an Adviser

At first, the direct assigning of limits and consequences should probably be left up to the bioparent, and you should avoid taking a direct role. Some say it takes at least two years for kids to begin to accept discipline from a stepparent. Two years is also about the time it takes to grow a strong, trusting stepparent/stepchild relationship. Any correlation? You bet.

During this adjustment period, defer to the bioparents (yes, plural). That doesn't mean you don't have a disciplinary role. Remember that discipline is the entire process of

Don't Be Wicked
Separate the evil deed from the not-so-evil doer. The problem is not *who* the kid is; it's *what* she's doing. Look for the positive intent behind the actions (see Chapter 11, "It's the Children!").

161

Don't Be Wicked

Wait until respect and affection are built before moving in like some terrible disciplinarian—and then *don't* move in like some terrible disciplinarian!

raising a child. You can and should model good behavior, treat the kids with respect, and encourage and reward them for things they are doing well. Leave the bioparent in charge of dealing with any major problems until you've gained their trust. Then you'll be able to assert yourself in a way they won't resent.

Bite your tongue. At times, and for certain people, this is going to be very difficult. Keep biting. Drag your partner into the bedroom to hiss disciplinary suggestions—that's cool. You have the right to voice your opinions, but let your partner be the final decision-maker and the enforcer.

Step 2: Protect Your Rights

Yes, leave matters of discipline to the bioparent for a while, but don't be a pushover when it comes to your own rights. You are a member of the household. You need privacy and consideration. It's also important that your stepkids understand that you and their bioparent are a disciplinary unit (remember the unified front theory?). As time goes on, they need to begin to see you, too, as an authority figure.

If you feel your rights or feelings are being stomped on, you *may* have to step in and assert yourself. Be prepared for conflict. Your partner should be your ally here.

Step 3: Enforce Established Rules

As you move into more of an authority role, you can begin to enforce already established rules and regulations. Continue to take somewhat of a backseat role by using reminders: "In this house, we all clean up on Saturdays," or "Josh, you know your mother insists you eat some vegetables before you eat dessert!"

Step 4: Join with Your Partner to Set New Guidelines

During this step, you begin to participate in family meetings, decide on the family values and rules, and help decide on jobs, duties, responsibilities, and expected behavior. You become one of the family decision-makers, and as an adult, your voice holds more authority than a child's.

Step 5: Make Spontaneous Choices

Back off on the discipline until the entire family is comfortable with one another. Once you've lived together for quite a while and are comfortable with steps 1 through 4, *then* you can begin to make independent decisions about discipline without deferring to your partner. It's appropriate to make spontaneous disciplinary choices in these instances:

➤ When the bioparent is not available

➤ When there are no established consequences for the misbehavior

Any decisions you make should be based on family values, rules, and limits.

Stepping Stones
It may take a while and some work for the bioparent to feel comfortable with you making disciplinary choices for his or her child.

Stepfamily Discipline Issues

This section covers a few of the most common disciplinary complications of living life "in step."

"You're Not My Parent!"

Resentment often boils out in those four little words. You might also hear, "You're not my mom, you can't tell me what to do!" These words hurt—they're meant to. Respond with calm authority in your voice, and you'll soon hear the last of this particular plaintive cry. Here are three not-so-snappy comebacks to help arm you:

➤ I live here and this is my house. You need to listen to me.

➤ I'm not your parent, but I am the adult in charge right now. I'm reminding you of the rules.

➤ I'm your stepparent, and you do need to listen to me.

Two Houses, Two Sets of Rules

When you have shared custody or a lot of visitation, it's very common for issues to come up about the differences in disciplinary approaches in each household. Take a back seat here, too. It's your partner's job to deal with his or her ex.

Kids are not always clear—or explicit—about what the rules are in their other household. Your partner and her ex should communicate about such matters, and then your partner can share the information with you. Unless it's unavoidable, don't rely only on the child's report.

Don't Be Wicked
Corporal punishment (spanking or hitting in any form) is never appropriate, acceptable, or effective. Spanking or hitting with an object is illegal.

You may fear that the kids will be very confused if they've got two households with two different sets of rules. Kids are smart; they adapt well. Remember that you and your partner have little control over what goes on at the ex's house. Make sure the child explicitly understands the values and rules in *your* household, and trust that the superior modeling you are providing will "take." If you feel, however, that there is some real physical, sexual, or emotional abuse going on in the other household, don't let it slide. *Get help.* (See Chapter 21, "Stepfamilies in Crisis.")

Combined Family Issues

When two families combine, there may be a collision of parenting styles, disciplinary approaches, limits, and privileges. There may also be conflicts between stepsiblings that require disciplinary action. Here are some tips for combining disciplinary styles:

➤ You and your partner need to actively work out your rules for behavior and discuss possible consequences.

➤ Move toward the middle. Ideally, the disciplinary approach of each parent should be similar, if not the same.

➤ Follow the Steps to Acceptance of Authority. Begin as an adviser to your partner, and remain the primary disciplinarian to your own kids.

➤ Make explicit your disciplinary expectations and who can say what to whom. This will help you avoid the "Don't treat my kid like that!" reaction that is common among parents married to a step.

I Kid You Not!

The first few years of stepfamily life are the most stressful. Forty percent of remarriages that end in divorce do so before the fifth year.

The Least You Need to Know

➤ Discipline means education. If there is no learning connected with it, discipline is ineffective.

➤ Effective discipline means establishing clear rules, limits, and consequences.

➤ Your disciplinary role as a stepparent will evolve over time.

Chapter 15

Surviving Visitation

In This Chapter

➤ How to prepare for a stepchild's visit

➤ Surviving the first time

➤ Tips for occasional visitation

➤ How to deal with terrible transitions

➤ What to do when a stepchild refuses to visit

Visits! There's an old saying that fish and house guests begin to stink after three days. But what if the house guest is your stepchild? And is a stepchild ever really a house guest? Should he be? What kind of parenting role should you take? This chapter focuses on the noncustodial visit (long, short, frequent, and infrequent) and looks at some of the big questions that arise whenever a stepchild who doesn't live with you appears on the domestic scene.

Visit Preparations

Even when visitation is a regular occurrence in a family, it brings tremendous disruption to the regular household routines. When visits *don't* occur often, the disruption can begin days or even weeks before the small fry arrives by car, bus, train, plane, or boat. Tension fills the household in anticipation of the big event. And everybody—bioparent, step-parent, other kids in the house, family dog—feels tense and anticipatory about different aspects of the impending visit.

Uptight Bioparent

The bioparent expecting a visit from a noncustodial child may knock him or herself out planning activities. After all, he wants the visit to be perfect. He already feels terribly guilty for not living with the child; now he fears the child's rejection of his new lifestyle, and he's worried about tensions that might erupt between everybody. At the same time, he's terrifically excited. Some bioparents feel the same kind of anticipation they used to feel before a big date. "Before Pierre gets here, I always feel tingly and nervous," says Cindy, whose son lives in another state and sees her every other month. "I want it to be a meaningful visit. I want it to matter, and I'm so nervous it won't!"

Uptight Stepparent

The stepparent is usually painfully aware, and often jealous, of how much the impending visit means to his partner. While the bioparent is excited *and* nervous, the stepparent is excited, nervous, filled with dread, and resentful of the amount of energy his partner is putting into the visit preparations. The stepparent tends to hold her breath and hope that the visit is pleasant. "I don't need it to be fun like Gary does," says Beverly. "He wants to have fun with the kids. I just want to make it through. Not that I don't like them, but it's just so much effort! All this planning. By the time they leave, I'm exhausted."

Other Household Members

The previsit prep can be hard on other kids in the house, too. They may pick up on the tension between their bioparent and the stepparent. They may also have their own concerns—including jealousy and anticipation—especially if they have to change their living space to accommodate the visitor. Once again, excitement wars with dread.

Here Come the Children!

Into this mass of roiling emotions wanders the stepchild (or stepchildren), conflicted and transitioning like mad between the two households.

The different players in this little drama all have different agendas, too. The bioparent wants joy, thrills, and closeness. The stepparent wants to make sure there is privacy and time with the bioparent. The kids…well who knows? Maybe one wants to have her stepparent take her shopping. Another one hates the stepparent and wants to see just the bioparent all weekend.

Yes, visits are complicated.

I Kid You Not!

Famous stepparent in musical history: Yoko Ono is the stepmother of John Lennon's son, Julian (and the mother of Sean Lennon).

The First Time

The first time that the stepkids come over for a sleepover visit (long or short) is a pivotal moment in the stepfamily's history. As a stepparent, you may feel desperate to please the children, to woo them, to go out of your way to make sure that you're accepted. You may also just want to casually greet them and go on with life, letting the kids fit in as they can. Both these emotions may exist at the same time.

Once the kids arrive, you may find yourself again conflicted. They may not be what you expected at all, even if you've spent casual time with them before. They may have been accepting, friendly, enthusiastic, and affectionate. Now that you are married or living together, you may find that the little ones have turned into little resentful creeps. They may be feeling so nervous that they've become inarticulate. They may be simply different from the kids you thought you knew, simply because kids change quickly as a natural part of growth and maturing. Or you may find that you like them very much, but that they take an inordinate amount of energy—energy you weren't expecting to spend.

This first visit probably has your partner flipped out too—either worried sick that the child won't accept the new arrangement or acting just a little bit strange or different, not as the lover you know so well. The tension the two of you feel may start to reverberate in your relationship. For the first visit, remember these pointers:

➤ Recognize that visits may be difficult at first, and just *be* with it.

➤ Take care of yourself. If you begin to feel emotionally overextended, take yourself out of the situation for a while. Take a walk, take a shower, or take a nap.

➤ Check in with your partner on a regular basis.

➤ Remain open for fun. Moments of supreme pleasure often follow moments of disaster, and vice versa. Enjoy the roller coaster ride.

Regular Visits

When visits occur on a regularbasis, things will get both easier and harder. It's a relief to settle into a schedule and to begin building a regular relationship with the kids. You can get a wonderful sense of family two days a week or even two days a month. Having the kids every weekend can also be a hardship for the couple who's busy working all week; there's no time for just the two of them. Be aware of the following trouble spots:

➤ Don't pander or grovel to try to gain a stepchild's acceptance; it won't work.

➤ Be pleasant and welcoming, but don't overdo it. The more you act like yourself, the sooner the child is likely to accept you.

Stepparent Visit Overload

During a visit of any length, you might find yourself in overload. Overloaded people do different things, depending on their temperaments. Some withdraw. Some just get weird—their mates look at them as if to say, "That's not really you! Where is the person I love?" You may find yourself unable to relax or, worse yet, find that you're acting wicked! When your stepchild is doing the same thing (which is common), the bioparent (who wants you two to love each other and get along) may panic.

The bioparent needs to cool out and stop forcing the two of you upon each other. You need to lower your expectations and goals for the visit.

The Abandoned Stepparent

It's not only the stepparent and the kid who start acting odd during visits. Your partner, the bioparent, is so happy or worried that the kids are there that she abandons you. Where is that intimacy? Where is the way she looks at you across the table, that combination of desire, affection, and disbelief at her good fortune? Now she's looking at her kids with the same intensity.

She might also start acting a little strange, talking in a different tone of voice, or snapping back into old behavior patterns. You may find yourself feeling abandoned and lonely, thinking, "I want my partner back!"

Here are some tips for the overloaded or abandoned stepparent:

➤ I know you're tired and somewhat miffed, but include yourself in at least some of the activities your partner is doing with the kids. Otherwise you'll begin feeling even more left out.

➤ Try to spend special time with each kid, even if it is on an occasional basis.

➤ Unless your time with the kids is very short (in which case you don't *need* a break), take a break for the two of you. You need your intimacy.

Occasional Visits

If you see your stepkids only once or twice a year or so, the transition periods can be very difficult for everybody. Don't plan too many activities, and expect *nothing* (I say this as though it's possible!). Remember that even several weeks can be a long time for a child, especially a little one. Kids can change drastically in a short period of time, so it can be like getting a whole new set of children each time they visit. Hey, it's an adventure.

Once the child arrives, give her a little time to adjust before plunging wildly into activities. Welcome her into the house as a member of the family, but make sure that she gets a refresher course on the way the household is run. Remind her of the family values and rules, and maybe discuss what the child remembers from the previous visit.

When you and your partner don't see a child for months at a time, there may be a tendency to treat her like a guest and stay on your best behavior. Stop it! It will work better for all concerned if you get real. Remember that you're not putting on a show here—this is family, and part of being a family is teaching family members how to be real with each other.

On the other hand, don't be too blasé: "Oh, yeah, Jim's here. Lay an extra place at the table, ho hum." Make sure you greet and treat the child like you are happy to see him; he needs the reassurance.

As you get to know the child, try to avoid playing "Quiz the Kid": "What are you into now?" "Do you have lots of boyfriends?" It's better to ask no questions for a while. For many kids, questions are not conversation—they are interrogation.

Don't Try to Fix Things

Your stepchild may arrive for the annual visit with language, manners, and clothing that you abhor. Though you may not like this evidence of his "other" house, or you may not appreciate these "new" behaviors that the child may be trying out on you, don't try too hard to change things. Yes, overt rudeness isn't acceptable, and neither is repulsive, gross behavior. When you can't stand it anymore, you can speak out by making a general assertion of the rules: "At our house we don't have food fights." But weigh effort and possible resentment against the possibility of having a nice visit, and move toward acceptance, enthusiasm, and encouragement.

You don't need to take on a parental role, but you do need to be an adult and a role model. Modeling appropriate behavior is an important part of being an effective stepparent, and that means setting limits on what kind of behavior you'll accept around you. That's true even if the visit is short. Also, try to be sympathetic to your mate, the bioparent, who may feel sad and frustrated at this visible evidence of this lack of control, influence, and input into the child's life.

Don't Be Wicked

Being "real" doesn't mean being rude. Courtesy and respect are an important part of healthy family dynamics.

I Kid You Not!

It can be tortuous to witness a visiting child exhibiting self-destructive behavior, such as smoking cigarettes, and to know that you have no control over his behavior. Remember that no parent, bio or step, *really* has control. You *do* have influence, though. Don't underestimate the power of good modeling, and let go of what you cannot change.

Don't Be Wicked

Pamper without money. A child's favorite dish for dinner, a cup of hot chocolate in bed, an inexpensive gift—there are ways to show you care without spending a bundle.

Avoid Overindulgence

When kids are only occasional members of a household, there's a tendency toward overindulgence. There's nothing wrong with a little indulgence, if it doesn't come at the expense of the other kids in the house, and if it isn't done with an ulterior motive, such as getting back at the nasty ex-spouse or trying to buy love from the child. When parents don't see kids except on vacation, they *want* to show them how glad they are to see them. Children should be treated with respect, courtesy, responsibility, accountability, and just a little pampering.

Semi-Combined Visits

When some kids live with you all or most of the time and the other kids come to visit, things can get even more complicated. "The visiting kids often feel like they are "intruders," and they may express great jealousy when they see the kids who are there all the time interacting with their bioparent. The kids who are "at home" may feel displaced both physically and emotionally, especially if they have to clear a space for their stepsiblings to sleep.

Don't Be Wicked

Kids who have two households, or who live in one household but visit another parent, are often hamstrung with loyalty issues. Don't ever use the child as a message bearer: "Tell your father if he doesn't pay the check on time this month, I'm seeing my lawyer again!"

In Angela and Ron's family, Angela's son Tony lives there full-time, and Ron's daughters come to visit on weekends. When they do, they sleep in Tony's room and Tony sleeps on the couch in the living room. "It's not uncommon for everybody to flip on us," says Ron. "Tony gets sullen and mean, the girls fight, Angela gets a headache, and I just can't stand it."

Semi-combined visits require a great deal of understanding on the part of the adults. It's not an easy situation, but it can get better over time as the kids form more of a bond.

Beginnings and Endings

Transition times (when kids arrive and when they get ready to leave) tend to be terrible. Some kids get quiet and withdrawn. Others act out.

"I can plan on at least two major blow-ups a week: one about two or three hours after Esther arrives, and one as she packs her bag to go back to her mother's house," says Carmina, who lives with her stepdaughter four days a week. "I've learned to take them in stride because they are so predictable."

Carmina is working on ways to lessen the tantrums. She's not asking too many questions, and she's establishing rituals around coming and going. When Esther arrives on Thursday afternoon, Carmina and Esther's dad Fred suggest a shower to "freshen up." Then Esther watches a video, and Carmina and Fred join her. The shower and video relax Esther, and the ritualistic aspect has come to be something she can rely on. As she packs to go home on Sunday night, Fred joins her for a special snack in her room.

The child who is changing houses—whether it is twice a week or once a year—is having to cope with new rhythms, rules, and patterns.

To help smooth the way, consider these tips:

➤ Allow some time for everybody to detox. Expect the worst, and maybe you'll be pleasantly surprised.

➤ Make yourself scarce for a while so you can "cool out" and work on your own tension levels. This also gives the child and the bioparent an opportunity to spend some time alone, rebonding.

➤ Establish rituals to help re-orient the child in your home.

> **Stepping Stones**
> Transitional times can be just as hard on the stepparent as the kid. Come to think of it, it's not so easy for the bioparent, either.

Visitation Schedules

Planning the visits, whether in the courtroom or over the phone, can be extremely stressful for everybody involved. (It usually entails dealing with the ex, and there's more on that in Chapter 16, "The Ex: That Other Birth Parent.") Though the best results happen when there's flexibility, this is not always possible. Unless it's utterly unavoidable, the bioparent should *never* cancel on a child. The child needs the security and reassurance of knowing that she's always welcome and wanted.

Visitation plans should incorporate the stepparent. Often the step feels out of the loop as the parent and the ex continue an intimate and often hostile relationship, planning times and setting up dates. Work with your partner so you don't feel forced into uncomfortable situations if relations are not fully cordial, such as waiting in the car outside the ex's house while the parent picks up the kids, or being the one to drop off the child.

Kids' Resistance to the Stepfamily

Visiting stepkids often have the most resistance to the stepfamily. They want to spend time with the bioparent they rarely get to see, but because they don't know you, they don't feel particularly close to you. Visiting stepkids often feel excluded from the family identity. Be sympathetic. Many shared experiences *have* occurred without them, so they have reasons for feeling left out.

You can help make a child feel more a part of the family by following these pointers:

➤ Creating a place for each child, even if it is a shelf (don't touch it—don't even peek!), a closet, a bed, a bureau drawer, or a corner. (See Chapter 10, "Your House, My House, New House," for more suggestions.)

➤ Give the child some public acknowledgment (but keep it subtle so as not to embarrass her). Try a small Welcome Home sign posted in the living room, or add the child's name to the mailbox: John, Jane, and Joshua Smith.

➤ Introduce your stepchildren to what you do in your daily life, whether it's a reading group, a bowling club, or a "take-your-daughter-to-work day."

➤ Try to spend time with each child alone.

Reassuring Your Own Kids

With stepsiblings visiting, your own children's reactions and ups and downs will certainly affect the whole family. If they're relatively happy and secure, it will make things easier for you. It may also make it easier on the visiting kids—they won't face hostility from your kids. The same rules apply whether your kids live with you all the time, part-time, or just visit. Here are some suggestions:

➤ Keep some space special and private no matter how crowded conditions get when the entire family is assembled.

➤ Help your child anticipate what the visit will be like by talking about it with her ahead of time.

Stepping Stones
Your job is to make your stepchild feel welcome. It's his job to test the boundaries you provide.

➤ Let your kid know that *nothing* has changed emotionally between you—the new kids are not crowding your affections.

➤ Sit down with your child and brainstorm ways to make the visiting kids welcome. By including your child in these kinds of welcoming activities, she'll feel a part of the events.

➤ Allow for grumpiness and plan to give her some space and time to be alone—and to be alone with you.

"May I Bring a Friend?"

Letting kids bring a friend along for an occasional visit can be a good idea, especially if you're having problems getting along.

➤ A friend can serve as an ice breaker, someone who might actually see you as a human being instead of a monster!

➤ You will get to see another side of the child—the side that giggles, hangs out, and plays.

➤ A friend is a bridge to the rest of the child's life.

When a Child Refuses to Visit

Sometimes a child might refuse to visit your home. Your partner, the bioparent, will feel wretched, but you, too, will probably feel rejected and hurt. (If things have been rough between you, you may also feel a little relieved.)

When a child refuses to visit, try to determine why. Here are some possibilities:

➤ You might have hurt the kid's feelings, or she may be hanging onto an old conflict.

➤ She might feel intimidated or teased by other kids in the house.

➤ She might feel that you cramp her lifestyle, that she isn't allowed to have friends over, listen to her kind of music, or dress as she prefers.

➤ She may be feeling pressure from her custodial parent to shun you.

➤ She may be frightened to leave her custodial parent alone because she or he is sick, or in bad shape emotionally.

➤ She might feel that she can't leave the custodial parent because she needs to be a protector in a violent household.

Even if your partner has visitation rights, you may not want to force a child to come visit. Encourage your partner to try to find out what's going on, offer an ear, and tell her you're ready to talk about it whenever she is. At the same time, both you and the bioparent should continue to encourage her to come visit. When she does show up, don't say a word, and don't hold it against her.

Post-Visit Blahs

When the visit is over, you and your partner may keep the postmortem going for days. You may have no idea of how successful the visit was. Your perceptions may be totally different from those of your Sweetie on this matter, too. I'll bet you feel utterly drained. Visits are exhausting.

When a Child Comes Back from Visitations

If you are the custodial family or you share custody, you may find that the kid comes back from visits to the other home in a terrible mood. It's very common for a returning stepchild to pick a fight with a stepparent, as if to prove to himself that you are not his *real* parent. Don't rise to the bait. Remember that transitions are brutal. Give the kid space.

The Least You Need to Know

➤ Visits of any duration bring disruption to the regular routine. Accept this fact as you prepare yourself and the rest of your family!

➤ Take care of yourself—plan time away from the stepfamily during visits if you expect stress.

➤ A little pampering can make a child feel welcome.

➤ Take time with transitions, and give the child leeway.

➤ Kids can change drastically in a short period of time.

➤ Publicly acknowledging the stepchild's role in the family can lessen resistance.

Chapter 16

The Ex: That Other Birth Parent

In This Chapter

➤ Working together with the ex to parent the children

➤ When the ex is intrusive, rude, or abusive

➤ Defeating your own jealous reactions

➤ How to meet face-to-face and survive

➤ The pros and cons of the ex's remarriage

Okay, *you're* not wicked, but sometimes you think the other bioparent—the one you don't live with and love—is. Coping with the ex is an exercise fraught with frustration for many, many stepparents.

Here's the scoop: Like it or not, there are no ex-parents, only ex-partners. As the step, you will likely have to deal with the child's "other" parent. Grit your teeth ('cause at times this may be just a teensy bit unpleasant) and take the high road. It's worth it. The kids will be happier if you all get along. Happy kids mean an easier home life. It's as simple as that.

In the interest of creating happy kids and world peace, this chapter deals with the ins and outs of you and your partner's relationship with the ex-partner of your partner. We'll also examine how your own Ex, if you've got one, enters into the mix.

How Much Co-Parenting?

When a marriage or relationship without kids breaks up, the exes usually stop having contact with each other. But alas, that's just not an option for parents. When kids are involved, the ex-partners usually maintain some kind of relationship forever.

The ideal relationship between ex-partners is a working relationship based upon mutual concern for the kids and mutual respect (at least regarding child-rearing). Sounds great, but how do you get there? How much involvement should the two ex-partners have with each other? What issues should they hash out together, and how much parenting autonomy should they each maintain? Ooh, these are hard questions, and there are no easy answers.

In general, a good working relationship is one that allows the kids to relate freely to all the parents involved, both step and biological. From your point of view, you and your Love should aim for a civil relationship with the ex (it may even be a caring relationship). Relax: Your mate is partnered with *you*. This relationship with the ex is no longer a love affair. As you and your mate discuss the ins and outs of co-parenting with the ex, here's some food for thought:

> ![Step-Speak icon] **Step-Speak**
> The *ex*, in this chapter, is a catch-all term for the ex-partner of your partner. The ex could be an old lover or an old spouse. Here, the ex refers to your stepchild's other parent.

➤ Joint custody or frequent visitation makes it harder to get along with the ex. This makes sense when you think about it—the more back-and-forthing, the more contact you'll have with the child's other parent. The more contact, the more opportunity for conflict.

➤ It is possible to have a good working relationship. Many, many people do (yes, even people who started with a *lot* of antagonism).

➤ Getting the balance right and the emotions settled takes time. Don't be surprised if it brings up old issues: "He's so flaky!" "She's a control freak!"

➤ While it's important to maintain strong, frequent communication, if the relationship is too tight (if it gets beyond the kids and into other areas) you may feel very left out. Too tight of a relationship between *them* can prevent real closeness between *you*. If your partner is hanging on too tightly, it can prevent you from fully being assimilated into the family. You *don't* want to be the odd dude out here.

> ![Stepping Stones icon] **Stepping Stones**
> It's best for the kids if the parents—biologicals and steps—get along. Do the best you can to be noble, suck it all in, and don't gossip or badmouth (in front of the kids, anyway). If adults can learn to work together, the kids gain, not lose.

➤ Too close of a relationship may mean that something isn't over there. Relax, I'm *not* talking passion or love. I mean that the full separation and mourning may not be complete.

➤ Too much fighting may also signify that there's some work to do, putting the old relationship in its new proper place.

How to Deal with the "Evil" Ex

The ideal working relationship is not always easily achieved. You may find yourselves frequently fighting about the ex(es). It may be that you and your partner have moved further along emotionally than the ex (and on some issues the ex may have something to teach you).

Intrusive Exes

Sometimes the ex is too much of a fixture in your life. If this feels like a problem to either you or your partner, look closely at what is going on. It may be that your Love or the ex is still not "over" the relationship. Insist that they separate. If your partner is having trouble with this, get help. A couple of sessions with a counselor may make a big difference. You are *not* number two just because your love and commitment came after the ex-partner's love and commitment.

It may be that you, too, are having a hard time with your own ex, if you have one. Divorcing couples go through three stages: holding on, letting go, and starting over. The ex-partners usually reach these stages at different times. That means that though you or your new partner may be *way* over it, your Ex may not be. Many people feel it would be easier to let go and start over if each ex didn't have to see the other. With kids, this isn't always possible—or desirable. Eek! Life is complex.

Marie, Steve's ex, lived just a few blocks from Steve and Brenda. Miranda, Marie and Steve's daughter, shared her time between the two households. Marie was alone, and more often, Brenda would find her voice on the answering machine, asking Steve for his help with a household calamity or wanting to discuss Miranda's science homework. Steve spent a lot of time helping Marie out, and Brenda seethed.

After Miranda's birthday (where Marie joined them at a local restaurant and spent the evening reminiscing with Steve about old friends, people Brenda had never met), Brenda was so furious she put her foot down— and almost put her fist through the wall. She told Steve she felt like the "other" wife. Steve confessed that he was having a hard time saying "no" to Marie—after all, she was still alone.

> **Stepping Stones**
> Even when the ex has died, your partner will need to complete the separation process of holding on, letting go, and starting over to fully *finish* the relationship.

Brenda and Steve needed a few sessions with a therapist before he was able to assert himself with Marie. The interesting thing is that once he stopped paying so much attention to her, Marie seemed to stop being so needy.

My Partner's Ex Badmouths Me to the Kids

It very well may be your partner's ex isn't *really* that bad, but it certainly seems so at times, especially when the ex is saying nasty things about *you* to the kids. Usually you'll only hear about those nasty things if the child tells you—oh, what a dynamic you have here! The child may want you to hear how you're being criticized or, more commonly, may want to bait you. It's your job not to take the bait.

Dealing with a nasty bioparent who is saying awful things about you to the kids provides you with a brilliant opportunity: You get to be the *good* stepparent! Model good behavior to the kids, keep them from running wild, and refrain from badmouthing the parent.

This advice is more than just a ploy to get you a halo. Badmouthing a bioparent (even if the parent is absent, abusive, or just rude) will backfire on you. Say your stepdaughter

> **Don't Be Wicked**
> The telephone is intrusive. Any time you pick up the phone, you run the risk of hearing your Love's ex-partner on the other end. Take three deep breaths and blow off the negative energy. Don't let it ruin your mood. And *don't* vent on the rest of the family.

Alicia is angry at her dad. Your saying he's a no-good scum will initially build an alliance with Alicia, but it's a phony one based on shared anger. Subconsciously, Alicia will feel that if her dad is bad, she must be, too. She'll resent you for pointing it out, and her self-esteem will suffer.

Alicia also is dealing with loyalty issues. The minute you say something nasty about her dad, she's gonna leap to his defense, no matter *how* angry she is at him. (There's more on this in the section "Loyalty Issues and the Kids," later in this chapter.)

If you can avoid responding to the provocation, you'll feel great about yourself. As you struggle to avoid taking the nasty ex's bait, seek empathy for the ex within yourself. If all else fails, sometimes it helps to try to pity the ex. Whatever it takes to do it, don't badmouth the ex. If you're guilty of doing this, stop.

The Prior Spouse Is a Creep

What if the ex is a creep? Sometimes the ex seems crazy, unpleasant, inconsiderate, oddball, sloppy, spacey, or rigid. What (if anything) you can do about this depends upon who the creepy behavior is aimed at. If it's aimed directly at you, you've got a choice—fight it or let it slide (don't rule out ignoring it; that doesn't necessarily mean you are relinquishing responsibility).

Say it's the child who is having trouble with the ex. If the child is eight years old or older (old enough to express herself clearly), let her handle it. That's between the two of them, her and her parent, to resolve. If the complaints are serious and they recur, let your partner be in charge of running interference. That's not *your* job. If you step in, you may very well make it worse.

Of course, all this supposes that no real emotional, physical, or sexual abuse is occurring. If you believe it is, *get help*.

I Kid You Not!

If you suspect child abuse, you need to take care of the situation *at once*. Call the National Center for Missing and exploited Children for advice. Get the child to a safe place. Call your lawyer. You can also call the Boys Town National Hotline at 800-448-3000. They provide 24-hour counseling for parents *and* kids.

When You Know He's a Creep but the Kid Doesn't

If you know that your partner's ex is a creep but the kid thinks he or she is a hero, shut your trap. You can't do anything about it anyway, and if you want to keep building your relationship with your stepchild, keep that trap shut. In an ideal situation, truth, justice, and the stepparent way will win the day. (Again, all this is assuming that your partner's ex is just an unpleasant person, not an abuser.)

Divorce expert Judith Wallerstein believes that children of divorce *do* understand their fathers' good sides as well as their bad sides, but they don't "as a rule, draw the conclusions that an objective observer would make from those records...." Wallerstein believes that teenage girls, especially, need to create the image of a protective, loving father and that "without any sense of contradiction, they are able to maintain a benign sense of the loving father side by side with a history of repeated rejections and failures." Later these same kids may think of their father as a betrayer. Of course, not only men are creeps, and both boys and girls will suffer from a creepy biomother's actions as well.

As a step, you'll do best if you give the ex the benefit of the doubt when it comes to parenting issues. People have different styles. Look for evidence of love and attention—ignore the clothes and manners and try to lead by example, not by attacking the ex's approach to life and parenting.

Jealousy

It's not unusual for stepparents to find themselves consumed with jealousy over the ex, even when they know they have little rational reason to feel that way. Jealousy is especially common in three instances:

➤ When you want kids of your own
➤ When your partner acts kind to the ex
➤ When your partner and the ex negotiate over parenting

When You Want Kids of Your Own

When you're deep in the throws of baby-want (and that can be a powerful, all-consuming desire) it's hard to feel charitable toward somebody who has what you so desperately need—the child of your mate. It's common for stepparents to feel insecure or inferior to the ex just because they've managed to reproduce and you have not. If you're having fertility troubles or your partner doesn't want any more kids, seeing the ex in the height of blissful parenthood can be a particularly bitter pill to swallow.

When Your Partner Acts Kind to the Ex

Usually the ex is spoken of with anger and bitterness. But there may be residual kindness and caring, and at the least, nostalgia. In many cases, you don't want to know about it. Perhaps she does him a favor or you overhear them talking on the phone in a familiar tone of voice. Out comes the jealous reaction.

Here's how this one comes about: Your partner wants to convince you that you are loved, that you aren't playing second violin in the orchestra of his life. He tells you that the ex was hateful and despicable to convince you. Then you see a more ambivalent reaction or get an insight into what made them fall in love originally. Whoa! Jealousy strikes. Will they get back together? Do they still love each other?

When They Negotiate Parenting

Just having your partner and the ex spend that much time talking about schedules and ways to deal with parenting problems is often very hard for the stepparent. You may feel left out or nonexistent, even though you *know* that a certain amount of time needs to be spent doing that kind of talking.

"It doesn't help that I know she hates talking to Jim," says Rodney. "I still get jealous. I feel totally left out. Aren't my opinions, my schedule, my money important? Yes, she talks with me before and after, and yes, she doesn't say a final 'yes' until we discuss it, but I still feel terrible. If they meet at his house I think they'll end up in bed together. If they meet here, I feel intruded upon. If they meet in a cafe, I feel sure that people are going to think they're a couple."

Defying the Green-Eyed Monster

Jealousy is ugly, it feels lousy, and there is no known cure for it except time and gaining trust. As you work through your own jealousy, try to keep these three points in mind:

➤ Your partner is with you because *you* are your partner's love interest. The ex is over.

➤ It takes time. Part of building a deep relationship is building deeper trust. Do your best to wait out the jealousy patiently while the trust builds.

➤ It's your job to bolster your own self-esteem. Do something kind for yourself. Do something kind for others. The better you feel about yourself, the less time and energy you'll have for feeling jealous.

Don't Compete with the Ex!

You can't fix what was wrong with your partner's previous relationship, and you can't make yourself into a better match. All you can do is be yourself and work to make your relationship the best that you can. It can be quite a temptation to learn all you can about the ex (what he was like in bed, what her body looked like), but steer clear! It's not going to improve your relationship; it will only make you crazy.

> **Don't Be Wicked**
> Be aware: Some ex-partners have a great working relationship when they are single, but the moment one of them has a new partner, watch out! There's a new *person* in the mix, and that "replacement" tends to bring out the worst in people.

Loyalty Issues and the Kids

The kids are not stupid. Actually, they are very sensitive. The rivalry between you and the ex, spoken or unspoken, has a strong effect on them. Whether or not you express it verbally, kids will recognize the conflict of loyalties from day one. This can (and often does, in fact) lead to some real schizo behavior on the part of the stepchild. One day he may really seem to like you a lot. "We're getting close," you say. The next day he cuts you colder than a winter wind in northern Alaska as he rebels against you and pulls away.

"I had a real hard time with my stepmom," Cathy says. "It wasn't anything about her. I just sometimes couldn't be around her. I felt like if I loved her that must mean there was something wrong with how I was treating my mom. I mean, my stepmom *wasn't* my mom, and though she wasn't really trying to be my mother, I felt disloyal to my mom."

Like many stepkids, Cathy dealt with her loyalty problems by talking about her mother to her stepmother at every opportunity. "I wanted to clearly let her know that I *had* a mother, and that my mom was much better than my stepmom."

> **Stepping Stones**
> If you're a woman with the same last name as the first Mrs., you may have some uncomfortable experiences as you're mistaken for each other. It can be uncomfortable being the second anything!

As a stepparent, it's vital not to play into these kinds of comparison games. Ignore them, keep a straight face, and pretend you are immune to them, no matter *how* you feel inside. Remember the positive intent of a negative behavior. Children are worried about loyalty, and their awareness of people and their feelings is very positive (and developmentally appropriate).

Money Battles, Visitation, and the Ex

Between custody/visitations logistics and money issues, the ex may hold a lot of power in your life. Though Chapter 22, "Legal Stuff," is all about the legal issues (such as custody and visitations), and Chapter 23, "Money Madness," is about money issues, it's important to note a few things here:

➤ Try not to let your animosity about the ex's actions and attitudes about custody and money affect how you feel about the children.

➤ Don't set yourself up as the antagonist against the evil ex. You and your partner are *partners*.

➤ Though you may have little control over these particular issues, you do have a great deal of control over how much emotional control the ex wields in your household. He is the past; you are the present and the future.

Face to Face

In an ideal world, your partner is over their relationship, the ex is over their relationship, and so are you. Everybody sets about co-parenting the children in a sensible, humanitarian fashion. If you can achieve this, bravo! A strong working relationship between the ex and the step is the best gift you can give the children. This kind of relationship is optional, however! If you are not ready or willing to be friendly with your partner's ex, you do not have to do it. It may be the ex who doesn't want to deal with you. Give it a shot, but if you're cut cold, pull back, baby.

➤ Try to keep a sense of humor when the ex throws a hissy fit if you're spotted in the same county where she lives. It's *her* problem, after all.

➤ You'll get mega-bonus points if you are gracious about attending social events where "He" is going to be. Remind yourself that *you* are the partner, take three deep breaths before entering the room, and imagine yourself as royalty. Treat yourself with respect in uncomfortable situations, and others will treat you that way, too.

➤ Imagination can be cruel, transforming unseen people into monsters, geniuses, or beauty queens. If the ex is taking on mythological proportions for you, sometimes the best thing is for you and the ex to meet. A couple of minutes together will remind everybody that most human beings are really just that—human beings.

I Kid You Not!

Sometimes it's the two ex-partners who can't be in the same room or even share a telephone line without hissing like angry cats at each other. And sometimes the step comes in to save the day, making the arrangements, running interference, and picking up the kids. You never can tell.

When the Ex Remarries

Many of the problems stepparents express about the ex disappear once the ex remarries. The relationships are more balanced, because instead of two against one (and a lonely one, at that) there are two happy couples. Relationships between exes and steps are often easier and less loaded with jealousy and resentment. The past is clearly past. The relationship is clearly over. Money issues often clear up, too.

But it's not always so easy for the kids. They have another relationship to accept, and a parent's remarriage is always a time of insecurity, especially if the new step has kids: "Am I still part of this family?" "What role will the new stepparent play?" "Will I even *like* the new stepparent?" It's important for you and your partner to reassure the kids just how important they are to you. A parent's remarriage often *does* affect how and where the child is cared for. You may be required to step in to do more active child-rearing. It can be a very hard time for a child.

The new relationship may also be a challenge for your partner, who may feel that the ex's new partner is a rival for the kids' affection. Be sympathetic. You already know what it's like to feel jealous or competitive in that way; share your wisdom and compassion with your partner.

Be prepared to deal with a little nostalgia. Fight your jealousy, and give it a little time to pass. No matter how evil or creepy the ex is now, she or he was once a person your partner loved and was making a life with. But now that era is over.

The Least You Need to Know

➤ Ex-partners should aim for a mutually respectful child-rearing relationship.

➤ Separating couples move through the stages of holding on, letting go, and starting over at different rates.

➤ Many stepparents feel jealous of the ex. Try not to compare—it only creates more trouble.

➤ Never badmouth the ex in front of the kids.

➤ The ex's remarriage may be glorious for you, but it will be hard on the stepkids. Be supportive.

Chapter 17

Birth Grandparents and Step-Grandparents

In This Chapter

➤ The role of grandparents—*all* of them

➤ Welcoming the grandparents

➤ Avoiding grandparent trouble

➤ When the grandparent is a stepparent

Grandparents play a very important role in kids' lives and in the life of a stepfamily. Whether they come bearing gifts, special attention, fancy clothes, and tickets to the ball game, or spankings, meddling, disapproval, and lack of attention, grandparents *matter* to kids. Grandparents often play a special role for kids whose first family broke up; they provide a sense of continuity.

The grandparents may also be big players in *your* life as a stepparent. On the one hand, you may feel judged by them ("I'm number two!"), yet they often help financially and emotionally. Lots of them provide child care.

More than that, increasing numbers of grandparents are taking on the role of stepparent or foster parent during and after their children's divorces. As you step into "stepping," you may find yourself relating to a grandparent who has also served in a custodial role.

This chapter is about the relationships between you, your partner, and your stepkids with the grandparents. That means all of them: your partner's parents, the parents of your partner's ex, and your parents! There's also a bit about grandparents *as* stepparents (a challenging role if there ever was one), and while we're on the subject, we'll talk a bit about what it's like when your stepkids start to have their own children and *you* become a grandparent.

Who Is What?

When we talk about stepfamilies, we're talking about more than the standard-issue four grandparents; it could easily be as many as six or eight. (How many cousins, aunts, and uncles? The thought boggles the mind, but with all those relatives running around, your stepkids have a pretty good chance of being *very* well loved.)

Grands, Other Grands, and Step-Grands

With all these grandparent words, we run the risk of getting confused here, so let's define some terms:

➤ We'll call your partner's parents the Grands.

➤ We'll call your partner's ex's parents the Other Grands.

➤ We'll call your parents the Step-Grands.

➤ All of them together are the Grandparents.

I Kid You Not!

Step-Grands tend to slip especially easily into a grandparenting role if the kids are very young when the stepfamily is formed. Who can resist a tubby little toddler? What's more, little children don't understand blood relationships. They respond to kindly, attentive, caring adults, whether Grand, Other Grand, or Step-Grand.

Naming the Grandchildren and the Grands

The name game continues. How should all those grandparents refer to the children? How should the kids refer to all those grandparents?

Paul's family has done a wonderful job of integrating everybody into family life. "I can't keep track of who's who anymore," says Paul, a Grand and a Step-Grand. "They're all just the kids; we call them all kin. The kids call each other brother and sister and cousin, and all of us have to think about it to figure out who belongs to whom. Why bother?"

Of course, not everybody is as able to selectively forget which child "belongs" to whom. But Paul's casual, accepting attitude is something to strive for.

You might encourage the grandparents to refer to them all as "the kids" rather than trying to keep it all straight—"my step-grandchildren" instead of "my daughter's husband's kids." Unless you're working on a genealogical chart, such clarification may not really be necessary.

As for the kids, there's lots of options for what they can call grandparents: Grandmother and Grandfather, Grandma and Grandpa, Nana, Nona, Papa, Pappy, Grams, Gram, Gramps, Gramp, Granddaddy, Big Ma, Big Daddy, Maw, Paw, yada, yada, yada. The kids can affix first names or last names, depending upon family style and comfort level. As with all naming, I suggest that any name you choose fit these qualifications:

➤ Be explicit (discuss it with the child and grandparent).

➤ Be respectful and agreeable to all.

Grandparents: Allies and Resources

Whether Grands, Other Grands, or Step-Grands, grandparents can be a real asset to the stepfamily.

In times when the kids are feeling resentful and challenged by the stepfamily arrangement, the Grands (your partner's parents) can play a strong part in creating a sense of family unity. When they demonstrate that they accept you into the family, they reassure your stepkids. In a combined family, when the Grands welcome your own children with broad smiles and open arms, they further the sense of one big family.

Welcoming the Grandparents

It's your job and responsibility to make sure that the grandparents feel welcome in your stepfamily. You may feel a trifle intimidated by your new in-laws (and you may feel more than a trifle intimidated by your out-laws, the Other Grands), but it's a good bet that they also feel a little intimidated by you. These are their *grandchildren* you're living with. You have power over how much they get to see their little Snookums. You can help them all feel welcomed and appreciated by following two hints:

➤ Telling them explicitly that you won't get in the way of their established relationship with the kids. Let them know how much they represent a link with the past and how much emotional security they provide the kids.

Don't Be Wicked

People have different styles of living, and the grandparents may present a completely different view of life to your stepkids than you do. Most of the time, it's fantastic for the child to be exposed to different approaches. But be aware! If you have concerns based on morals or physical safety, it's vital that you step in with a complaint and, if necessary, remove the child.

➤ Being aware that they may do things different ways. Their whole style of living may be vastly different from yours. Be flexible and tolerant.

➤ Giving grandparents photos and school schedules, especially if they live out of town. Encourage them to be part of the children's lives.

➤ Encouraging the kids to send the grandparents notes, make them drawings, and invite them to events.

➤ Showing your appreciation when they help you out with the kids.

➤ Not abusing their willingness to help out.

➤ Understanding the impact that all this (separation, divorce, remarriage, and general stepfamily dynamics) has on them.

Trouble in Grandparent Land

Sometimes the going isn't so blissful, the wrinkled faces aren't as crinkled with smile lines as they are with frowns, and the kids are little monsters.

Bonded—Against You

Grandparents and grandchildren may form a tight unit and exclude everybody else. This often happens with the Other Grands; most parents will side with their own child in a divorce, and some have been known to encourage their grandkids to look at the new stepparent as the wicked impostor. But it can also happen with the Grands. If your stepkids are having a hard time with the situation or with you, the doting Grands (your loving partner's parents) may well side with the kids against you. Of course, by doing this they're siding against their own child's choice of a mate, but hey, people don't always act rationally now, do they?

Measuring Up Against the Ex

It's never a clean slate with your in-laws, the Grands. They've dealt with your forerunner(s), and they usually have an opinion about how you measure up. In the best of circumstances, they will politely keep that opinion to themselves. In the worst of circumstances…well, in that case, it's up to you to enlist your partner's help and support to say (and mean) "Knock it off, Pa, this is the love of my life. Now be *nice!*"

Being measured against the ex doesn't always mean you'll come out looking lousy. But any kind of measuring isn't fair. Jeanette married Bob, the dad of three teenagers. Bob's dad, Jeanette's father-in-law, was ecstatic that Bob had married Jeanette, not just because they were great together, but because Jeanette and Bob were from the same cultural background and Bob's first wife had not been. Jeanette basked in the glow of her father-in-law's acceptance. Sounds great, doesn't it?

Guess again. Just think about how Bob's kids felt. Their mother had never been fully accepted, and then after the divorce and her former husband's remarriage she felt like a nonentity to the family. People were polite to her but made no special effort toward her. The children's loyalty was with their poor, put-upon mother (as well it should have been), and Jeanette had a much harder row to hoe with them—all because her father-in-law thought she was fantastic!

Morality and Judgment

Values and morality can sometimes get between the older and younger generations. It's very painful when your parents, the Step-Grands, disown you and ignore your stepkids because you married a divorced person, or when the Grands take the side of the ex (particularly ex-wives) and disown their own child. It does happen. Sometimes people cannot be convinced of the validity and importance of your stepfamily. When this happens, it's a tremendous loss to all.

When Partners Fail Each Other

Sometimes stepparents' complaints fall on deaf ears. You complain about your in-laws and hear, "Oh honey, you've just gotta try harder!" or, "You're too sensitive."

Perhaps your Sweet Baboo is nervous about making a scene with the parents and so tells you, "Grin and bear it, honey. He's old and we don't see him that often."

None of this is fair. It's often hard to stand up to your parents (it doesn't matter *how* old you are), but unity within the partnership is vital. You need your partner to be your ally. Your partnership will *not last* unless you are on each others' sides.

Grandparents and Biokids/Grandparents and Non-Biokids

Combined families can get complicated. Say Betsy and Brian are married. Betsy has a son, Amos, and Brian has a daughter, Amy. They all live together. What's the relationship between Amos' Other Grands and Amy? Nothing, right? But if Amos' Other Grands or his Grands (who are Amy's Step-Grands) bring attention and gifts only to Amos and ignore Amy, is that fair? Amos is their grandson, but is it okay to play favorites in front of Amy? Is it okay for them to say they love their grandkids more than the other kids?

Then there's your parents and the stepkids, their stepgrandchildren. Your parents may be reluctant to accept your partner's kids. Hey, many can't even accept the new partner!

All these complications can lead to some real resentment and misery. While you can't expect Step-Grands to care as much about their stepgrandchildren and the stepsiblings of their grandchildren, they *do* need to show courtesy and respect to your family unit. It's up to you and your partner to assert yourself on these matters and to request equal treatment. "Ma, cool it and be nice to the kids—*all* of them!"

Stepkids Ignoring Step-Grands

Sometimes it's the other way around: your parents are a dream, but your stepkids are impossible! If the kids are being overly chilly to your parents, the kids might not realize that it's okay *not* to love them. They may have picked up a complaint against them from you or your partner (watch your tongue, now!), or they may be worried about betraying their own grandparents. So they pout and ignore.

Reassure the kids that they don't have to love or even like your parents. Increase familiarity by telling them a little about each parent. Seek shared interests or character traits. "You know how much you like magic? Well, Arthur, my dad, used to be a magician. He never tells his tricks, but if you asked him to help you learn to palm that ball, I bet he would."

On the other hand, if your stepkids are being rude to your parents (or to their Grands or Other Grands), it's time for a talk. We all know kids can be cruel, and kids can be snooty. If it's not respectful, it's not acceptable. They need to know that.

Other Grands and You

The Other Grands are still a part of your stepchildren's family, and they always will be (even if the ex is deceased). You may never meet these people, they might act neutral, or they might be mean and try to poison your stepkids against you. You can try to resolve any problems, or you can let it slide, hoping, once again, that truth, justice, and the stepparent way will win out again. Whatever you do, remember that you can't divorce the children from their grandparents, even if your partner has no relationship with those grandparents anymore.

Don't Be Wicked
Remember the obvious: Half of your step kids' grandparents are the parents of that evil ex—they're the Other Grands. Their loyalties lie with that ex, and that's where they should be. They'll see *you* as a challenge, so be welcoming. Don't damage or limit their relationship with their grandbabies.

If you and your partner have custody of the kids, the Other Grands may feel cast aside, not considered, and very sad about the loss of their grandkids. They may want visitation with the kids. It's important for the kids to be able to maintain a relationship with all their grandparents.

The level of involvement is largely up to you (see the following section for details on grandparent visitation and custody rights). If you don't want to have personal contact with them, suggest that they take the kids out alone. If you're very open-minded, you might include them in a family event or holiday.

It may feel a little odd at first, inviting the parents of your partner's ex over, say, for dinner. There are no rules about what is right or wrong; go by your own comfort level. While you'll never feel comfortable hanging out with the ex's parents, people are pretty decent and will rise to the occasion in most cases.

I Kid You Not!

Long live the American family! The demise of the American family has been prematurely announced. Think about all those grandparents! It's not dead; it has just changed form.

Conflicts Between Grands, Other Grands, and Step-Grands

Rivalry isn't just about siblings. Sometimes grandparents get competitive with each other, and because there are so *many* grandparents in a stepfamily situation, the squabbles can get quite extensive. I'm tempted to say that you should simply butt out and ignore them. They're all grown-ups. You don't, won't, and shouldn't have control over how these people are treating each other. But unfortunately, if there's a fight between them, *you* (and your mate, and way too often the stepkids) are the ones who are going to be caught in the cross-fire.

Steer clear! Avoid taking sides. If it gets too horrendous, then the solution is to call a therapist for yourself and maybe for the kids. Talk with the kids to make sure they're hanging in there. Assure them that you care about them.

Separation Is a Last Resort

Grandparents are *so* important to kids, and kids are *so* important to grandparents that it's imperative to try to work out any and all problems. A lot of the burden here is on you; you need to be explicit about what kind of behavior is needed from everyone involved.

Grandparents may be a bad influence on the kids, they may say nasty things about you and your family, and they may have different beliefs and try to impose those on the children. Take a leap of faith—you have tremendous influence on your stepkids. That influence may be challenged, but it's not threatened, by the grandparents. The world is full of people who have other things, both good and bad, to offer. All you can do is teach kids your own values the best you can and then let them go.

➤ Don't let yourself feel left out of the family dynamics. This may mean you have to resist the urge to mope in the corner. Enlist your partner's help.

➤ Don't push intimacy into your relationship with the Grands and the Other Grands. For a while, consider them your stepkids' grandparents. You can't expect instant intimacy. Give it some time.

➤ If things are going terribly, you might need to consider separation, keeping the kids from spending time with the Grands and Other Grands. This should be used only as the last resort, though.

I Kid You Not!

What do Bill Clinton, Mary Tyler Moore, Oprah Winfrey, Maya Angelou, and Jack Nicholson have in common? They are all on TV a lot. But besides that, all were raised (at least partially) by grandparents.

The Rights of Grands and Other Grands

Grandparents don't have a lot of legal rights, though they do have a few. In all states, the courts can grant visitation rights to grandparents (Grands or Other Grands). But just because they petition doesn't mean they will win—it's gotta be in the best interest of the child. Sometimes the grandparents have to prove that they have a deep and lasting relationship with the grandchild. Sometimes they'll gain visitation if the child lived with them for a while. And sometimes the courts will turn them down, saying that recognizing their rights would compromise the parents' rights of choosing with whom their kids can associate.

Here's the scoop on the Other Grands' rights when their grandkids are adopted by a stepparent: Normally stepparent adoption cuts off all ties between the adopted child and their biological family, and that includes the Other Grands. The courts have granted visitation rights to Other Grands in stepparent adoption in many, but by no means all cases. Other Grands have the best chance for visitation when the stepparent adoption follows the death of their child and parent of the grandchild (rather than relinquishment or abandonment).

Stepping Stones
Step-Grands must be explicit in their wills if they want their step-grandchildren to inherit from them after their death.

Occasionally custody fights ensue between grandparents and parents, usually in the case of abandonment. Sometimes, when neither parent is able to take care of a child, a custody fight between grandparents occurs.

The Grandparent During Divorce

Grandparents are commonly called upon to bail out the parents during a divorce by taking care of the kids. In tumultuous times, grandparents can provide an anchoring influence. But many times, that anchor is dislodged when the parent remarries and reclaims the child.

When the child moves from Grandma and Grandpa's house to the new household with her parent and new stepparent, the grandparents can easily feel displaced or unappreciated. If you're the stepparent in a situation like this, be aware that the Other Grands may take out their hostility on you. Make sure that you and your partner express your appreciation and your respect for them. Your job is to build bridges, not burn them.

I Kid You Not!

More than three million children in the United States live with their grandparents or other kin, not their parents.

The Grandparent as Stepparent

Frequently, grandparents are becoming stepparents to their children's children if the parent is too young to be a responsible, full-time parent. Often it happens when a parent wants to give up a child for adoption and the grandparent will have none of it. Other times, a parent gets into trouble with drugs or crime and can't take care of the child.

Grandparents who stepparent their grandchildren have extra complications:

➤ The relationship with their own kids is often damaged, strained, or nonexistent. Many grandparents don't want (or else actively fear) contact or involvement from the birth parent. Some long for it and don't have it and must then grieve for their child as they would grieve for a death.

➤ There's little legal assistance for relatives who take on a relative's children.

➤ Grandparents may also have health complications due to age. (Chasing a toddler when you've got arthritis is no walk in the park.)

➤ Resentment comes with the territory. It's hard to raise a whole new family when you expected to be finished with such responsibilities by now.

Stepping Stones
The Grandparent Information Center, a division of The American Association of Retired Persons (AARP), puts out a newsletter called *Parenting Grandchildren: A Voice for Grandparents*. You can contact them at 202-434-2296.

The Step as Grandparent

When a stepparent becomes a step-grandparent, things often shift for the better. A new baby tends to bring a family together anyway, and when your stepkids have children, they often gain a sudden understanding of how challenging stepparenting (indeed, parenting of any kind) can be. All of a sudden, you might get a little *appreciation*. There's a tremendous amount of joy when a baby begins to recognize you.

If there's an unusual age difference between child and grandparent, the little one won't even realize it. When Ami was 31, her step-granddaughter Colleen was born. Ami has no children of her own, but at an age when most of her friends are answering to "Mommy! Mommy! Mommy!," Ami is answering to "Grandma!" Colleen doesn't understand that her Grandma is younger than her mother—and for Colleen at age 6, it wouldn't matter if she did know. Anybody over age 18 is a senior citizen for a child!

The Least You Need to Know

➤ Grandparents provide a sense of continuity.

➤ Grandparents should be encouraged to treat all the children—bio and step—equally.

➤ Grandparents are *vital* to kids, and vice versa. Do your best to encourage strong relationships with them, to avoid separations, and to resolve problems early.

➤ Increasing numbers of grandparents are parenting their children's children, which often presents a challenging responsibility.

➤ If you have a troublesome relationship with your stepchild, wait a while (alas, maybe a long while). Stepkids often mellow to stepparents when they become parents themselves.

Cross-Cultural Stepfamilies

This chapter is about life in a cross-cultural stepfamily. Diversity rules!

What do I mean by cross-cultural? Well, a cross-cultural relationship isn't limited to people from different countries of origin. Most people come from (at least slightly) different cultural backgrounds. Cultural differences can include different socioeconomic classes, races, and religions. Even genders have different social cultures! Looked at that way, *most* love relationships and stepfamilies have cross-cultural aspects, and that can lead to complications best resolved through communication.

The ideas and exercises in this chapter focus on cross-cultural challenges, but they can help *everyone* communicate more effectively, inside *and* outside their stepfamily.

Step-Speak
Culture can refer to a person's ethnic background, place of birth, religious upbringing, or social class.

Step-Speak
Cross-cultural communication means communication (written, verbal, and nonverbal) that occurs between people who come from different cultural backgrounds.

Living in a cross-cultural family, you're on an adventure of discovery. The kids are, too. All this means that you and your stepfamily have to talk about your differences in experiences, beliefs, values, and culture. Broaden their minds, and broaden your own. You're bridging the world with understanding.

Child-Rearing Cultural Differences

Child-rearing practices vary from culture to culture. If you've got a stepfamily where more than one style of child-rearing is taking place, watch out! You may be in for some misunderstandings. This chapter talks about some differences in approaches, both to child-rearing and to life. Different isn't bad—it doesn't mean anybody is particularly right or particularly wrong. We're just talking about a difference in style.

In some cultures, young children are indulged in every whim until they reach age 5. Then the party's over, and the children take their place in the grueling school system (and later in the dog-eat-dog work world). In other cultures, children are expected to be "seen but not heard." Think about whether you have heard variations on these themes: "In my town, it was *rude* when a child didn't address adults by Mr. or Mrs." "Why won't that child give me a hug? Am I such a monster?" Some cultures believe in corporal punishment, and some do not.

Bring a stepparent who believes in "spare the rod, spoil the child" into a family whose culture never lays a hand on kids, and you're in deep for some culture clashes.

Learning Your New Family's Ways

Whenever you have a relationship in a cross-cultural situation, you have to communicate effectively. Intercultural communication consultant William Sonnenschein believes that effective cross-cultural communication requires self-awareness, respect, tolerance, flexibility, empathy, patience, and humor. That's quite a list. Let's break it down:

Self-Awareness

Your cross-cultural communication will be improved by your willingness to really know yourself and to understand your reactions. Your perceptions of the world and your values affect your interpretation of what other people are saying and doing. You have to understand yourself and what you are bringing to the stepfamily (good points, old baggage, values, expectations, and beliefs) to understand the others. You can improve your self-awareness in so many ways (and I'll give you one way in the "Slants and Rants" exercise later in this chapter).

Respect

One of the biggest complaints by people from nondominant cultures is lack of respect. But you will find that just trying to understand and learn about the differences between your culture and your stepfamily's culture leads to increased respect and improved cross-cultural communication. (These differences can be as basic as how often you brush your teeth or whether you are allowed to blow your nose at the table.) Try to learn about your stepfamily's culture in specific ways. You can read and research, ask questions, or maybe even learn the language. (I know, Hungarian *is* hard.) Active listening works here, too. (Active listening, my cure-all for what ails you, is explained in Chapter 4, "Moving In Together.")

Step-Speak
A *nondominant culture* is a culture that is in a geographical area culturally dominated by another culture.

Tolerance

People's behavior can have ambiguities or mean more than one thing, depending upon what culture the person is from. There are ambiguities in language, style, and behavior. When an African-American child looks at you and says "You're *bad*," she may not be saying you're a naughty stepparent. An Asian-American child's refusal to look an adult in the eye will be interpreted as "shifty" in some cultures, but merely respectful in his. You'll improve your cross-cultural communications if you remain tolerant of behavior that may change meaning from culture to culture. Haul out your "positive intent" (this theory of looking for the good intent behind people's actions was discussed in Chapter 11, "It's the Children!").

Flexibility

You'll do best in life when you remain flexible, particularly in situations that are new or challenging. Go with the flow, babe, ease with the breeze. Here's where your self-awareness of your own values steps in again. If you really understand yourself, you'll be able to relax when things are going differently from expectations, as long as it doesn't threaten your real values.

Empathy

Feeling what another person feels, and walking a mile in his or her shoes (ouch, blisters!) is really important for cross-cultural communication. Try feeling what someone who is different from you might be feeling in new or strange surroundings. It may give you a whole new perspective on the world.

Patience

Cross-cultural communication (and living in a cross-cultural stepfamily) can be difficult. Be patient. Family growth takes time.

Humor

Miscommunications can be funny! Laughter is essential in a family when you have to learn new customs as well as get used to living with a whole bunch of new strangers. When you lose your sense of humor, you lose your sense of humanity as well as your perspective.

Slants and Rants, an Exercise

Remember how I said self-awareness is essential for good cross-cultural communication? Here's an exercise that will help you understand more about your own biases and perceptions. On the left are a bunch of behaviors. On the right, you jot down what you might assume if you see or experience this behavior coming from one of your stepkids (or your partner, or your partner's parents or extended family, for that matter). When you're done, I'll explain how behavior can reflect cultural differences.

If a member of my stepfamily…	I might assume…
Speaks very softly	
Speaks very loudly	
Is always late	
Stands very close	
Stands too far away	
Never hugs or kisses me	
Never laughs at my jokes	
Doesn't ask questions	
Giggles too often	
Doesn't make direct eye contact	
Has a soft handshake	

Now take a few minutes and think about why the person behaves that way. Do you think it's intentional? Is it due to a personality or cultural difference? Why do suppose you make the assumptions you do about their behavior? Are these assumptions based on things you've learned from your own culture? From past experiences? From the way you were raised?

Cultures Are Different

In the preceding exercise, you observed your own reactions to people's actions. But not all cultures are the same. Biologically, yes, and in terms of potential, yes, but in terms of how different cultures act and react to different circumstances, no, we are *not* the same. Here are some ways that cultures may differ in their approach to life. Keep in mind that I'm dealing in generalities—sometimes huge ones.

As you read through these, ask yourself, "What am I like? How about the members of my stepfamily?" You'll soon get a sense of your similarities as well as your differences. There is nothing intrinsically wrong with any of these styles; they're just *different* (and, I insist again, different is *not* bad!).

Why So Formal, Dahlink?

Americans tend to be informal ("Nice ta meet you, Joe") and to shake each other's hands. Other cultures may be more formal ("Very honored to meet you, Mr. Howard") and use hugs and kisses as well as handshakes in their greetings. You may *think* your stepdaughter is walking behind you because she's embarrassed to be seen with you, but she might be showing you respect—in some cultures, that's a way of honoring you.

"You're Pushing Me!" "No, I'm Not Even Close!"

Cultures differ in their sense of personal space. People from northern European cultures like to stand further away than people from southern European cultures. If you're in a stepfamily with people from a more southern area, they may (wrongly) consider you cold or uncaring just because you're not as kissy and huggy as they are.

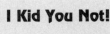

I Kid You Not!

A friend from Nairobi, a young black man, was visiting the States. He got onto a public bus that was almost empty; there was only one other passenger, a middle-aged white woman. In Nairobi, it would be rude to ignore a person sitting alone on a bus. It would be like saying that the person was somehow offensive. So our friend sat down next to the woman. She perceived his gesture of goodwill as threatening and hostile.

Language: Straight Up or On the Rocks?

Some cultures like it all spelled out as explicit, direct communication, with the emphasis on the content of the speech. "Say it like it is, man." They believe that it's what you *say* with words that matters. Other cultures put the emphasis on the entire atmosphere around what's being said. (Were her eyes downcast while she said it, or did she stare at you? Did he wine and dine you before or after making the proposal?)

Food: Fuel or Fantasy?

Food can be a sacrament, a chance for socializing, or a refueling session, and some of how people approach eating and dining is cultural. Religious rules also figure in to eating habits (and I've got more on that later).

"Time to Go!" "Stop Rushing Me!"

"Hurry, hurry! Time is money! Don't be late!" That's one cultural approach. Other cultures work on "rubber time," which is a more elastic sense of time. Get the two approaches together in a household, and you'd best be aware of the differences or you'll all be feeling a *lot* of stress.

You're My Family

Even the perceptions of friends and family can be different in different cultures. The dominant American culture tends to focus on the nuclear family. In other cultures, the family unit is the extended family—uncles, aunts, third cousins thrice removed, and their best friends from grade school. Loyalties are different; self-responsibility is highly valued in some cultures. In others, people believe more in their loyalty and responsibility to their family. In some cultures, the elderly are given status and respect. That isn't true everywhere.

Bumper Stickers Do Not Lie

Beliefs and attitudes vary widely between cultures: "Liberty! Fraternity! Equality!" "Show your respect and know your place." "A woman without a man is like a fish without a bicycle." "Question authority!" "Children should be seen and not heard." "That's a man's job."

Yes, some of it is personal, but all of us are affected by the culture we grow up in. How many of your ideas are based on tradition? How about for your stepfamily?

Teach Your Stepfamily About Your Culture

A strong family identity is a foundation for everybody in the family to stand on. Building a family identity is more than a matter of deciding on the family rules and family style. A family also has a sense of shared history. In a stepfamily of any kind, you're suddenly a family, and you have to *build* your history through shared experiences.

In a cross-cultural family, you need to do more. You need to learn about your stepfamily's culture and teach them about yours. As you build your family identity, your customs and background may be incorporated into your stepkids' lives, becoming a part of their own sense of history, continuity, and future. Here are some tips for letting them all know who you are.

Acknowledge and Celebrate Your Background

It's not just where you live or where you were raised; it's also who your ancestors were, and which values and customs you've kept from their cultures. Let your stepkids know *why* you have a hard time giving them compliments ("If I don't tell you how gorgeous you are often enough, it's probably because my Grandma always said not to tell a child she's beautiful. It might put the double whammy on them. I'll try to do better, but understand where I'm coming from, okay?").

Link Your Stepkids with the World Community

Giving your stepkids a sense of your culture broadens their minds and gives them a sense of mutual humanity, an understanding of something they share with other people in distant parts of the world. "I'm giving you these red beads for your wedding day because it's a Nepali custom. Married women wear red beads. See mine? In this culture, people wear wedding bands. Same thing."

Teach Them the Lingo

Language *is* culture, say many communication experts. Teach your stepkids your language, or at least give them a taste.

Invite Your Stepkids into Your Community

An Anglo-Saxon child may have no idea of the beauty of a gospel church in full swing. An African-American child may be blown away at your family's annual North Coast Indian pow-wow. Your Japanese-American stepchild (and your Japanese-American partner) may never have pigged-out at an all-you-can-eat smorgasbord that's just like the one you left in your home town in the Midwest.

Cook for Them, or Take Them Out to Eat

They may squirm at Vietnamese pho the first time, but soon they'll be begging for it. Compare your matzo ball soup with their won ton soup (broth with dumplings are fabulous the world over!). Explain *why* you love mayonnaise and white bread sandwiches. Make a family cookbook for holiday gifts (and I don't mean just Christmas or Hanukkah; I'm talking Diwali, Santa Lucia, Solstice, and Kwaanza).

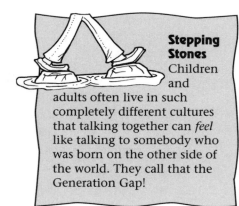

Stepping Stones
Children and adults often live in such completely different cultures that talking together can *feel* like talking to somebody who was born on the other side of the world. They call that the Generation Gap!

Play Them Your Music

Persist gently when they scream at you for imposing Karen Carpenter on their delicate ears. Musical taste—and breadth of taste—takes time.

Share Your Cultural and Personal Stories

Stories gently teach values and consequences, as well as provide a way for your family to get to know and understand you.

Cross-Cultural Communication Skills

Okay, it's hands-on time. Here are some clues to improving your own communication with people from other cultures. If you model it, they will come. These tips are for communicating with stepkids where there's a language barrier as well. Use these tips whether you're speaking in your most comfortable language, their most comfortable language, or a shared language that's not native to either of you.

Speak Slowly and Solidly

Keep it simple. Use simple words, short sentences, and enunciate! Don't chew those words! Don't use slang, and don't be so sarcastic (okay, this tip is for *all* stepparenting). And, above all, don't assume that they understand *what* you said *when* you said it just *because* you said it. If there's even a smidgen of a doubt about understanding, ask them to repeat back to you what you said.

Listen, Listen, Listen

Listen actively. Listen for the meaning, not the lousy grammar. Listen for the positive intent. Suspend your judgment. Hold your horses and *wait* before responding. Listen with your eyes as well as your ears; watch for cues in facial expressions, gestures, and body language.

Question and Query Quizzically

A yes or no answer is often not enough. Ask for more than that because you wanna make sure you guys are understanding each other. Don't assume smiling and nodding means understanding or agreement (in some cultures it might mean only that the person is respectfully listening). You don't want to be asking negatively phrased questions now, do you?

Don't ask convoluted questions such as: "Do you want to go to the store with me and get milk, or would you prefer chocolate milk, after your room is cleaned, unless, did you clean it already?" "Huh?"

Giving Instructions

Break it down step-by-step, and don't explain all the steps at the same time. Ask for questions (and be ready and happy to answer them).

Don't assume that you have been understood, even if the yesses are flying fast and furious. Check out the action. Has the child understood?

"I Don't Get It"

If you're not clear about something, repeat what you have heard and ask for clarification. Then repeat what you believe she meant. You think your stepkid is suicidal because she's standing there with a worried look on her face saying she wants to jump out the window. Don't call 911 instantly; get some clarification. "So you mean you want to jump out the window? Oh! You mean you want to go to the neighbor's yard and jump on that trampoline you can see when you look out your bedroom window! I'll call Carolyn and ask if you can come over."

Nonverbal Cross-Cultural Communication Skills

Lots can be communicated without words. You might be thinking, "Hurrah! That'll make life in a two-language household easier." Well yes—and no. Gestures are not always the same in different cultures and ethnic groups. Try to become aware of cultural taboos, too: Don't put your hand on a Thai child's head; it's insulting. So is pointing your chopsticks at somebody from Japan. In some cultures, touching may not be acceptable; in others, walking with arms around each other, holding hands, or hugging between members of the same sex is groovy. Eye contact can be interpreted as a challenge, a sign of disrespect, or the sign of an honest, forthright person, depending on what culture you come from.

Adjusting to Differences

With differences in values, lifestyle, and approaches to child-rearing, you and your partner have a lot of communicating and problem-solving to do. But you do have an advantage over stepfamilies where the differences aren't so obvious. Because the differences and conflicts are so visible in cross-cultural stepfamilies, you're more likely to put in the time and energy to get to know and respect each other's ways. Doing this increases your chances of having a successful stepfamily.

Food and Dietary Restrictions

Life in a bicultural stepfamily makes dinnertime interesting. "I *hate* cornbread." "Have you ever tried it?" "Well, no...." Unless there are physical reasons (such as an allergy) or religious or moral reasons (such as Muslims or Jews not eating pork), aim for broadening everybody's palates.

Where there are dietary restrictions, whether for religious or moral reasons, it's vital to respect them. Never plop a hunk of gristly meat on a vegetarian's plate and force him to eat. It's cruel and disrespectful (and that's true no matter what age that vegetarian is).

At the same time, respect's gotta go both ways. The vegetarian isn't being respectful if he chants "baby killer" to you at dinner just because you're eating a lovely veal parmagiana. Flexibility is key. You may end up having several sets of pots and pans (one for meat, one for dairy products, and one for the nonkosher vegetarian), but at least you'll have some mutual respect in the household.

Families often have conflicts over how much to eat and whether a child should be forced to clean her plate. It's a challenge for most of us to relax, to present healthy food, and to let children regulate their own intake. People of all cultures should realize that food isn't an area you can effectively regulate. Setting boundaries and limits around your child's eating patterns will only lead you to trouble. Don't go there.

Religious Differences

Interfaith families are increasingly common, and not just for stepfamilies. In some families, one "side" converts; in others, Mom and Dad try to raise the kids with a little of both religions ("They can choose when they are older"). Some throw up their hands and give up on official worship, and some split down the middle and have two camps.

Rachel, mom to two and stepmom to another two, says, "On Saturday my kids and I go to temple. On Sunday, Chris and his kids go to church. We've asked all the kids if they want to explore, but they haven't been ready to do that yet. My kids think of going to temple as a special thing they do with Mom, and I think that Chris' kids feel the same way about their Sunday morning Mass."

You may want to talk with your spiritual leader about solutions for interfaith challenges. Many organized religions run interfaith groups and classes. No matter what approach you take to religion, it's essential that other people's religious choices be respected. You won't have much of a marriage (or a family) if essential beliefs and moral values are disrespected.

Socioeconomic Differences

Culture isn't just a matter of what country your people come from, or what religion you practice. Socioeconomic differences, if they exist, can lead to vastly different approaches to living. It's not just a matter of how much money you make every year, either (though you or your partner may need to adjust to having more or less money, now—see Chapter 10, "Your House, My House, New House"). Socioeconomic differences can include different values around how you talk about and spend money, your attitudes toward credit, your "breeding" and manners, your family's emphasis on education, and so on.

As a member of a new stepfamily, you'll find it helpful to discuss which attitudes of your own and your partner's (not to mention the kids) are based in your socioeconomic cultures. Understanding is key to tolerance.

Generational Cultures

It may sound strange, but even a few years between partners can make a cultural difference. Every generation has its own cultural references—TV shows, music, even attitudes toward life. In our stepfamily, Bill is a child of the '60s, I'm a child of the '70s, his kids are children of the '80s, and the cultural "wars" between Hippie, Punk Rocker, and Gen-X'ers sometimes rage.

If there are age differences between you and your partner, you may find that there are things you don't understand about each other. I don't really *get* it when Bill talks about the sense of community and shared purpose he and his friends felt in their youth. He'll never really understand what it was like to grow up in an in-between generation, feeling too young and too old for all the action. On the other hand, generational culture differences can provide wonderful opportunities to stretch and grow. No doubt your stepfamily will have friends of all ages, too, each bringing their own generation's perspectives to share and learn from.

Holiday Traditions

A stepparent who has different holiday traditions from the rest of the family—especially a stepparent with no child of his or her own—can feel left out in the cold. Any family's traditions have force. It's vital for *everybody* to be considered when planning holidays. (There's a whole lot more on this in Chapter 19, "Holiday Conflicts and Vacations," coming right up.)

I Kid You Not!

How did these two all-Caucasian-from-the-Midwest adults start celebrating Diwali, the Hindu festival of lights? Blain was originally married to an Indian woman from Bombay. They had two kids and then divorced. Blain got remarried to Linda, a woman who had grown up in Peoria with him. Even though Blain and Linda's backgrounds were both Christian, they kept some of the Hindu holidays in their lives, first because of Blain's kids and then because they'd simply been incorporated into the family traditions.

Don't Bring Us Down!

Cross-cultural families can feel pressure and resistance from people both within and outside the family.

Family Pressure

It's hard enough to be a stepparent sometimes. Under any circumstances, it can hurt terribly when your stepkids don't accept you. When there is a racial or cultural component, it has it's own particular sting. Here are a couple of things to remember (before you freak out, cry, and refuse to talk to anybody in the family ever, ever again):

➤ Your race or culture may simply be an easy target. If your stepchild is in the mood to attack you (from resentment, jealousy, or simple moodiness), your culture may simply be a pretext. It doesn't make it okay, and it doesn't make it easier to know this. It just gives you an approach for response. Respond to the impulse, not the insult.

➤ Racial or cultural biases may be a matter of education, or lack thereof. Use it as an opportunity for education. Remember that discipline means teaching; rather than *punish* your stepchild for being cruel, educate her.

When the Larger Family Judges You

Racial and cultural divisions can pull extended families apart. Perhaps your parents-in-law are bigots; what, then, are they saying about you to the stepkids, and how can the stepkids react to their Grands?

Societal Pressure and Judgment

Interracial and intercultural families often face uncomfortable outside pressures. The kids might react in a number of ways (you might, too):

➤ General anger. Anger at you for entering their lives and causing all the problems, or anger at the outside world for being unfair and bigoted.

➤ Fear, regression, and withdrawal from social activities.

Helping Kids Deal with Bigotry

Take a proactive approach. You and your partner will need to present a strong and united front against the world. Talk with your stepkids about what is happening, in age-appropriate language. Seek out other biracial or intercultural families.

The Least You Need to Know

➤ Almost all stepfamilies have cross-cultural components.

➤ Different only means *different*, not better or worse.

➤ In a cross-cultural family, you need to actively learn about your stepfamily's culture and teach them about yours.

➤ Respect is the cornerstone of a thriving cross-cultural stepfamily.

➤ Flexibility is key!

➤ Healthy cross-cultural families are more likely to put in the time and energy to get to know and respect each other's ways.

Chapter 19

Holiday Conflicts and Vacations

In This Chapter

➤ Holiday hoopla and hell

➤ How to plan so everybody wins

➤ Presenting the presents

➤ The keys to surviving family events

➤ Vacation planning with and without the kids

Vacations, special events, and holidays: Rather than being filled with fun and fabulous frivolity, they're often (too often in a stepfamily) filled with high expectations, as emotionally laden as a woman carrying triplets, but doomed, doomed, doomed to disappointment. Let's try to change all that, shall we?

This chapter is about holidays, special events (such as birthdays and Mother's Day), and vacations, all of which should and can be fun!

Planning the Stepfamily Holidaze

Deck the halls, spin the dreidel, roast the turkey, light the candles; it's holiday time! You've been through the wedding and you thought the worst was over! Now it's Christmas, Hanukkah, Kwanzaa, Thanksgiving, Passover, Easter (otherwise known as "the trial-by-fire holidays"), and you know the truth: It's not over, and it will never be over. Holidays are one of the most difficult transitions for stepfamilies to deal with. But come now, not so glum, please. There *are* ways to enjoy yourself and help ensure that the rest of the family has a good time, too.

Expectorating Your Expectations

Let's go back to square one and review the destructive power of expectations. Because holidays are so imbued with ritual (and rituals *aren't* rituals unless you do them over and over), we all expect certain things to happen during the holidays. But what happens when the rituals change? Whoops! We're still expecting them. Alas, we find ourselves back in the lava pit of disappointment, bubbling and melting away. Ouch.

Stepping Stones

"Unrealistic expectations are the biggest risk," says Emily Visher, founder of the Stepfamily Association of America. Don't expect that your holidays will be the same in your new stepfamily as they were before.

The longer you are together as a family, the easier the holidays will feel as you develop your own rituals and traditions. But at first, the crunch of expectations and disappointment can make holidays pretty rough. Each of you in your stepfamily has an internal sense of what feels "right" for the holidays, and this sense is built from your past experiences. Every family does things slightly differently, even if they celebrate the same holidays (remember that cross-cultural families have more complications—refer back to Chapter 18, "Cross-Cultural Stepfamilies," for evidence of *that!*).

Winter Wonderland? Not!

The winter holidays, which for most Americans are the big holidays of the year, can be rough. Be aware! Issues that have been brooding under the skin of the family tend to come to a head and erupt during these times. Expectations are high—often way too high. People have unrealistic images of what the holiday season should be. Think about it: All of our cultural images about what the holidays should look like in a family are based on the nuclear family: Mom, Dad, the kids, the dog, flannel pajamas, the fireplace, the smiling faces.

Memories...

And then there are the memories of how things *were*. Ah, memories of blissful childhood holidays when Mom and Dad were together and everybody was so *happy*.... Whoa, reality check! Were they *really* so great? Things get misty in retrospect. It's true, in some families, holidays are a time when people set aside their problems. But in many others, people get depressed, get drunk, fight, and feel miserable. The holidays are the times of the year when people are most likely to commit suicide. For many families, it's the worst time of the year.

Despite this, kids and adults alike feel nostalgic about the past, even when the past included unhappy family times. Kids want to hold on to their rituals, no matter what they are. After all, rituals are part of who they are.

It's the Little Things

"But we always open our presents in the morning!" "What? No pot roast on Hanukkah? And *we* always eat sour cream, not apple sauce, with the latkes!" Sometimes life is lived in the details, and it's the absence of tinsel on the tree or not having the dog around to sneak the turkey skin that makes people most painfully aware that there have been major changes in their lives.

"Superficialities take on symbolic meanings at holidays. Solutions that can please both sides are a good bet," writes Cherie Burns in her book, *Stepmotherhood: How to Survive Without Feeling Frustrated, Left Out, or Wicked.* To go for the give and take, and to try to create solutions that will satisfy the soul of each family member yet move the stepfamily into the future, people have to understand which details really resonate for them.

Understanding and re-creating are two different things. Many times it is inappropriate to try to re-create somebody else's ritual. "I'd never thought about it, but the first time it was Valentine's Day morning and my parents weren't standing together over my bed serenading me with 'Let Me Call You Sweetheart' was the moment I realized that my mom was really dead, and that nothing was ever going to be the same," says John, whose father remarried the next winter. "I'm totally glad my stepmom didn't try to do that with my dad; I would have lost it."

The loss of holiday rituals is something to mourn, and it takes time—and probably a few holidays without the ritual—to fully heal.

I Kid You Not!

Our holiday rituals usually are associated with an image of an intact, first-marriage nuclear family. When their family doesn't match the image of what a family should be, stepfamily members may feel disappointed, left out, or even embarrassed.

You'll do best if you discuss holiday plans ahead of time and include everybody's input. Negotiating a family holiday is a big reminder that there are other people involved in your family, each of them deeply wedded to their own traditions. Time for a family meeting! Here are some suggestions and advice for revamping the holidays for your new stepfamily.

➤ Plan ahead. Don't let expectations go unspoken, or otherwise somebody will be doomed to disappointment. If your partner has converted to Judaism and the kids think Santa's coming and he's not, you've got a *big* problem on your hands.

➤ The first few years, try to lower your expectations. Get real Zen about it and expect nothing.

➤ Don't assume holidays will be calm and peaceful if daily life is full of strife. There's no holiday from mixed feelings, and you can't force fun, gaiety, and family spirit.

➤ Don't expect holidays to be as they were in the past. Also be aware that the loss of the old ways of doing things is a disappointment for the kids, as well as for you.

➤ Discuss how holidays *used* to be for each of you, and have each person define which rituals are most important to them. This can be hard to hear (especially if you're having some troubles coping with your partner's ex), but it's very important. Incorporate into your holidays a few of these important old rituals.

Stepping Stones
When your family fights over holiday customs, problem-solve by mixing and matching: one of yours, one of mine, one of little Joey's, and three new ones that we've never done before!

➤ The winter holidays are traditionally a time of family togetherness. You and your partner can have some private time, too (eggnog and a hot time in front of a hotter fire), but always take the stepkids into consideration.

➤ Acknowledge that you are starting from scratch. There is something exciting about having the opportunity to create holidays as you'd like them to be. Then create a few new family rituals, things that *none* of you has done before. Aim for creating your own holiday spirit (with additions) and welcoming kids into it.

➤ Don't try to re-create somebody else's rituals. You can't make it as it was, you don't want it as it was (because that was before you!), and you'll only make people unhappy if you try. It will backfire, I guarantee it.

➤ Be flexible and encourage flexibility.

➤ If things are *really* tense, don't force get-togethers, or minimize the amount of time spent together.

➤ Remember to celebrate. You *are* a real family.

Ease into It

Holidays are most enjoyable when the stress is less. Take the pace down a notch. Make it easy on yourself. Instead of cooking a huge meal, go out to dinner. If you're cooking at home, have everybody pitch in. Having several people agonize over whether the turkey is done or whether the little red thing that pops out is broken fosters a sense of togetherness between them. They'll have a shared sense of accomplishment, and sharing the work load will reduce the resentment load. Hallelujah!

Holiday Logistics

So who's gonna spend the holiday where? Sometimes holiday plans are predetermined by custody agreements, but sometimes there's flexibility built in. If you've got some options, discuss them with the kids and try to be flexible about their desires. Rigidity won't help.

Some families split up the holidays each year ("I'll take Halloween, you take Thanksgiving"), and some try to do both (Christmas Eve with Mom and "Uncle" Morrie, Christmas Day with Dad). Some people celebrate twice, once with each parent (this is more true for birthdays than holidays).

In our family, because we're Jewish and Aaron and Rachel's mom is not, they do Christmas with her and at least one night of Hanukkah with us. Thanksgiving? Bill's ex is alone, so the kids celebrate it with her, and we do it with my folks. Later that weekend we usually get together for a second feast (this way everybody has two chances to pig out!).

Don't Be Wicked
Rigidity makes you brittle, and if you are brittle you will break. Remain fluid, flexible, bendable (and forever young!).

I've even heard of families where he spends holidays with his kids at his parents' house, and she spends holidays with her kids at her parents' house. It doesn't matter *how* you divvy it up, as long as it feels pretty fair to everybody.

The Semi-Combined Family Holiday

Watch out for trouble on the stepsibling front when some of the kids have different plans. Stepkids can feel left out if there are "whole" kids in the picture. Try to keep the presents even, and have as much of the major festivities take place when all the kids are around. Lots of discussions (and hugs of welcome) are definitely in order here.

Creating New Holidays

If all the holidays seem to be taken up with stress and other people's claims ("But Thanksgiving is *mine!*"), you can always select another one (Cinco de Mayo, Arbor Day, Stepparents Day) to become an annual blow-out holiday. Give gifts! Decorate the house! Host a party! Host two!

Adult Stepchildren and the Holiday Season

The more adults in the family, the more confusion and chaos there is in terms of holiday logistics. When stepkids partner up and start their own families, the number of adults who aren't quite related and who have their own family holiday traditions will grow incrementally. Talk about logistical nightmares! Once you get it organized ("Joe is doing Christmas, Anthony and John are having their annual midnight Solstice candle lighting, we're all piling over here for the first day of Kwanzaa, and Molly and her kids get to do New Year's brunch this year"), you'll probably have a very merry and *very* busy time.

When there are lots of subfamilies, there's a tendency for people to sit together in cliques at large family parties. And in every family there's at least one diplomat who probably talks too much but who serves as the cross-over member, making everybody feel welcome (or at least united in their annoyance at the diplomat).

Guilt and Loyalty

Stepping Stones
If your partner is without the kids, he or she will feel lonely. Create an alternate festivity for yourselves. Don't just stay home and mope. Don't force false cheer. This may be a time for the bear skin rug, the sexy underwear, and the champagne toasts. If you celebrate Christmas, put the "ho ho ho" back into Santa Claus' laugh.

Holidays can be brutal for the children of divorced parents. Kids very often feel incomplete. If they spend the time with you and your partner, they'll no doubt feel torn about not being with poor Mom or Dad. Try to respect the fact that the kids are thinking of their other bioparent and that their nostalgia for the past is *not* a direct shot at you. Yes, it's true, you don't picture into their fantasies of parental togetherness. It's nothing personal.

Virtually all kids have these fantasies, especially around the holidays. They like the idea of their parents together, even if in reality their parents can't spend two minutes in the same room without making the children want to run off to Katmandu and drown their sorrows in Tibetan yak butter tea and ganja.

If the kids spend the holiday with their other bioparent, they will be missing your partner—and they may even be missing you!

Special Days to You

Mother's Day, Father's Day, your birthday—there are lots of opportunities for agony and martyrdom for stepparents! But don't succumb; a bad attitude will get you nothing but grief. Moping around because nobody remembers your birthday isn't fair. You have to *tell* people, "Hey, my birthday's on Friday and I want us to all go out to dinner." Tell your partner that birthdays are important to you, and strongly suggest that your Love talk to the kids about at least making you a card.

Mother's Day and Father's Day, "Hallmark" holidays or not, can feel like particularly high hurdles to cross, especially the first one. Don't leave it to chance; discuss your feelings with your partner before you get disappointed. Then it's your partner's job to get the kids to call you or make you a card.

Before special events or days that mean something to you, take the initiative:

➤ Be clear about your plans. Anticipate problems and discuss them with the kids.

➤ Tell them your expectations. They aren't mind readers. Talk with your partner.

➤ Don't expect a major deal about Mother's or Father's Day. The kids feel conflicted enough as it is. Acknowledging it is important, but celebrating it may be too painful.

➤ Yes, of course it hurts to be ignored or snubbed. Try to understand the positive intent behind it. It's not meant to hurt you; it's about guilt and loyalty to the other bioparent.

Gift Giving

Gift giving, whether for birthdays or holidays, can be another one of those stepfamily expectation minefields. You're blithely walking through a meadow, and "boom!" And you didn't even realize the expectation was there.

For their first holiday season together, Elisa knocked herself out making hand-woven sweaters for her fiancé's kids. She wrote each one a little letter, expressing how much she enjoyed them and how delighted she was to have them in her life. How she slaved! They opened the sweaters, shrugged, read the notes with blank faces, tossed them down and attacked the rest of the pile. Elisa couldn't believe it. She expected at least a little graciousness from them, a little acknowledgment of the effort she'd gone to.

When it comes to stepkids and gifts, remember these points:

➤ Don't expect *anything* from them. That way you can be pleased as punch if they whisper "Happy Birthday" and seem to mean it.

➤ Don't try to "buy" their love with expensive or large gifts. It won't make a whit of a difference in terms of how accepted you are, and it easily can cause resentment (from the kid or from your partner's ex).

➤ You and your partner should discuss expectations and realities with the kids *before* the holidays. Financial matters may have changed. If kids are used to a lot, let them know ahead of time if things are different now.

➤ Kids often can't bring themselves to offer thanks to a stepparent.

➤ Many kids (stepkids or not) are rude and thoughtless. Others are simply blunt: "I *hate* red. Why did you get me red? Red is for *babies*." How you handle their rudeness is up to your partner and you, though I think it's vital that your stepkids act graciously if your family gives them gifts.

➤ Be fair! In a combined family, spend equal amounts on each child. This kind of fairness is *more* important than it would be in a natural family.

I Kid You Not!

It's easy to snap and lose it when a stepchild looks up from the piles of loot and asks, "Is this all there is? Dad will get a lot more for me." Of course! It pushes all your buttons, that you're not caring enough, not rich enough, not liked enough…. It's vital that you don't bite, because that's bait on the hook. Take a deep breath and say, "I hope you enjoy your presents, Anna. We chose things that we thought you would especially enjoy this year." Leave it at that. Excuse yourself. Go to the bathroom and cry. Things *will* be better next year.

Coordinating Gifts with the Ex

Tommy really wants a dump truck, a computer game, and a bike. Who's going to get what loot for him, Mommy or Daddy? Sonia really wants a Barbie doll, and while you and your partner hate the idea of her playing with such a sexist, materialistic toy, your partner's ex is all for getting her three, plus a Barbie Dream House.

What to do, what to do? Alas, coordination, conversation, and compromise with the ex is in order here. Once wee Tommy and Sonia have made their wish lists, it's time for the two bioparents to talk together to arrange which, who, and how much. This can be uncomfortable—it gets into big, bad money issues.

Encourage your partner not to get into a one-upmanship situation with one partner topping the other's spending. You guys should be the model of restraint; perhaps the ex will follow suit. Very often, reasonable behavior is actually met with reasonable behavior. Don't encourage your partner to buy joint gifts with his ex. Coordination, conversation, and compromise only go so far—joint gift giving falsely signals reunification, and it tends to confuse kids by blurring family boundaries. Your family is your family, the ex's is the ex's, and that's that, birthday or no birthday.

Where Do the Presents Get Opened?

Where should the child open the gifts? All of them on the actual day, no matter what parent she's with, or at separate celebrations, even if that means on a nonholiday? If you opt for all on the day of the holiday option, the nonresident parent won't get to see the gift opening, and it might be uncomfortable for the kid, and the ex. If you opt for separate ones, then the child's celebration is split. There's no strictly correct option. The only thing strictly correct is to discuss it with the ex and with the child, and come to a mutually agreeable solution. Nothing is carved in stone; just because you do something one way once doesn't mean you're doomed to do it that way forever!

Weddings, Graduations, and Other Special Events

They're the times of celebration and rejoicing: family weddings, graduations, your partner's parents' 50th wedding anniversary. But complications also loom. Who'll host the graduation party, Mom and her partner or Dad and his? Both? Can they really get along that long? What about weddings? Who'll stand up with the bride, her biodad (who she's seen two weeks a year since she was 3), or her stepdad (who taught her to ride a bike, shoot pool, bake cookies, solve an algebraic equation, and water ski)?

Catch my drift? You *should* be celebrating, but instead your dentist is threatening to put you in a jaw brace to keep you from grinding your teeth in your sleep.

You, the new step, may be on informal trial, or at least close scrutiny. Everybody is watching to see what the exes do when they see each other. So what's to be done?

➤ Choice #1: Opt out of the big family hoopla and do a couple of smaller family hooplas.

➤ Choice #2: Do the big family hoopla, plan within an inch of your life, and then practice your meditation and *let go of the results.*

If your partner and the ex can agree to disagree enough to negotiate who gets what event (he'll do their son's baseball awards ceremony, and she'll do their daughter's godmother's second wedding), the calm will do the kids a world of good.

Who's Coming to the Party?

If there's acrimony between the exes (as there often is), relatives and friends of both exes have a tough choice. Which one to invite? You and your partner may find yourselves excluded from other people's special events at times. It's tough deciding whom to exclude, and it's hard to cope when you're the one who hasn't been invited. Try to be generous. The choice is often made not on a basis of whom the host likes better, but for many other reasons. Try not to hate the host, and don't use the disappointment as an excuse to become hermits. Get out and do something *else* fun! There are, no doubt, events where *you* make the A list and the ex does not.

Snubbed and Heartbroken

How *can* you take it when you, the step, is snubbed by your stepchild for the bioparent who didn't put as much time and energy (or money) into her uprising? It's hard to be left out of the graduation pictures and the wedding party. But it *is* the child's choice. Enlist

Stepping Stones
Remember that "parent" is not just a noun—it's also a verb.

your partner for understanding, love, and support during this tough time. No matter how hard you try, and no matter what you do, you are *not* the parent. It hurts. Try to suck it in and act noble.

Being Gracious When Nobody Else Is

Wanna chalk up some good Karma? Here's an opportunity to show how noble, sophisticated, big-hearted, mature, and elegant you are. There will be times when you *must* attend an event with the ex. Rise like yeast dough above the rest, practice your serenity, and be utterly and infallibly gracious. You'll drive the petty ex wild and gain major points with everybody else. You'll also give a wonderful lesson in modeling to the kids.

Stepping Stones Maybe the honoree (the birthday girl or the graduation boy) can celebrate twice! Mom and her partner can host the pre-dinner, and Dad and his partner can host the post-dinner—this way, the kid gets *lots* of attention.

When Not to Attend

Sometimes you'll all be invited to an event and, for whatever reason, you know it would *not* be a good thing for you, your partner, and the ex to be in the same room. It may be too hard on you, or it may be too distressing for the kids. This can be particularly hard when it's a child's special event, such as a wedding, graduation, birthday, or award ceremony. Sometimes your partner should go and you should not.

If you and/or your partner decline, send something along to show that you are thinking of the child at his or her special moment. It's easy for a child to interpret physical distance as a lack of caring, and that certainly is *not* what you want the child to feel.

Your Partner's Funeral

Hopefully some issues in this section will never affect you.

When your partner dies, you'll probably be in charge of the funeral plans. Try not to be petty about the ex attending. The children may need their remaining bioparent for strength. If the kids are young, you may need to have a discussion with the other bioparent about whether it's appropriate for the kids to attend the funeral.

If things are very strained between you, perhaps you can call upon a friend to act as your emotional bodyguard, to keep the ex from getting near you and to try to remove the ex if he or she decides to throw a scene.

Sometimes grown children want to be involved or take over the funeral plans. Your grief and shock may make it hard for you to resist. Express your feelings as best as you can. Try to listen. Deaths often bring family members together rather than split them apart.

What about when the going gets even rougher? There are times (and families) where things are so bad between the step and the stepkids and the ex that the step doesn't feel comfortable or welcome at his or her own partner's funeral. That's ridiculous, childish behavior. If there's a family get-together afterwards, you can politely excuse yourself, but you are absolutely within your rights to attend your own partner's funeral.

➤ If things are rough family-wise, make sure that you have at least one friend with you to escort you to and fro.

➤ Funerals are for mourning. Ignore over-zealous mourners who express bitterness to you.

➤ Plan a private ceremony later, a time to say good-bye in a private way that would be significant to both of you. This could be a walk on a favorite beach, crying over a *Casablanca* video, or a ceremonial toast with your partner's favorite sherry.

Vacation Vagaries

Vacations can be rough to negotiate. Between school schedules, work restrictions, and visitation arrangements, it's a surprise that they ever happen at all. So here you are, with your annual two-week holiday looming. What are you going to do, where are you going to go, and (here's the $64,000 question) will you take the stepkids?

➤ With or without the kids, you've gotta plan well in advance so that everybody (including the ex) is in agreement about dates and (if you're taking the children) destinations.

➤ Always establish Plan B. People get sick, and emergencies occur.

With or Without the Kids?

Are you going to take the kids along? If you've got a semi-combined family with two sets of children, you may not have a choice. Say it's summer. Hers go off to the biodad, and here come yours! There's never *nobody*. You can try to arrange it so that everybody goes on vacation together, and this has one real advantage: True family feeling is built through shared experiences. Any vacation will have its ups and its downs, and sometimes the downs provide the most interesting war stories (in retrospect) and a sense of "all of us against the world." A group vacation can be excellent treatment for the stepfamily without much of a sense of togetherness.

Taking just some of the kids can be advantageous, too, especially if you don't usually get to spend much time with them. Once again, it's the shared experience thing.

Where To? And What to Do?

There are endless possibilities for vacation destinations, depending upon your time restraints, budget, and interests. In general, gear your activities toward the lowest common denominator, the youngest kids. You can usually supplement with activities for the older ones, but, for instance, a 4-year-old will *not* get much from a European wine tour (and therefore, neither will you). Try for Euro-Disney with time arranged on the side for the adults to visit a couple of caves.

Check out family resorts with baby-sitting services. Not all of them are terribly expensive. It's important to spend some time alone, just you and your partner. You could also go early and have the kids shipped to you, or stay late and ship the kids back.

Be aware that the ex might flip out and demand the kids back, or manipulate them so that they *want* to go home. It's been known to happen, even on brief trips.

Without the Kids

If you decide to take a little jaunt without the kids, watch out for sabotage by the other bioparent ("Oh gee, I can't take care of Jimmy after all, so sorry!"), and have another plan set up for emergency baby-sitting. Perhaps the Grands?

The Least You Need to Know

➤ Holidays are one of the most difficult transitions for stepfamilies to deal with.

➤ You cannot and should not re-create somebody else's holiday traditions. This is your time to start fresh, perhaps blending a few old rituals with some new ones.

➤ Communication and advance planning can help create holidays the whole family will enjoy.

➤ If you want a birthday party, *say so*!

➤ Being excluded from a special event is not always personal.

➤ Stepfamily vacations can help create stepfamily unity.

Gay Stepparenting

Gay stepparenting is basically like stepparenting of any kind, but with a few unique twists. A gay stepfamily is, in some ways, similar to any cross-cultural stepfamily in terms of the pressures mounted against it by the world, and by the family. But being a gay stepparent brings in a whole host of different—and often very difficult—cultural issues into play. As in any stepfamily, the gay stepparent has to define his or her role.

Stepparenting in a gay or lesbian partnership is often complicated by legal factors. Face it: Much bigotry remains, and when it comes to custody and visitation rights, the court system is *not* on your side. Unfortunately, it's almost impossible to look at gay stepparenting without considering the legal issues and ramifications. In this chapter, we'll look at those, too. This chapter focuses on gay and lesbian stepparenting, where a child is born into a heterosexual relationship and one parent later becomes involved with a same-sex partner. This is how most children traditionally end up with gay and lesbian parents.

More and more, gay and lesbian couples are having kids "from scratch," through alternative insemination, adoption, or surrogate mothers. I'll touch briefly on this kind of co-parenting, but it's largely subject matter for a different book (see the recommended readings in Appendix A for suggestions).

Gay and lesbian stepparenting is a huge subject, and all I'm going to be able to do is give you a quick scenic tour. Hang onto your hats, here we go!

I Kid You Not!

With the increase in gay and lesbian couples having (or adopting) babies together comes an increase in another kind of gay or lesbian stepparent. Say Rosie and Posie have a baby, Sam. Rosie is the biomom, and Posie adopts Sam. Rosie and Posie, both legal parents of Sam, break up, and Rosie gets together with Reeva. Reeva is a lesbian stepparent to Sam, and though her legal status is as iffy as *any* stepparent's would be, at least the other legal parent, Posie, won't be fighting for sole custody on moral grounds!

The Gay or Lesbian Stepparent

Here you are, a gay or lesbian person in love with a parent. What is your relationship to your partner's child? Are you a friend, an "aunt" or "uncle," or a stepparent? Because legal marriage is not yet an option, it's a little trickier to answer that question than it might be in a heterosexual partnership.

We're talking emotional and financial commitment here. Because there's no judge or clergy to pronounce you married, family becomes a state of mind. Only the two of you can answer the question of when you are a family.

Let's assume that this isn't just a dating situation, but that you're deeply in love and building a life together. Who are you to the kids, and what's your role? That's gonna depend. Gay and lesbian relationships have the same long-term success rates as heterosexual relationships, so that's not an issue. There's that legal stuff looming, especially if the other bioparent does not approve (as is often the case). We'll look at that in a moment.

Then there's the "in the closet or out" question. What's it like to be out of the closet and see your stepkids suffering from bigotry and ignorance? How can you be a stepparent to somebody who doesn't know you're gay?

In or Out?

Making the decision to go "public" with your life and sexuality is a huge personal decision. There's no one right answer.

In some gay and lesbian families, everybody is already out of the closet. In some ways, this makes life easier (no lies, no subterfuge) but, then again, life can be harder if you experience outside prejudice. Much of your experience in this regard will be geographically based. Life in San Francisco's Castro District or in Manhattan will be a lot less stressful for you and the kids than it would be in the Bible Belt (well, unless you're talking about rent and parking).

In some families, coming out of the closet is not an option because of career, environment, family, or legal considerations. In that case, you need to figure out whether the kids should know. Some of that depends on their age, and whether or not you and your partner are living together (yup, some people are totally committed but unable to live together because of legal custody issues).

Young children who haven't been exposed to bigoted ideas accept gay and lesbian relationships with no problem. That's the good news. The bummer is that young children may not be able to keep their mouths shut when they need to. Older children may already have biases that need correcting, and they may suffer more from peer problems. They may also have trouble keeping it a secret, and they may suffer from having to keep something so vital to their lives (such as who their parents are) quiet.

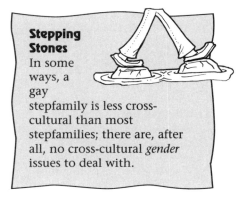

Stepping Stones
In some ways, a gay stepfamily is less cross-cultural than most stepfamilies; there are, after all, no cross-cultural *gender* issues to deal with.

Coming Out Is a Process

For most people, coming out is a process, not an incident. Many people are "out" with their friends and the gay or lesbian community long before they decide to tell their children. They may be "out" with their kids long before they tell their ex. (Sometimes they never tell their ex, for fear of custody or visitation consequences.) Little kids don't understand sexuality and just take it in stride. So Mommy loves Alice, so what?

Many people are delightfully surprised at the love and acceptance their kids of any age express to them when the truth is explained. Often, though, older kids are initially distressed. It can be brutal for parents to face the wrath of their nonaccepting children.

Stepping Stones
There's Something I've Been Meaning to Tell You, edited by Loralee MacPike, is an interesting and moving collection of true stories by parents who've come out as gay and lesbian to their children. Check it out!

223

Kid Reaction: Fear!

Kids of the same sex as a gay or lesbian parent sometimes react to the news of their parent's sexuality with fear. They fear that the new partner will take their parent away from them (this is common in heterosexual relationships, too), and they also fear that because their parent is gay, that will make them gay, too.

➤ Your partner should reassure the kids that *nobody* will ever take the child's place in the parent's heart and life. (You, too, can participate in this important conversation.)

➤ Sexuality is random throughout the population. Reassure the kids of this fact, even if they don't ask.

The Kids' Reaction to You

How will the kids react to you, their new stepparent? If their parent has come out as gay or lesbian *before* you two got serious and decided to make a life together, the issues you'll face will be very similar, if not identical, to those that heterosexual stepparents face.

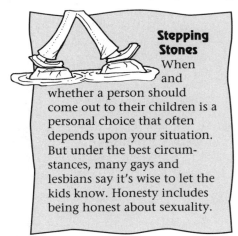

Stepping Stones
When and whether a person should come out to their children is a personal choice that often depends upon your situation. But under the best circumstances, many gays and lesbians say it's wise to let the kids know. Honesty includes being honest about sexuality.

If your partner comes out to the kids at the same time that he or she presents you as the big love of his or her life, there may be a very different reaction. The kids may have known you as a friend of their mom's or dad's for a long time, they may love you in that capacity, and yet they may flip out and reject you now that they understand that you play a more intimate role in their parent's life than they had realized.

Don't feel bad; this kind of reaction is common in many heterosexual cases, too ("You mean you and John *do* it, Mommy? That's terrible!"). And the closer you've been with the child, the more she may feel betrayed by you. Nope, she'll think, he's no longer my friend; he likes my daddy better than me!

Your Role

So, who are you going to be to the kids? As in any stepparenting relationship, your role will be defined by you, your partner, and the stepkids. Here are some ideas to get you started thinking about your role. (Now's a good time to go back and review the steps to acceptance of authority in Chapter 9, "New Family Structures.")

➤ The "traditional" model of the gay stepparent (if such a thing can be said to exist) is to use an aunt or uncle as a model. You can be tough and eccentric "Uncle" Bobby, who hangs out with Dad. How about wild "Aunt" Lizzy? Of course most aunts and uncles don't sleep with Mommy or Daddy, so it's not quite the same thing. But being a concerned, semi-involved adult is never a bad place to begin.

➤ What do you do when you're an in-the-closet stepparent? How do you stepparent when the child doesn't know? Whether or not the kids understand the situation, you can participate in their rearing as a responsible, involved, and concerned adult. You don't need to claim the title of "stepparent" to have a real impact on their lives.

➤ Your role as a stepparent is even more open to interpretation than it would be in a heterosexual relationship. You're not facing the same wicked assumptions, so in some ways, you may not have as many struggles. You can parent deeper, sooner, and more broadly.

Co-Parenting

Although most children of gay parents are born into heterosexual relationships, the incidence of "turkey baster," sperm bank, and surrogate-mother babies born to gay and lesbian couples is rising. A co-parenting situation differs from a stepparenting situation in that there is no other bioparent to participate in child rearing or provide emotional input in the child's life.

One of the challenges of being the non-biological co-parent is fixing the concept in people's minds (including your own) that you are an equal parent, and you've got to do this all without the benefit of the law. Consider signing a co-parenting agreement (there's more on this below). Writing the agreement will help you clarify your role. Also, in more and more states, non-biological co-parents are securing their legal rights to their children by adopting them. There are more details on gay adoption in Chapter 24, "In Addition, There's Adoption!"

Don't Be Wicked
Don't ignore the kids just because you don't understand them. People who haven't spent a lot of time around children (and this includes many gays and lesbians) often feel uncomfortable around children. Give it time. Go to the library and read up about child development.

Step-Speak
A *co-parent* is one of two equally responsible participating parents in a child's life. A co-parent is not necessarily a biological parent. The term is often used to designate one of a child's two parents when the parents are gay or lesbian.

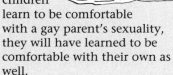

Stepping Stones
When children learn to be comfortable with a gay parent's sexuality, they will have learned to be comfortable with their own as well.

The Courts and Custody

Here are some details about the legal situation specific to gay stepfamilies. (Turn to Chapter 22, "Legal Stuff," for more general legal advice.)

It's scary to be lesbian or gay with a family and children when the custody situation is as precarious as it often is. Archaic ideas and rigid court systems have led to many life-long partners who feel that they're not free to live with each other, for fear that one will lose his or her children. Things are improving for gay parents, but they still aren't easy, and in some places the laws are fairly draconian. Homosexual sex (as well as sex between unmarried partners of any kind) is still a crime in some states!

If your partner's ex (and the family of your partner's ex) is liberal and accepting of your partner's sexuality, breathe a very big sigh of relief. You're very fortunate. There will be no custody battle unless one of the ex-partners declares one.

Big Bad Courts

Custody decisions vary widely from state to state and jurisdiction to jurisdiction. This means that you and your partner need to do research about your rights and the legal precedents. Yup, if there's a custody battle a-brewin' (even if it's just a teeny black cloud off in the distance), it's time to get some *good* legal advice before you've got a tornado in your front yard.

The traditional advice to parents in the middle of a custody dispute is to be discreet in your sexual activity. This holds true and should be doubly stressed for lesbian and gay parents. It's possible that you may be able to live together and pass as roommates, if people don't know you are gay.

Historically, evidence of homosexuality has been sufficient to deny custody to a parent. The stigma of homosexuality (combined with the court's false assumption that just because you're gay or lesbian, you live a promiscuous lifestyle) has produced this reaction. Now, it's true, courts are changing for the better, but the system still isn't great.

There's some good news: Increasingly, the burden is on the heterosexual parent or couple to prove the connection between a gay parent's lifestyle and harm to the child. There's also some bad news: You partner can use anything (including the fact that your stepkid might be teased at school) to prove that the kid won't be comfortable, happy, or safe with you.

If your partner wants custody of the children, he or she should be *way* discrete in lifestyle. If your partner has custody, remember (how could you forget, with these ugly threats hanging over your head) that custody and visitation terms can always be changed. This may mean that you're a hush-hush matter.

Can't live with that? If you two are living openly together as a gay or lesbian couple and you want to openly stepparent your stepchild, you should be prepared to testify in court. Then it's up to the judge.

Stepparenting in Absentia

In some states, when the ex objects to the presence of a gay or lesbian parent's partner, the courts will restrict visitation to times the partner isn't there or, if the gay parent and the partner are living together, will disallow overnights. Other states are more reasonable, allowing the usual visitation unless harm to the child is demonstrated.

When your partner has kids and you are not allowed to spend time with them, it's hard to be an active stepparent, now, isn't it? When you and your partner are very close and share all aspects of your lives together, being cut off from such a big piece of your Love's life can feel destructive, and just plain sad. Your role shifts to support system and Big Ear for your partner.

Just because you can't see or get to know your stepkids doesn't mean that you should ignore they exist. Talk with your partner about the visits. Live vicariously. It's important to your relationship to maintain some kind of link, even if it is purely emotional. Remember, too, that things will change over time: The kids will grow up, and the legal atmosphere will shift. Never give up hope.

Your Rights as a Gay Stepparent

You've been together seven years and your stepson is nine. Now you're breaking up. Can you get visitation rights? Not usually. Unless you've adopted your stepchild, you've got no parental rights (you've also got no parental responsibilities!). There have been a few new rulings in Wisconsin, Pennsylvania, and New Mexico that may show a change in rights in those states.

Be prepared to prove you've acted as a parent in all ways (including financially), and you may have a chance. While you're together (and deeply committed to parenting the little Snookums in question), it's a good idea to draft a co-parenting agreement.

A co-parenting agreement is a document that clarifies the stepparent's role, including making explicit the expectation that, should the adult relationship dissolve someday, the stepparent will continue to play a role in the child's life. It may, or may not, hold up in court. A co-parenting agreement is not directly enforcible—it merely shows intention. But there is growing support among the legal community for the idea that a child suffers when removed from contact with people whom she loves, and who have played a parental role.

Co-parenting agreements can be short, or they can be very detailed. The National Center for Lesbian Rights at 415-392-6257 has a free sample co-parenting agreement. It's geared toward sperm-donor situations, but can easily be modified.

> **Don't Be Wicked**
> Just because you're together and lovey dovey *now* doesn't mean you'll always be. Protect your rights! Sign a co-parenting agreement.

Coping with the World's Reactions

Most lesbian and gay parents find that the world, for the most part, is helpful and kind. Many, many lesbian and gay stepparents have felt only support from members of the communities where they live and work. Yet there's enough cruelty and ignorance in the world to make anybody feel weary and outraged at times. It can also be exhausting to have to constantly explain your family configuration to strangers.

"It isn't easy being green," as the song goes, and being publicly identified as a lesbian or gay stepfamily isn't always easy either, especially for the kids. Certain places are more gay- and lesbian-friendly than others, but even in the least homophobic areas of the country, kids (and you) may be targets for bigotry.

It's an odd paradox, but at the same time that many gay and lesbian couples want to be less visible in the community for legal reasons, the fact that they are raising kids together makes them *more* visible. PTA meetings and Little League, pediatrician visits and school bake sales—as a stepparent, you may want to be involved in your stepkid's activities, and these activities will bring you into public view.

Your position and the perceptions of you within the gay and lesbian communities may also shift now that you're involved in raising a family.

➤ Explain your family configuration in a cheery, matter-of-fact tone. This will disarm most people and make it difficult for them to respond in a negative fashion. April Martin, author of *The Lesbian and Gay Parenting Handbook*, writes about the confident exterior attitude she projects: "My aim is to convey the unspoken message that anyone worthy of my respect and friendship will simply not have a problem with gay and lesbian parents."

➤ The lesbian or gay stepfamily will need to be especially aware of school situations and run interference: "Yes, John *does* have two Mommies. Call either of us if there's an emergency, please."

➤ Know your legal rights. You, your partner, and the child have the legal right not to be harassed.

➤ A child being teased at school needs support, respect, and a show of pride. It's hard work being an advocate for justice. Celebrate him. It will help.

➤ Create a place of peace, self-esteem, and mutual respect within your home. A child raised with respect will have the strength to dismiss bigotry, not internalize it.

The Least You Need to Know

➤ Most aspects of gay and lesbian stepparenting are identical to heterosexual stepparenting.

➤ There are pros and cons to coming out to the kids, but if circumstances allow, it's best to let the kids know.

➤ Kids may feel resentful of you and jealous of your relationship with their bioparent (so what else is new?).

➤ The courts are getting more lenient about awarding custody to gays and lesbians, but don't count on it.

➤ You'll probably find that most people are kind, open, and accepting.

Chapter 21

Stepfamilies in Crisis

In This Chapter

➤ Figuring out when trouble means TROUBLE!

➤ Kids and self-abuse, substance abuse, and eating disorders

➤ How to respond when your stepkid is in trouble

➤ Dealing with violence

➤ Incest and other sibling issues

➤ Finding a good therapist and good therapy

Life around the house is no fun. You dread coming home from work. Nobody is talking to anybody, though there's a lot of screaming going on. Snarls have replaced smiles (if there ever were any in the first place). Maybe the stepkids are acting up, in trouble at school or with the law. Maybe they're depressed, destructive, bulimic, or lethargic. (Maybe your partner is. Maybe you are.)

Normal stepfamily life is stressful, but there is stress and there is stress, if you know what I mean. Sometimes the day-to-day complexities of living together erupt into a crisis. If you, your partner, or any of the kids are at each other's throats all the time, are having trouble coping with daily life, or are just so miserable that you wonder whether it's worth it, it's time to take a serious look at the situation.

Stop tossing and turning with vague anxiety all night, and face the truth: Things stink, they look hopeless, and you feel utterly overwhelmed. "Warning! Internal combustion engine about to explode!" I have a sneaking suspicion it might be time for some outside intervention. This chapter is about problem-solving (for the stepfamily, you, and your partner) on an individual and a family level.

Stepchildren with Problems

A stepchild with problems creates problems for the entire family. High-stress behavior never happens in a vacuum; even one member of the family "losing it" is one too many, and this affects the stepfamily as a whole.

Divorce, death, remarriage, a new family configuration—these are all very hard things for a child to adjust to. Children of divorce are at risk for depression and stress, and this can sometimes turn into self-destruction, violent behavior, failing in school, and addiction. Most kids will show some signs of stress, so don't immediately leap to thinking your stepkid is having big trouble. Give it some slack time, but be wary.

How will you and your partner know if the adjustment is happening? If you are new in your stepchild's life or not very emotionally close, watching for changes in behavior may be difficult for you. After all, you don't know the child! Here's where your partner will need to take a leadership role.

How can you and your partner tell if a kid is in trouble? There are several key telltale signs to watch for, including these:

➤ School problems
➤ Peer relationships
➤ Problems at home

School Problems

Your stepchild's response to school is an excellent indicator of how things are going. Watch for a sudden drop in grades, change in interest, or increased absenteeism. It may be that something nasty is happening at school, or it may be a reaction to stuff going on at home. Either way, you and your partner will need to deal with it.

Peer Relationships

Check for a change in friends. Is your partner's pretty little Miss-Goodie-Two-Shoes-straight-A-girl suddenly piercing her midriff and hangin' with the bad crowd? If she's still getting those A's, she may just be playing with new styles of living. If she's losing her old friends, acting belligerent, and messing up her grades, it's time to check it out. How old is she? Might it just be the tumultuous tides of adolescence? Or perhaps you're all living in a new community and your stepson is having trouble making new friends. Is he usually shy?

If you don't live with the child, it's going to be especially tough to figure out how the peer relationships are going.

Problems at Home

You'll get your best sense of how a stepchild is adjusting (or not adjusting) by how he or she acts at home. Yes, expect sullenness, especially toward you. But if you're seeing evidence of self-abuse or addiction, if the child is committing crimes, or if things are unbearably strained, your stepchild—and the family as a whole—may need some additional help.

> **Stepping Stones**
> It's hard to admit that your stepkid is in real trouble—it's human to try to deny it. But it's better to look at it now than suffer the consequences of letting it go too far.

Self-Abuse, Eating Disorders, and Addiction

Watch out for signs of serious trouble, depression, or self-abusive behavior, especially in the teen years. (You may want to take a look again at Chapter 12, "Stepteens: The Brutal Years," which is all about these crazy teen years.) Keep paying attention to what's going on, even if they initially ignore you—the more trouble they're in, the more they *will* ignore you. Part of good stepparenting (indeed, parenting of any kind) means persisting in showing your care, concern, and positive reinforcement, even as the child cuts you cold. Believe me, they do hear the care in your voice, and it matters. Giving a child a sense of his own strengths will help him learn to respect his body, respect and care for himself, and feel confident enough to resist peer pressures.

Here's a list of things to look for as you assess whether your stepchild can use some outside counseling:

> ➤ Self-abuse includes cutting, burning, extreme risk-taking, and other self-destructive behavior. While pierces, tattoos, and branding may be the style, there's a difference between minor risk-taking and keeping up with the crowd, and major self-damage caused by depression.

> ➤ Eating disorders, including anorexia (self-starvation) and bulimia (bingeing and purging), are common among teens and younger children. If your stepchild is developing an eating disorder, you may be the last person to notice. An anorexic's loss of weight may be so gradual that you don't notice. Many bulimics maintain a normal weight. Eating disorders require professional help, so don't try the do-it-yourself approach.

> **Stepping Stones**
> School involvement (for you, your partner, or both) is a good way to keep an eye on your stepchild's well-being. If the teachers know you as a concerned parent, they'll be more likely to keep an eye on your child to see how he or she is doing. Call for a general chat; don't wait for conference time or to be called into the office!

➤ Substance use is different from substance abuse, and many kids do some experimentation in their teen years. When a child or teen is already stressed, however, substance use can easily turn to abuse. Substance abuse is rarely so obvious or glaring as trash baskets full of empty gin bottles, track marks on an arm, or scary people tromping through your house bearing syringes and burning all your spoons. Look for other signs: plunging school grades, change in weight, loss of interest in life. By the time a child is addicted to a substance, there are usually a lot of other visible troubles—hey, problems leak.

Violence: in the Child, in the Household

Violent tendencies seem to be part of human nature, but that doesn't mean it's acceptable in your stepchild or in your household. To reduce such tendencies in your child, you'll need to take personal responsibility to reduce his exposure to violence inside and outside the household. Raising gentle human beings is difficult at times. Think about how glorified violence is in our society: Saturday morning cartoons, bloody video games, action and horror flicks, the seductive and frightening qualities of gangs. At school and after school, the toughest kid often gets the most respect, and this, too, can make a child become violent, especially a child who is frustrated and dismayed by a shake-up in his home life.

Don't Be Wicked
Never threaten violence out loud, whether or not you mean it. "I'm gonna KILL you!" might merely be words, but it can be extremely threatening to a child. On the other hand, *thinking* "I'm gonna KILL you!" might actually relieve some of your tension—just keep it to yourself.

In a stepfamily where you may not live with the child, or where you share the child's time with another family, it's tougher to reduce violent influences. But within your own household, you and your partner can do a few important things:

➤ Reduce TV time. The average American preschooler watches up to six hours of TV a day. By the time your stepchild is 14, she'll have seen 11,000 murders! There's a lot of evidence that TV desensitizes kids to violence and encourages violent behavior.

➤ Model nonviolent behavior. If you or your partner is having trouble controlling your emotions, if there has been child abuse of any kind (or there's any danger of abuse), get help immediately. Parents Anonymous has groups throughout the country. The National Office at 909-621-6184 can refer you to the group closest to you.

➤ Discipline without corporal punishment. Violence of any kind escalates and tends to create more violence. A child who gets hit at home may well take out her frustration on another child.

Reacting to Trouble

Stepparents react to a stepchild in trouble in a variety of ways. It's common to feel angry. Anger is normal, natural, and very often an appropriate emotion to feel when somebody is messing up and the mess is affecting your life. Stepparents also talk about wanting to put emotional distance between themselves and the troubled child ("He's your son, you deal with him!"). For stepparents who aren't very experienced in parenting, a child in trouble can feel utterly overwhelming.

Blame Doesn't Help

It may feel momentarily gratifying to blame your partner's ex for your stepchild's problems ("Well, of course he's a delinquent. Just look at his crazy mother!") or to blame it all on the divorce (this is a symptom of guilt that your partner may express). Neither of these reactions helps anything. Blame clouds reality and takes up a lot of emotional space. Lose it.

A Bit About Anger

When you and your partner first find out about a child's troubles or misbehavior, you may be furious. Hey, everybody flips their lid sometimes, and there are good things to be said for expressing righteous anger. When you show your anger cleanly, it demonstrates to the kids that angry feelings can be expressed in a way that doesn't harm or hurt.

The trick is in figuring out how to use—not abuse—your anger and how to manage it, redirect it, and problem-solve your way out of conflict.

➤ Remove yourself from the immediate situation, if necessary, and either vent your anger (pound a pillow or scream into the wind) or practice some relaxation (breathe deeply and meditate). You may need to do both.

➤ Make sure that you're not redirecting to your family the anger you feel at the guy who ran the red light and almost crashed into you on the way home. If you're in a foul mood and ready to growl at anything, warn the family that a large bear has just entered the house and that you aren't really angry, just very grumpy. (But such a warning isn't enough—you still shouldn't take it out on everybody!)

➤ Express your anger clearly, using words to show your expectations, emotions, values, and needs. State what you are angry about. Tell your stepchild what you would like done about it. Use "I" statements.

➤ Try to respond effectively, no matter how strong and angry your first reaction was.

➤ Pay attention to yourself. Are you still angry even though the immediate problem has been resolved? Hash it out with a friend, or write it down in a letter (you don't need to send it). It's important to acknowledge how you feel so that it doesn't explode in your face in the future.

Stepfamily Problems

As we've learned, problems leak. It's rare that only one person in a stepfamily is troubled or sad. People affect each other. Then there are all the interdynamics of living together....

Problems in Your Marriage

With all the usual strains of a stepfamily, it's no wonder marriages have such a high failure rate. Pay attention to your marriage, and keep your priorities straight. Go back and review Chapter 8, "Your Marriage." Watch for problems. Sometimes they can sneak up on you when you aren't looking.

It took an affair for Joe and Sue Ellen to get their priorities in order. They'd been so busy dealing with Joe's son's resistance to Sue Ellen and Sue Ellen's daughter's plunging grades that they'd stopped celebrating life and each other. Joe, desperately needing a break, began a brief affair with his boss at work. After several months of crisis (and some good counseling), Joe and Sue Ellen were back on track. This time they were paying attention to their marriage, as well as to the kids' problems.

Resolving Stepsibling Hostility

Stepsibling hostility is a normal part of living together in a family. Have you ever known sibling children not to fight? You have? Then I promise they aren't spending time with each other.

When you are trying to resolve stepsibling (or sibling) conflict, try to stay neutral and avoid taking sides. Think of yourself as a referee, or let them resolve it by themselves.

One disciplinary approach is to have all the kids take responsibility for a conflict or problem. (Remember, you don't need to be punitive.) There's a bonus if they all get annoyed at you for holding them all responsible: They'll ally themselves together (against you, yeah, but at least they're in agreement now!).

I Kid You Not!

There's a trick I learned back when I was a drama student. The cast of the play just hadn't gelled. Nobody liked each other much, and there was no sense of camaraderie on stage. The play stunk. The night before opening night, the director (a wise and experienced man) called us all together and chewed us out so thoroughly that we all left furious and hurt, but bonded against him! That was exactly what the show needed to give it that needed oomph. We were a hit!

The Specter of Step-Incest

They're not related, technically. They haven't been raised together, so they don't have the built-in taboo family members have against having sex with each other. Susie hasn't seen Bobby in his dirty dydee…. You get the picture. He's a boy, she's a girl…uh oh. Trouble.

When I was in high school, the following horror story happened to two kids (I knew them both) who were going together, and had been for about a year. A year-long relationship means a very serious relationship in high school. John and Kelly were one of the most popular couples around. John's parents were divorced. Kelly's parents were divorced. John's dad and Kelly's mom—you guessed it. They met through the kids, fell in love, and rapidly got married. Now John and Kelly (who had been having a sexual relationship) were suddenly living together like brother and sister.

This story struck chills into every kid's heart in high school (it still gives me the shudders). What could the kids do? Poor John and Kelly. Two months after the marriage, John and Kelly were barely talking to each other. Sixteen was too young for them to be living together as lovers, and living together as siblings was unbearable for them. For each of them, this had been their first love relationship. Friendship felt out of the question. The emotions were too intense. (And what I want to know is, what were those adults thinking of? I know, they weren't thinking at all!)

If you have kids in the house of preteen or teen age, consider these:

➤ You're not the thought police, but it's a good idea to monitor potential incestuous situations and keep the bedrooms as far apart as possible.

➤ Watch for intense feelings between them. "I hate her!" might be covering up intense attraction.

➤ Don't ignore any sexual charge you see; it won't just go away.

➤ Discuss it with the kids, even if you don't see anything between them. Assure them that it's normal to feel sexual feelings but that it's not okay to do anything about it.

➤ Stress the risks: disease, pregnancy, family breakup, emotional breakdown.

➤ Little kids are more likely to develop the normal sibling taboo.

➤ If it's occurring under your roof, you have a say in what is and isn't allowed. It is up to you. If the kids are adolescent, sexually involved with each other, and unwilling to stop being involved, one or both of them may need to move out for the health of the entire family.

➤ Adult stepsiblings in their 20s or 30s are adults. You cannot control their behavior, but you have a right to react and respond.

➤ Don't be afraid to get counseling. The hormones are normal, the situation is difficult, and a therapist may be able to help.

Incest Across Generation Lines

Incest or sexual abuse between parents and children (step or biological) is, unfortunately, a huge problem (you'll find a brief section on this in Chapter 11, "It's the Children!"). It is completely unacceptable and very damaging to the child and the family. If it is going on in your stepfamily (or even if you suspect it is), you need some help getting through this very difficult time.

I Kid You Not!

Famous stepparent in literature: Humbert Humbert, the evil pedophile in Nabokov's *Lolita*, was her stepfather. He arranged to have her mother killed while she was away at summer camp, then picked sweet Lolita up and seduced her. Talk about incest!

S.O.S! Save Our Stepfamily!

Assessing the situation is the hardest part. Once you've made the decision to get some help for your family, you'll find that there are lots of resources available. Therapy is a tool; it's a way to learn, take care of yourselves, and heal old wounds. Therapy is positive. Just because you're seeking therapy doesn't mean that you're nuts, that your family is a failure, or that you've done something wrong and need punishment.

When you've decided to get help, you may have to push the issue with the rest of the family. Just because they are initially resistant doesn't mean you should give up the idea without trying. Go by yourself for the first couple of times, if necessary.

Finding the Right Person

There are many different types of therapies and many types of therapists. You'll need to think (at least briefly) about the therapist's type of training and personal style. Hang on, it isn't as bad as all that! Besides, I'll help you figure it all out right now!

Where Will You Find One?

When you are looking for a therapist or other mental health professional to help you and your family, you can begin by following these tips:

➤ Asking friends and family members. Got a sister who's been in therapy for years? Ask her to ask her therapist for a referral to somebody who specializes in stepfamilies.

➤ Checking with social service agencies, family service agencies, and the National Association for the Advancement of Psychoanalysis (212-741-0515). All these can give you referrals to therapists in your area. In some parts of the country, mental health professionals advertise in local weeklies or monthlies.

➤ The Stepfamily Association of America trains and certifies therapists in the work of stepfamilies, and maintains a list of organization-approved therapists who have been trained by the SAA or another reputable source. You can get a referral from them by calling 800-735-0329.

When you first call a mental health professional, you'll probably spend a few minutes on the phone briefly describing your family's problems and getting a sense if this is the right therapist for you. Don't feel shy about asking questions. In the normal course of therapy, you won't be asking questions about the therapist, so get your initial questions out of the way now. Remember that *you* are hiring the *therapist*, not vice versa.

Here are some suggestions for questions to ask:

➤ What's your training and experience? (See the following section for a brief description of what all that alphabet soup after their names means.)

➤ What is your experience working with stepfamilies? (You want somebody who specializes or who has had experience in stepfamily relationships. It's not taught in grad school. There are particular dynamics to stepfamilies, and you cannot use the same therapeutic approaches, methods, or information that you would for a nuclear family.)

➤ Are you affiliated with any national or local stepfamily support system?

➤ What are your rates? Do you have a sliding scale? How often do you generally meet with your clients? Will you meet with us individually, or primarily as a group?

➤ How will you evaluate my family's problems?

➤ How do you approach the problem I'm seeking help for?

➤ Have you had success with short-term as well as long-term therapy?

Listen to how the therapist answers the questions, as well as what she answers. Does she really seem to hear your family's situation, or does she jump to conclusions? You may need to talk to several people before you find one that feels right. Just having the right letters after a name doesn't mean someone scores well on the empathy, wisdom, and insight scale.

If all feels right on the phone, schedule an initial session. Keep an open mind. You may trust the therapist, but your partner and/or stepkids may not. Each person attending the therapy has to approve of the person. (In the case of a reluctant stepkid, you and your partner may need to put your feet down and insist that she attend. She does get approval of who, though. Therapy builds a very tight relationship between client and therapist.)

239

What the Initials Mean

Mental health professionals come in a variety of flavors. Here's a brief breakdown of what all those initials mean:

An M.D., otherwise known as a medical doctor, is called a psychiatrist when he or she specializes in psychological treatment. A psychiatrist can prescribe drugs. This means that if a pharmacological approach is recommended by a non-M.D. mental health professional, a psychiatrist will be involved as a secondary care giver.

A Ph.D. holds a Ph.D. in psychology. She may also have other clinical training or certification, for instance, in psychoanalysis or another therapeutic approach. Special note: Any old Ph.D. (a Ph.D. in Meso-American archaeology, for example) does not qualify as a person to mess with your mind. You're looking only for that Ph.D. in psychology or a related field.

M.F.C.C. stands for marriage, family, and child counselor. To get this certification, the therapist must earn a masters degree and then counsel people for about a zillion hours under supervision. Then he takes an oral and a written exam, and if he passes, he's certified. Keep in mind that not all M.F.C.C.s will have the same approach. (Hey, not all mental health workers of *any* kind will have the same approach!)

A L.C.S.W. is a licensed clinical social worker. To get this certification, the therapist goes through a process similar to the M.F.C.C.s. She earns a masters degree in social work, counsels people for gobs of hours under supervision, and takes an oral and written exam.

An intern is a candidate for an advanced counseling degree of some kind who is completing her counseling hours while using the license and under the supervision of a certified therapist.

Stepfamily Support Groups and Organizations

As the number of stepfamilies in this country has boomed, so has the number of support services. You are not alone! Check out Appendix B for Web sites focusing on stepfamilies.

As an alternative or an addition to private therapy, you and your family might be interested in checking out some of the stepfamily support systems. The Stepfamily Association of America (402-477-7837) is a non-profit educational organization that holds support meetings in chapters all across the country. Also check out the Step Family Foundation at 212-877-3244.

Alternative Alternatives

For depression, stress, addiction, guilt, or other yucky feelings, consider combining your therapy with some alternatives, such as a massage, a hot bath, ice skating, acupuncture, or a manicure. Caring for the soul means providing it with fun and pampering, too.

The Least You Need to Know

➤ All stand or all fall. A problem with a stepchild is a problem for you.

➤ Substance abuse and eating disorders may be difficult to see when the child doesn't live with you.

➤ Expressing your anger cleanly and clearly shows kids that angry feelings can be expressed in a non-harmful way.

➤ It's normal for similar-age stepsiblings to feel sexual feelings for each other. Don't do anything about them unless such feelings turn into action.

➤ Good therapy is not a punishment; it's a tool for healing and growth.

Part 4
Legal Schmeagle

As a stepparent, you have little legal standing and few legal rights, so it's important to understand your situation and to know what measures to take to protect yourself and your stepfamily.

This is the part of the book where we steer our way through the heavy stuff: money, laws, adoption. How do you deal with medical consent forms? Do you need a will? Are you responsible for supporting your stepchild through college? Should you adopt your stepkids? How do you go about adopting? If your marriage breaks up, can you get custody of your stepkids?

Gnarly questions, and sometimes gnarly answers. I'm no lawyer, but I can't stand it when things aren't clear. Here, then, is the legal schmeagle side of stepparenting for the complete idiot.

Details, details, details inside.

Chapter 22

Legal Stuff

In This Chapter

➤ The real scoop on custody and visitation rights

➤ All about stepparent rights and responsibilities

➤ Medical consent

➤ Wills, taxes, and other inheritance stuff

➤ Finding a good lawyer

You live with the child, you care for the child, yet in the eyes of the law, you're complete and utter strangers. In a few states, there is some assumed connection for inheritance rights and custody—but which states? Well, it changes. There's also some inconsistency within state law. Confused yet? *Everybody is!*

The legal situation within stepfamilies is *way* bizarre, baroque, and just plain bad. I've included this chapter on legal stuff to help you understand what's going on, but remember, I'm no lawyer, and though I'm doing my best to get accurate information, this is *not* intended to be legal advice.

Stepping Stones

It's up to you and your partner to know your rights and responsibilities. Check out *Every Parent's Guide to the Law*, by Deborah L. Forman. It's a good place to start learning the right questions. Questions before answers, folks.

What You've Learned So Far

If you're living with somebody who is going through a divorce, go back and review Chapter 4, "Moving In Together." If you want information on grandparent rights, see Chapter 17, "Birth Grandparents and Step-Grandparents." Gay or lesbian stepparents should check out the information in Chapter 20, "Gay Stepparenting." Money matters (including child support) are discussed in Chapter 23, "Money Madness," and, in Chapter 24, "In Addition, There's Adoption!" you can find adoption information (a lot of material in that chapter covers legal issues, too).

Whatcha Mean, "Custody?"

I've been talking about custody issues all through the book, but now that we're here in the legal chapter, let's take a moment to really look at some more detailed definitions. Unfortunately, words mean different things in different places (and I'm *not* talking about France, New Zealand, and Sumatra; I mean that definitions change from state to state). It's up to *you* to know the laws and terminology in your state. Go to the library and ask the reference librarian for the family law statutes—and bring along a lot of coins for the copy machine!

Step-Speak

Legal custody refers to the decision-making authority for a minor child. *Physical custody* is the right of a parent to have the child live with him or her. In *sole custody,* the parent has been awarded full legal and physical custody. In *visitation,* the parent has been awarded time with a child but has no decision-making authority. *Shared* or *joint custody* refers to an arrangement in which both the care and authority are shared by both parents.

What Is Custody, Really?

When a kid has two biological parents who live with each other, both parents are responsible for making choices: where the child will live, whether she goes to public or private school, if she can play with that rude girl Eleanor, and what to pack in her lunch box.

Say the parents split up (it's been known to happen); then who makes those choices about the child's life? (Of course, the older the child is, the more choices he's making himself, but as long as he's a minor, many of those choices are being made for him.)

Whoever has *legal custody* is in charge of decisions about the child's upbringing. *Physical custody* is the right of the parent to have the child live with him or her. A parent might have joint physical custody, with the child living in both houses, but have sole legal custody. Or, in some states, parents might have shared legal custody, in which case, both are responsible for making decisions about their child.

Sometimes, one parent has *sole custody*, that is, that parent has been awarded full legal and physical custody. The parent who doesn't have sole custody usually has *visitation*, the right to spend time with the child without the authority to make decisions.

More and more, people are arranging for *shared physical and legal custody*, which means that all the responsibilities, caretaking, and decisions about the child are shared.

Deciding on Custody

If the two ex-lovebirds decide to go their separate ways and agree on custody issues, life's a breeze. There's no legal problem; the courts won't even ask you about your arrangements.

But if complete agreement can't be reached between them, then there are usually custody battles. Such battles (an apt name!) can be expensive and emotionally trying for the parents, and they definitely take their pound of flesh from each child. If the exes can do one thing right in life, it would be to resolve custody issues amiably, or at least privately. Kids have a hard enough time adjusting to the split-up and spending time with each parent separately. They suffer terribly over custody battles, especially when the battles end up in court. Fortunately, only 2 percent of custody battles actually go to trial.

> **Stepping Stones**
> You don't really need an attorney; you can do your own custody and or visitation agreements, and it's probably better for everybody if you do. For help (and suggested agreements), check out *Mom's House, Dad's House: A Complete Guide for Parents Who Are Separated, Divorced, or Remarried*, by Isolina Ricci.

Custody Is Always Renegotiable

Keep in mind that no custody (or visitation) arrangement is final. Any decision made (whether individually or by the courts) can be changed or renegotiated if circumstances change. And hey, guess what, Stepparent, you're a circumstance!

All custody decisions should be made with the best interests of the child in mind, and this criterion is used by all courts (should you end up there). It's what most custody battles focus on. But how the courts *apply* this best-interest clause varies widely. Talk about a mixed-up mess to explain! Policies and treatment of custody disputes vary from state to state and jurisdiction to jurisdiction, and they continue to change and evolve. I can't tell you what the law is like where you live because I don't know!

Visitation

Now let's talk about visitation rights. When one bioparent is awarded sole custody of a child, the other bioparent is generally awarded visitation rights. That means that he or she gets to visit with the child.

The terms and schedules of visitation are sometimes determined by the parents and sometimes by the court system, and there's great variation among them. The most typical schedule for parents who live near each other grants the noncustodial parent visitation every other weekend, from Friday to Sunday evening. When parents live a long way from each other, schedules like this may not work. Instead, the child may spend extensive time during summer and winter vacations.

Visitation, like custody, can and will be changed as needs change, or if circumstances change. (In the case of a gay parent, for instance, visitation *may* be curtailed if the parent begins living with a partner; see the details in Chapter 20, "Gay Stepparenting.")

I Kid You Not!

How bioparents react to the divorce is crucial for the children, and primary custody and visitation (versus shared custody) is not always in the best interests of the child. In her book, *Mom's House, Dad's House*, Isolina Ricci says that "sole custody arrangements with visitation to the other parent can leave boys and girls with 'responsibility mommies' and 'recreation director daddies' or, worse, with overburdened mothers and dropout fathers."

Stepparent Responsibilities and Rights

Are you cool with all that custody and visitation stuff? Okay, now what happens when the parent who has primary or shared custody gets married or forms a serious partnership? What about the stepparent? Legally, where do you fit in? And what happens if you and the bioparent split up? What kinds of rights do you retain to your relationship with your stepchild?

Stepparent Child Support

Just because you're married to a parent, you aren't legally obligated to support a stepchild. If, however, you voluntarily assume a parental role (in terms of support), you *may* be obligated to continue that child support if your partner dies. If, on the other hand, you get divorced, your relationship with your stepchild legally ends. This doesn't mean you can't (or shouldn't) continue to participate in your stepchild's financial care. It just means you won't have to.

Stepparent Custody and Visitation

So you've split up with your partner. Can you get custody of your stepkid? Chances are small—it doesn't matter that you changed Bobby's diapers, spent hours helping him with his social studies homework, sat with him when he had the stomach flu, and held his hand when Suzy Sears broke his heart in sixth grade. You may be closer than two anchovies in a can, but despite the court's claim that custody decisions are made "in the best interests of the child," they tend to believe that a child belongs with his biological parents. You may, however, have a strong case for visitation.

If you're divorced from the bioparent of your stepkids, you may be able to get some legal visitation rights. (This is assuming you can't work out some visitation arrangement with your Ex first.) The courts will consider the child's best interests here, and many states recognize that kids may view stepparents as parental figures and form strong attachments to them.

Your lack of legal status regarding your stepkids also fouls up the works should your partner die. A few states have enacted laws that allow custody by stepparents (especially if the child is left orphaned).

I Kid You Not!

In a few court cases, stepfathers who (wrongly) believed that they were the biological father have been granted the right to seek custody and visitation. It's been a mixed blessing for these men because they've also been mandated to provide child support, something that, as stepfathers, they would normally not be required to provide!

Wills, Taxes, and Benefits

Unless you're fairly explicit in legal documents, your stepchild will not be as fully protected money-wise as your biochildren are. But there's some good stuff to report: If you (or your partner) are the primary support for your stepchild, you can claim her on your income tax as a dependent and get the full dependent deduction. Your unmarried minor stepchildren may also qualify for your social security if you become disabled or die. (If they qualify, they'll be covered as long as they are high school students, or until age 16 if they are not.)

Will You Get a Will, Please?

If there's one thing that writing this book has taught *me*, it's to make a will! If your spouse dies intestate (that means without a will), you will generally inherit between one-third and one-half of all the estate, and your spouse's biokids will split the rest. If there are stepkids (in this case, your own biokids) involved, things might get hairier. Generally, stepkids cannot inherit from a stepparent.

A few states now allow a stepchild to inherit, but you must prove that the relationship began when the child was a minor, that it continued all the way until the stepparent's death, and that the stepparent intended to adopt the child but was foiled by legal snafus. In a few other cases, stepkids have been named heirs when there's been nobody else except the state to inherit.

Who's the Guardian?

Dying without a will is crummy for another reason that has nothing to do with money. The most important function of a will is to enable you to choose a guardian for your children. In a combined family, things get even sadder when the two parents die together in a flaming plane crash—the kids all go to their other bioparents, splitting your new family in two. There's little you can do about this. When a parent dies, custody automatically goes to the noncustodial parent. If the other bioparent is already deceased, you've *especially* gotta make other arrangements.

Step-Speak
Intestate means dying without a legal will. *Probate* is the legal process by which the court ensures that an estate is properly distributed to those entitled.

No matter what's been agreed upon informally within your network of family and friends, it's far better to make a will. Otherwise when the whole shebang goes to *probate*, the courts will have the right to choose the children's guardian, the survivors will be caught up in a court case, and any money may be tied up for years.

Medical Consent

Because you have no official legal status, the medical community may not allow you to authorize medical treatment for your stepchild. And because, legally, stepparents have no authority, care providers have developed some policies to deal with the issue.

Say you walk into Emergency with Billy, who is choking to death on a cherry-flavored popsicle stick. Yes, they'll treat him no matter who brings him in; delay would cause serious damage or death. And if you bring him in with a broken arm, they'll *probably* treat him at your request, though they may try to delay until they reach a bioparent. They may very well *not* treat him if he needs major surgery—at least until a bioparent can be located.

I Kid You Not!

You're lucky if you live in Missouri, at least in terms of medical consent laws and stepparenting. There's a statute on the books that empowers parents to consent to a child's medical treatment—and it defines "parent" to include stepparents.

You can get around this system partially (or at least save Billy some pain) if you have your partner grant you power of attorney, or if your partner (and your partner's ex) have signed a form authorizing you to represent your partner when consenting to medical or dental procedures. You may want to carry copies of these forms with you, as well as file them with your pediatrician and your local hospital.

Power of attorney forms and medical consent forms vary in their language from state to state. You can get free blank forms at any local hospital and many doctors' offices. You'll need witnesses.

Following is a simple medical authorization form to be given to the physician in charge. (You can use this for baby-sitters, too.) It puts the physician in charge, and, as such, it's not meant as a final solution. Both bioparents must sign the form (contact an attorney if you can't get agreement from bioparent #2), but it should work for emergency situations and can tide you over until you get the *real* forms that give *you* rights to consent:

Medical Permission to Treat Minor Child

To Whom it May Concern:

As regards our child:

Name:_____

Address: _____

Date of Birth: _____

Social Security Number: _____

In the event that during our absence at any time, any illness or accident should happen to our above child that in your opinion shall necessitate x-rays, a surgical operation, the giving of anesthetic, or any other surgical or medical treatment, we hereby consent to the taking of x-rays, performance of such operation or operations, the giving of such anesthetic, of giving of such treatment by you or by any surgeon or physician designated by you.

This permission is granted with the expectation that you would make all possible attempts to communicate with us in the event of any serious accident or illness, and that you would act under this consent only in an emergency; but at the same time, we want to make it clear that you are to be the sole judge of the practicability of such communication, or the existence of an emergency and of the necessity of an operation or other treatment. You are authorized to call an ambulance if necessary. If hospitalization is necessary, please take child to _____ Hospital. We hereby assume all financial responsibility for such service.

This consent shall continue in force until we give you written notice of its revocation.

Known allergies (to food, medication, etc.): _____

_____

_____

Child's regular doctor is: _____

Child's medical insurance (company, policy number): _____

Parent's signature: _____

Parent's name: _____

Address: _____

Telephone at work: _____ at home: _____

_____
 (Notary Public)

_____
(Date)

_____
(Commission Expiration Date)

Parent's signature: _____

Parent's name: _____

Address: _____

Telephone at work: _____ at home: _____

_____
 (Notary Public)

_____
(Date)

_____
(Commission Expiration Date)

Note: This letter must be notarized

School Days, Rule Days

Say you go to pick up your new stepchild at preschool one day, the teacher asks for your ID, and then refuses to release the child to you. You feel ambivalent—yes, you're mad, but you're also pleased that they're protecting your stepchild. Do you really want just anyone to walk off with her? Of course, it's a bummer. How can this be avoided? On the school emergency form, there is usually a space where the bioparent can list the people who can pick up the child, or who should be called if the child is ill or injured. Get your name inserted there.

Finding a Lawyer

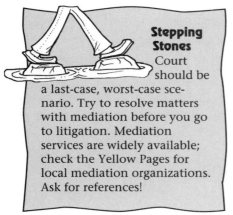

Stepping Stones

Court should be a last-case, worst-case scenario. Try to resolve matters with mediation before you go to litigation. Mediation services are widely available; check the Yellow Pages for local mediation organizations. Ask for references!

Lawyer jokes and slurs abound: Lawyers are greedy, unscrupulous, slimy, rich, manipulative, and opportunistic. But then again, jokes are merely jokes. There are a lot of decent people practicing law out there, and sometimes you need one. Keep in mind that lawyers charge a lot (between $150 and $250 an hour) for advice and information that is often available elsewhere. If you want to do it yourself, check out Nolo Press; it publishes a slew of how-to books on legal matters and is designed for nonlawyers. If you're involved in a contested court case in which the other side has a lawyer, you believe your rights are being seriously violated and big bucks are involved, or a child's custody is being seriously contested, consider getting a lawyer (either as a coach or to handle your case).

Getting a Good One

How do you find an experienced, competent, and available lawyer? There's no guarantee of quality even if you do follow these suggestions, but it's a place to start. Make a list of potential people, then get on the horn and start honking:

➤ **Ask your friends.** Lawyers *do* specialize, so find out what kind of problem prompted your pals to use the lawyer. Ask your friends not only if they *won* but how they were treated on a personal level, how confident they were with the lawyer's experience, and how unbelievably expensive it was (no, you don't need to know numbers). If this lawyer can't help you, she may refer you to one who can.

➤ **Bar Association referrals.** Find these in the phone book under "Attorney Referral Service" or "Lawyer Referral and Information Service." These listings are *not* screened, so get references. Also keep in mind that many times the most established and well-regarded law firms have more than enough business or get most of their new clients through personal referrals. They may not need to advertise.

➤ **Legal plans.** You may be enrolled in a prepaid legal plan that allows a certain amount of advice for an annual fee. That's great, so get your money's worth. Two things though: The lawyer isn't making much dough off of you, so be careful that you don't get short shrift or that he doesn't encourage you to get involved with additional unnecessary procedures. Also, be aware that the lawyers helping you may know *squat* about stepfamily law.

➤ **Law schools.** Many law schools run free or reduced-cost law clinics. Many focus on services for low-income clients. You can begin here, but you may not get the stepfamily law specialist you need.

➤ **Advertisements.** Well, you can certainly find a lawyer this way, but do you really want to trust "Fast Freddy Frumble, We'll Settle in 30 Days or Your Money Back"? Stick with the other resources unless you have no other options.

Getting the Right One

Here are some considerations when tracking down the right lawyer:

➤ Your lawyer should be experienced in handling stepfamily issues. Ask first before you waste time and money with someone who's not really up on the specifics you need.

➤ Your lawyer should be able to provide good references to people who've used his services.

➤ He shouldn't drain you dry completely. Ask about cost, and keep in mind that there are usually lots of extra fees.

➤ Look for a lawyer who's supportive of alternate resolution, such as mediation and arbitration before litigation.

➤ Do you like this lawyer? How accessible is he? Does he seem threatened when you ask questions? If so, watch out!

➤ A lawyer best suited as a coach (one who gives you advice and helps you prepare legal forms) may not be the best one for you if you have to go to trial.

➤ There's no reason to hire (and pay the fees of) Clarence Darrow or Johnny Cochran if you just need to file a few forms.

➤ Sleep on it. Make no decision before its time.

> **Don't Be Wicked**
> Watch out for lawyers who try to sell you services or expensive legal procedures you don't need. Get a second opinion before you turn over the keys to the vault!

The Least You Need to Know

➤ Your legal rights and responsibilities as a stepparent are slim to none.

➤ Legal rights and precedents vary widely from state to state; know the law where you live!

➤ In rare cases, stepparents can get custody. Visitation rights are granted more commonly.

➤ Write a will! Write a will!

➤ A lawyer is not a lawyer is not a lawyer. Find one who specializes in stepfamily law.

Money Madness

Money makes stepfamilies insane. Within the stepfamily and between the exes, everybody is complaining, whining, stressing out about money, and begging for more of it. If your stepfamily suffers from money madness, you're not alone. Money is the wedge that drives many stepfamilies apart.

The top reasons cited for second divorces are children and money, in that order. As Claire Berman says in her book, *Making it as a Stepparent*: "Nor are these necessarily two separate issues. Child care expenses (especially where there are offspring from more than one marriage) take a major bite out of any family's budget."

Money madness: Its bitterness can spread and poison everybody and everything, including kids, partners, and decisions. In this chapter, we'll take the demon dollar by the collar and give it a good shaking (watch out for flying coins!). C'mon everybody; show me the money!

The Stepparent and the Family Checkbook

As stepparent, your partner's money matters matter to you. Before you link money and your financial future with your own true love, you should know the facts. What's your partner's income? Does your Honey pay alimony or child support? What are the costs of your stepkids' educations? Are there any mortgages on the monthly bill list? What's your Darling's debt situation?

You also need more than the facts. You and your partner will need to make some decisions about money matters— how will your family handle your own internal financial matters? You'll also need patience to put up with money tensions between your household and the ex's household, because money and child support make people crazy. Knowledge, decisions, coping with life—let's take them in order.

Getting the Goods on Your Situation

To understand reality, you'll need to know just what's coming in, and what's going out. If you're as unclear as most people about where it all goes, try charting your spending for a few months. Write down what you spend daily (keep a tiny notebook with your wallet). Once a week, combine all the groceries into one sum, the bridge tolls and parking meters into another, total the drinks at the neighborhood bar, and so on. Once a month, combine the weekly lists. Charts are available in many books on personal finance, or you can use a computer program (Quicken is good).

Bill and I made our own charts and charted our spending for seven months, but unless you're both self-employed as we are, you probably can get a good handle on your spending in three months. Yes, writing down every penny you spend takes some time, but it also removes that panicky, out-of-control feeling from the pit of your stomach. You'll know how you're doing, will be able to clearly determine where to cut down, and (if you're digging yourself into a debt pit), will know how much extra you need each month.

Money Come, Money Go

Here's a questionnaire for you and your partner each to fill out, one that will give you the bigger picture so that you know the reality behind your mutually misty eyes and high hopes for the future.

What's your monthly income?

_____

What are the details on your savings, investments, and other assets?

_____

What's your retirement income?

_____

What about life insurance?

_____

Do you pay alimony? If so, how much?

_____

Do you pay child support?

_____

How much do you pay directly to your Ex?

_____

Do you receive child support? How much?

_____

Does this child support include medical expenses? If not, how much do you pay in medical insurance and expenses?

_____

How much do you receive for medical insurance and expenses?

_____

How much do you spend on other expenses for the kids (including clothing, toys, books, toiletries, dance classes, and sports activities)?

_____

How much do you spend on other areas of expense (including summer camps, birthday parties, and gifts for the child's friends)?

_____

Do you take your children as tax deductions? If so, how many child deductions do you take?

_____

Does the deduction status change from year to year?

_____

What joint assets do you hold with your Ex (including property, pending property sales, and other assets)?

_____

If your assets with your Ex are being liquidated, how is that being handled?

_____

_____

_____

Do the kids go to private schools? If so, who pays?

_____

_____

_____

What's the deal on college? Are you paying? Sharing? Letting the kids handle it if they want to go? (College costs include tuition, living expenses, books, and incidentals.)

_____

_____

_____

How old will the kids be when the gravy train stops chugging and support ends?

_____

Child Support

As a stepparent, you have no legal obligation to support your stepchild (unless you adopt the kid, in which case, you aren't a step anymore!). Reality is far more complex, however. Child support and other financial decisions between your partner and your partner's ex are major decisions, often determined during the divorce. Like custody decisions, financial decisions can be altered as situations change—and you certainly are a situation!

If your partner gets child support for your stepkids, your financial earnings shouldn't alter the amount your partner gets. If, however, you're providing a lot of the support (food, shelter, and clothing), the ex can make a case that your partner now has a higher amount of income available to raise the kids and might try to get child-support payments reduced.

If the stepkids are of college age and are applying for financial aid (loans, grants, or scholarships), be aware that the amount of parent contribution the colleges expect is often figured on the total household income. If you are concerned about the effect of your finances on your partner's child support or your stepkid's financial aid, consider signing an agreement to keep your finances separate.

No matter what, you're probably going to be very affected by financial arrangements for your stepkids. After all, it's money coming in or going out of your household.

Stepping Stones
If child support (or alimony) is part of your life, you'll often find yourself deeply enmeshed in the financial life of your partner's ex. (I know, this is not exactly where you want to be.)

How Much Child Support?

Many states provide guidelines, such as tables, formulas, and other ways of determining who pays what and when. Your partner's child support will be figured by looking at the child's needs (including education, insurance, day care, and special needs of the kids), the income and needs of the custodial parent, how much the parent paying child support can afford to pay, and the standard of living before divorce or separation. (This last consideration is a goal, not a guarantee; the courts understand that everybody's standard of living usually drops after a divorce.) Here are a couple of things to remember about child support:

Don't Be Wicked
Deadbeat-ism isn't just for men— biomothers can be just as deadbeat as biodads. All parents, whether male or female, have a legal and moral responsibility to care for their children financially.

➤ Child support isn't tied to custody or visitation arrangements. That means that a parent isn't allowed to withhold support payments, even if he or she disagrees with the ex, or even if the ex is out of line and forbids visitation. If there's a visitation problem, your partner should go back to court to get the visitation enforced. Withholding support only hurts the children.

➤ A parent must support kids until they are of legal age (and this age varies by state), unless they are on active military duty, the child is legally declared emancipated, or the parent's rights and responsibilities are terminated.

What If the Support Is Late?

Exes often fight over support checks, and lateness is a common complaint. As a stepparent, you'll keep everybody's blood pressure lower if you don't butt in when support checks are late. Leave it up to your partner, and try not to nag or complain too much.

Late support checks are sometimes a form of emotional testing by the ex. If the ex hasn't fully disengaged from the relationship, he'll sometimes test to see if his contributions still matter, if the family still cares. There's more about this kind of power play later in this chapter, in the section "The Great Money Toss."

Step-Speak
When a parent doesn't pay his or her child-support payment on time, the overdue amount is called an *arrearage*. Arrearages will rarely be forgiven. If your partner can't make a child support payment, get thee to the courtroom immediately for an adjustment!

Understanding why the checks might be late doesn't make it okay. If the ex is chronically late with support checks or the checks stop coming, call the District Attorney's office. Being a deadbeat parent is highly illegal. If the custodial parent owes more than $1,000 in child support, that information may be reported to credit bureaus. Other consequences for a deadbeat parent may include blocking her driver's license or professional license renewal, garnishing her wages or tax refunds, seizing her property, finding her in contempt of court, or putting her in jail.

Child Support, a Taxing Issue

Child support is tax-free to the receiver, and it's not a deductible expense for the payee. Only one household can claim a child as a tax exemption each year. Some exes trade off. Legally, the person who has custody of the child for the longest part of the year is eligible for the deduction unless the other parent pays more than 50 percent of the child's support. (If you're taking a deduction for a noncustodial child, you'll need a claim form (IRS form 8332), and you'll need the other parent's signature.) Either way, the exes will have to cooperate. "What, again?" Yup.

Don't Be Wicked
A true-life wicked stepmother story: Marcy and Renee lived with their biofather and stepmother. Their mother, who was supposed to contribute to their support, hit a dry streak and was sending nothing. One day, Marcy and Renee went to visit Mom, who gave them each a crisp $5 bill. When the little girls excitedly showed their stepmother their gifts, she took the money from them for child support.

Household Money Decisions

Now that you know the gory money details, you can make some decisions and some adjustments.

One Pot or Two?

How should you deal with household finances within your stepfamily? Should you pool your money or keep separate accounts? With one pot, all money is joint money and all earnings go into mutual expenses, investments, and savings. In the two-pot system, each partner pays for his or her own expenses and contributes an equal amount to the household (or an equitable amount, based on relative incomes). If you're keeping your money separate, you'll probably file separate tax returns, too.

There are reasons and arguments for both systems. Your situation may be begging for two pots (talk to a financial adviser for advice on your situation), or you may be fine (and emotionally satisfied) with just one. You should also know that the laws on family money differ from state to state, and in some places, you will not be *able* to keep your money separate, even if you want to!

According to James Bray, a researcher and clinician in the department of family medicine at Baylor College of Medicine, couples who use the one-pot method show higher family satisfaction than those who keep their money separate. However, before you throw caution to the wind and lump it all together, also consider these:

> ➤ Differences in spending patterns

> ➤ Differences in income and assets

> ➤ Emotional feelings about having separate money

Stepping Stones
Tom works for a non-profit foundation and brings in $19,000 a year. Rebekah is an engineer making $50,000. Rebekah and Tom believe his contribution is as valuable as hers, even though it's considerably less money. They lump it all together as "their" money, and base their one-pot budget on a family income of $69,000.

The two-pot system is a little more complicated. There are two basic approaches to handling shared living expenses.

Just as with housing costs (it's covered briefly in Chapter 10, "Your House, My House, New House"), you can divide shared costs down the middle (or by a percentage, based on how many kids each adult has). Or you can decide that each partner's contribution is equal to half the effort, decide what percentage of each person's earnings should go for each expense ("I think we should each pay 80 percent of our net toward the household." "Nah, make it 75 percent, and you're on!"), and leave the rest for each person's discretionary spending or saving.

The percentage approach works best for partners who want to keep their money separate and who highly value each other's work but have a gross disparity in income.

If you decide to keep your money separate, consider signing an agreement to do so. It may help if your partner ever has to go to court over the kids' financial situation.

You and Your Partner: Merging Economic Lifestyles

When you and your partner have different earning power and different economic lifestyles, you may be in for some tension as you adjust to living together.

Don't Be Wicked

In combined families where the partners come from families of different financial classes, the Grands and Other Grands may send expensive presents to their own grand-kids and none to their step-grands, setting up a "class" situation among the children. You and your partner should take steps to make sure neither set of kids feels left out or like second-class citizens.

Standards of living usually change when there is a divorce and a remarriage. It's a hard adjustment when you're used to living high off the hog and your family income is now reduced, or when you've been a wild-and-free single person and you're now taking on family financial responsibilities. It's also hard (but not as bad) to get used to a higher standard of living. If you're moving in with a wealthy partner, it may be hard to avoid feeling as though you're the poor relation sponging off somebody else's wealth. If you have kids, too, and they (or your Ex) aren't sharing your new goodies, you're a prime target for major Parent Guilt. No matter how much child support and alimony you pay, you may face the fact that it doesn't feel like enough.

Then again, if your kids' other bioparent partners with somebody with more money, that can be hard, too. You may feel guilty that you aren't paying your "share," and you may feel bad that you aren't the prime supporter of your kids.

Economic Choices

Economic hardships in a stepfamily often lead to hard, ugly choices. Maybe the stepmother who wanted to stay home with the kids now needs to get an outside job to help pay alimony. The stepfather who wanted a baby of his own may reluctantly conclude that having another kid will put the family over the edge.

"We fight about money and where it goes," say Mary. "It's more complicated than if there were just two of us." Watch for emotional creepers; you may think you're okay with the decisions you've made (after all, they're based in reality, right?). But disappointment and resentment are not rational emotions.

Don't leap to conclusions if it makes the two of you unhappy. Try problem-solving for alternative solutions (there's an exercise in Chapter 13, "Family Talk," that may help). Keep in touch with how you are feeling, and search for other solutions if you're unhappy. You want this relationship to last, but it won't if you are miserable.

Money Crazies and the Ex

When it comes to money, watch those emotions fly like hard-hit tennis balls between you and your partner, between your partner and your partner's ex, and between you and your partner's ex. (If you're a combined family, you may also face problems between you and your Ex too!) All the experts suggest trying to separate financial and emotional problems between the exes so that they can be dealt with individually.

Back in Chapter 16, "The Ex: That *Other* Birth Parent," you read a lot about the ex. But here's a little more about money specifics (you can't get too much advice in this troublesome area).

The Ex Is Always There, Somewhere

Jon is fed up with his wife's ex and voices it clearly. "He's part of our life, and I don't want him here. My wife and I are building a home together—I'm raising her kids. Why does this man, who I have nothing in common with and don't respect—I despise how he treated my wife and the kids—why does he have to be a part of our financial decisions? I feel as though he's taken up invisible residence in the corner of our living room."

It's hard knowing you don't have "all" of your partner. It's hard to remember that she had a history before you and that the "history" involved kids who now have a big impact on your life. It may be a difficult mouthful to chew, but because there are kids involved, your partner's ex's financial matters are your financial matters, too.

Keep these points in mind:

➤ It's your partner's job to work out the money situation with the ex (after all, it's not your Ex, though sometimes you put so much energy into worrying about the creep that it feels that way).

➤ Pettiness and hassles go hand-in-hand with exes and money negotiations. Be cool, even though you may find nasty things being said about you as well. "I struggle with these kids, and he's off buying a fancy computer and going out to dinner! Where does he get off!" says your partner's ex, ignoring the facts that this same ex refuses to work more than part-time, that you use your "fancy" computer for your work, and that you entertain clients at restaurants as part of your business.

➤ You stay out of it.

➤ You have little or no control over how money is spent in the other household. Here's a complaint so common it verges on stereotype: No matter how much child support you and your partner send, the kids turn up on visiting day in threadbare clothing. This is a battle you will rarely win. Decide if it's worth fighting. Tolerance and an ability to remember to breathe deeply are wonderful assets for stepparents. Try to cultivate them.

➤ Medical and dental care should be included in a child-support agreement. Stepmother Emma argues about toothbrushes and dentists. "Can't their mother share the cost and responsibility of taking care of her own children's teeth?" Emma growls. "Then again," she says in a catty tone, looking around to make sure nobody can hear her, "you should see her own teeth. I guess she just has different priorities."

➤ Money is the great cover-up and catch-all. Other issues, namely emotional ones, hide behind money arguments.

I Kid You Not!

Theresa and Joe's relationship with his ex is strained, at best, and many of their fights are over money. One day, Theresa slipped her stepson Tom $10 as he got on the commuter train to go back to his mother's house. Tom's mom called Theresa in tears and screamed at her that she was trying to buy her son's affection.

➤ Money arguments can be an excuse for rehashing the old relationship and hanging onto old ties (even if the relationship has turned ugly). Lynette's partner has almost daily contact with his ex as they squabble about money arrangements. "They're still bonded in this totally weird way!" she complains.

➤ If your partner pays child support, the ex may feel dependent. This is not a good situation. When people feel dependent (or are dependent), they tend to get odd.

➤ It's hard but necessary sometimes to ignore and put up with an ex's "poor little me" syndrome. Be fair, make arrangements your conscience can live with, and ignore the rest.

➤ While some exes and new partners manage to plan their finances all together, this is not possible or even desirable for most families.

The Great Money Toss

Throwing money at a problem doesn't make it go away. There's a set of unfortunate syndromes known as D.D.S. and M.M.S.—Disneyland Daddy Syndrome and Moneybags Mama Syndrome. The primary symptom? Too much generosity when it comes to the kids. D.D.S. and M.M.S. are usually suffered by noncustodial parents, and these are usually their causes:

Step-Speak
Disneyland Daddy Syndrome (or Moneybags Mama Syndrome) is a condition suffered by parents who feel guilty, resentful of their ex, and/or estranged from their children. Its primary symptom is being too generous with the kids in terms of money and material things.

➤ Guilt and loneliness. The Disneyland Daddy misses the kids, and when he does see them, he uses money to substitute for daily care and affection.

➤ A desire to one-up the ex. Moneybags Mama is furious at Dad. "I'll show him what a good parent provides!"

➤ A need to feel important and loved. Disneyland Daddy never sees the kids, barely talks with them, and has little emotional connection. "A new Nintendo 64 will make Junior love me!" he thinks.

Of course, parents with D.D.S. and M.M.S. are hopelessly deluded. Pampering a child with money or expensive gifts solves nothing. It won't bring the child closer to them (either emotionally or in terms of time spent together), it frustrates the custodial family's sense of what is appropriate, and it teaches kids how to use manipulation to get what they want.

Junior, the Guilt-Broker

The stepkids often get in on the money act (especially if there are already money tensions in the household). Don't be blackmailed by cries of "My Mommy would let me have it." Kids need to learn that different households have different priorities. You can be gently assertive about this without trashing the other bioparent. ("In our house, we don't buy expensive electronic toys. We'd rather spend the money on good books and outings together.") (Trashing the other bioparent is *never* a good idea.)

Always talk about money in a straightforward fashion. Kids adjust well to less money and privilege if you communicate the situation in a respectful fashion and in ways they can clearly understand.

I Kid You Not!

Men have been the traditional money-earners in our society, and though this has changed dramatically, many old attitudes hang on, trailing like toilet paper stuck to a shoe. Many men feel guilty, irresponsible, and unmanly if they aren't supporting all their children in the style to which they were once accustomed. Remember that moms are just as responsible as dads for their children's support.

Jealousy, Again

Money envy is normal. You may agree in theory that financial affairs between your partner and your partner's ex are not your business, yet you may feel agitated about the time your partner spends negotiating. You may feel envious of the possessions and privileges of your partner's ex, especially if you are struggling to help support your stepkids. You may even feel envious of the presents your partner buys for your stepchild. Try to remember that envy and jealousy are emotions that rarely make you feel better in the long run.

A Healthy Money Mind

The emotional impact of money problems can be enormous. To keep them from killing your marriage, it helps to foster in yourself a healthy, forgiving, slightly removed, and bemused attitude. When the going gets tough, think of yourself as an earning partner and a contributor to the stepchildren, rather than as a victim. As with many things in life, money fights can be like thunderstorms: loud, scary, windy, and wet. But despite all the booming and banging at the time, they usually do little real damage.

The Least You Need to Know

➤ Money problems are a dangerous force; they can (and often do) split up stepfamilies.

➤ Understanding where you stand financially is your first line of emotional defense against financial stress.

➤ Standards of living usually change when there is a divorce and a remarriage. Prepare to adjust.

➤ Money issues (including child support) between exes often remain loaded. There's more than money here; there are emotions!

➤ A good money attitude will help keep your stepfamily strong.

Chapter 24

In Addition, There's Adoption!

In This Chapter

➤ Why to adopt your stepchild

➤ Getting parental consent

➤ The adoption process, step-by-step

➤ Gay and lesbian stepparent adoption

Tired of existing in legal limbo? Ready to make the big commitment to your stepchild? As a stepparent, your legal status is nonexistent, your social status is iffy, and you always have to defend yourself against the charges of being "wicked." When you adopt your partner's biochild, you lose your stepparent nonstatus, drop the step, and become a full-fledged parent with all the rights and responsibilities of a biological parent.

About half of all U.S. adoptions are by stepparents. But of course, stepparent adoption is not for everybody. If your stepkid already has two living, concerned, involved parents, adoption is probably not in the cards.

This chapter is specifically about stepparent adoption: the reasons to do it, the reasons not to do it, and the steps you'll need to take. Once again, I'm messing in business not my own—the legal field. For any adoption, you'll need to consult a lawyer. Wanna adopt your stepchild? Make that call to the lawyer first to see if it's possible in your situation!

Stepparent Adoption

Stepparent adoption is a form of "relative adoption," which is adoption of a child by somebody who is related to the child by blood or marriage. (Another common type of relative adoption is adoption by grandparents, but stepparent adoption is far more common.) Legally, there is no difference between an adopted child and a biological child for consent, surnames, custody, child support, inheritance and property laws, incest, criminal law, and so on.

In most adoptions, the relationship between the child and the bioparents is usually terminated, over, kaput. In a stepparent adoption, only the noncustodial parent loses parental rights. (The noncustodial parent occasionally keeps visitation rights, and I'll talk about that a little later.)

Why Adopt Your Stepchild?

There are few reasons why you *need* to adopt a stepchild. In this country, people can choose to live with whomever they want, they can support anybody they want, and they can love whomever they want. But there are many reasons why a stepparent might *want* to adopt a stepchild.

For some, it's a matter of protecting the child from legal snafus around inheritance. For others, it's an attempt to give equal status to all kids living in the household. Or the action itself may be a ritual of public commitment, like a wedding ceremony. For others, it's just making legal what's already a reality; the commitment, and the actions of parenting, have taken place long before.

If your stepchild's other bioparent dies, you may want to solidify your legal relationship. Thus ends the wishy-washiness. It's all settled—medical release, names, inheritance, and guardianship questions.

What happens if you haven't adopted your stepchild and your partner dies? As a stepparent, you have no legal relationship with your step-little-one. Unless you adopt (or are named guardian in advance), the court will be appointed guardian in such a circumstance. Your stepchild may be sent to live with biological relatives, and you may not be able to gain any visitation rights. (Of course, all this is true if the other bioparent has not died. In that case, if your partner dies, your stepkids automatically go to the noncustodial parent.)

Here are some other reasons to consider adopting your stepchild:

➤ If the other bioparent is living but has abused, neglected, or abandoned the kids, you two and the kids may want to sever that hideous relationship.

➤ Adoption is a demonstration of affection and commitment. It's not just legal; it's also highly symbolic because the child literally becomes your child. And it certainly stops all those arguments that begin with, "You're not my dad! You can't tell me what to do!" (Hey, but that's not a real reason; the tensions will simply pop up elsewhere.)

➤ Adoption can help enforce those incest taboos between siblings.

➤ You may consider adoption if you've got shared biochildren and you want the stepchild to have status and rights that are indistinguishable from the other kids. Adoption also helps reduce sibling jealousy.

➤ Adoption is permanent. Adoption provides emotional security for the stepchild (and for you!). Adoption is a ritual that says, "You're mine forever—I choose you."

When Not to Adopt

There are also many reasons not to adopt your step-child. Here's a dose of ugly reality to spoil your day:

➤ Before starting proceedings to adopt a stepchild whose other bioparent is living, consider very deeply. Adoption is permanent and severs the relationship with the bioparent.

➤ Adoption cures nothing. Although it might ease sibling jealousies, it doesn't erase all tension around your house. Adoption won't automatically solidify your family. Don't use it as medicine.

➤ If there's any doubt about the health or longevity of your partnership, hold off! As you are well aware, partnerships can break up, but your relationship as parent—be it biological or adop-tive—doesn't end.

➤ A contested stepparent adoption is awful for everybody, especially the child. Do you want to put everybody through that kind of scrutiny?

> **Don't Be Wicked**
> Is it really in the child's best interest to cut him off from his other bioparent? Stepparent adoption may leave the child with a sense of loss and guilt (ah, those loyalty issues), especially if the bioparent has been involved in the child's life. Even when the parent isn't around, adoption is a very serious thing. This is the kid's parent you're talking about!

Other Options

Many legal protections provided by adoption can be obtained by stepfamilies with a little bit of extra work. Adoption is not always necessary, and the choice to adopt should not be made just for pragmatic reasons. Taking a child as your own is an emotional commit-ment, too.

If adoption is impossible, unfeasible, or undesirable, consider becoming your stepchild's legal guardian. A guardianship establishes a legal relationship between you and your stepchild (for things such as medical consent and providing education, food, shelter, and clothing), but the parents remain the parents. This option may work for you if you are a custodial stepparent. In this case, you'll need the consent of the other bioparent, but you may face less resistance than if you were requesting consent for an adoption. If you decide to become your stepchild's legal guardian, consider acknowledging this important step in your relationship with a family ceremony.

Adoption Step by Step

Adoption is one area that's easier to navigate for stepfamilies than it is for non-stepfamilies. (We found an easier area! Hurrah!) Adoption after a parent has died is simplest. It can get confusing—not to mention legally and emotionally complicated—if the birth parents are both living and are either divorced or never married to each other.

Adoption is regulated by states, and there are some significant differences between how things are done in, say, New Hampshire and California. Fortunately for us, some things are the same, and some general principles and concepts don't vary too much from place to place.

Lawyers! Yes, Indeed

Lawyers are not always necessary in life, and many people feel they get more work than they should. They're essential, though, for adoptions. If you're beginning the journey to stepparent adoption, you'll need some support and lots of information to get through the snarls of legality. Review the guidelines for finding a good lawyer in Chapter 22, "Legal Stuff." Make sure you ask how many adoption cases your lawyer has done and whether he or she specializes in family law. This is the most important thing you can do for yourself.

Familiarize yourself with your state laws and precedents. If you are willing to spend time in a law library, you may not need a lawyer for this. (If you have decided to get your information through a lawyer, consider hiring a research lawyer because they usually charge less than a trial lawyer.)

Getting Consent

If the other bioparent is still living, he or she must consent to the adoption unless his or her parental rights are terminated. Consent procedures differ. In some states, the birth parent must sign a form in front of a social worker. In others, the birth parent must appear in court.

What if you can't find the birth parent? Haul out the phonebook and turn to "Private Investigator." Unwed fathers (if they were never married) must be notified in most states and, in many states, must give consent to the adoption as well.

Once you have consent, you can skip down to the section "Filing the Petition." If you can't get consent (or cannot locate the parent), read on!

Stepping Stones
It may sound silly and obvious, but your partner (the custodial parent) must also consent to the adoption. That means no holiday surprises: "Guess what, darling? Your little Joey is now *our* little Joey!"

Terminating Parental Rights

If you can't get consent from a child's parent, you must go to court for a Termination of Parental Rights hearing. (Okay, time to bring the lawyer in, right about now.) You're going to have to prove that the parent has given up his or her parental rights to the child. The laws are inconsistent from state to state on this one, but generally the court decides on parental rights based on both the parent's previous behavior toward the child (abandonment, abuse, or neglect) and character concerns.

Here are some representative conditions the court may consider. (I include them here so you can get an idea before you call your lawyer—which you do need to do!):

➤ *Abandonment.* Has the parent maintained an active interest in the child's life? What if the parent hasn't supported the child but sends cards on a regular basis? In some places you must prove that the parent intended to abandon the child. In other places, the parent needs to have deserted the child for more than three months. Abandonment (as with all consent law) is decided by the court. "The court" means the judge you get and the state you live in. Judges and states vary widely. Do your research before you claim abandonment to find out how things in your neck of the woods generally go.

➤ *Abuse and substantial neglect.* The court may need to see that abuse or neglect was significant, and that it happened more than once.

➤ *Failure to support.* In many places, failure to support a child is considered a condition only when the parent could pay but didn't ("Hey, I had to buy a boat, man!"). In other places, chronic underpaying makes parents eligible to lose their parental rights. Some deadbeat parents who are reluctant to consent to an adoption have made deals to avoid having to pay their child support in arrearage (the amount of back child support they owe).

➤ *Failure to protect.* Neglecting to protect a child from known dangers is another condition that may cause a parent to lose his or her parental rights.

➤ *Character issues.* Depravity, open and notorious adultery or fornication, habitual drunkenness, and drug addiction are all conditions that may be considered as just cause for a parent losing his or her parental rights.

As you might imagine, court cases discussing these matters can be pretty brutal for everybody concerned.

I Kid You Not!

Stepparent adoptions may sometimes permit the non-custodial parent to continue to have visitation rights after the adoption. Grandparents also sometimes retain visitation rights, especially if the adoption occurs after the parent's death.

Filing the Petition

After the child is free for adoption, you must file a petition with the adoption court. Your adoption petition (which your lawyer will help you draft) will supply this information:

1. Your name, address, age, date of marriage, and other details.

2. A description of the relationship between you and the child to be adopted.

3. The legal reason that the birth parent's rights have been terminated. This is either because he or she gave consent, or is the result of your Termination of Parental Rights case.

4. A statement that you, the adoptive parent, are the best person to adopt this child. (This is where you may include the length of time you and your stepchild have been living together.)

5. A statement that the adoption is in the best interests of the child. You may need to justify this (your lawyer will advise you).

You (and your lawyer) will also include in your packet the consent forms (or the court order terminating parental rights) and the official name change request, if you're changing the child's surname.

I Kid You Not!

In most states, you can change your name simply by using it in all aspects of your life. You can call yourself anything you want, unless it's rude or intentionally confusing, capitalizes on the name of a famous person, or is chosen with attempt to defraud. Even though your stepchild or adopted child can use any surname she wants, she may have trouble getting it accepted for medical, school, or other identification reasons. It's a simple process (especially during an adoption) to file a name change request with the court.

When the petition is filed, it will be a few months before your hearing. Some adoptive stepparents are free to sit back and wait until then; others need to jump more legal hoops to establish that they are "fit" to be parents. In these situations, stepparents must pass the home study and the waiting period.

Are You Fit?

Okay, you're physically fit. You can bench press 250 lbs. and run three miles without becoming winded, but does that make you *legally* fit to be a parent? In most adoptions, being declared "fit," which includes a home study and waiting periods, are part of the standard process.

Most stepparent adoptions skip this "fitness" step. I repeat: Most people will not need to be declared "fit" as parents. In some cases, especially in the case of second-parent adoptions (see "Gay Stepparent Adoption," later in this chapter) or if your adoption is being contested, you will need to be declared a fit parent, and go through the home study process. I'm including the information here just in case.

The Home Study

The need for a home study is determined by the situation, your state, and who lives in your household. Home studies and waiting periods are often waived if the adoption is uncontested and if it's just you, your partner (the bioparent), and the child at home.

The home study is an investigation of your home life to verify that you are fit to raise a child. It's conducted by a state agency or licensed social worker. If you are required to prove your fitness, the agency worker or social worker will tour your home and will ask you questions. She'll then prepare a short report for the court, to be reviewed with your petition, name change request, and so on. (Some states don't require the home study to be submitted to the court; then it's up to the agency or social worker to determine your fitness.)

What will they look at?

➤ They'll try to determine if your partnership is stable.

➤ They'll look into your health record, both physical and mental.

➤ They'll look at the money: how much you have and, more importantly, whether your financial situation is stable. (No, you don't have to be rich; they just want the situation to be adequate and safe.)

➤ They'll check out your lifestyle (and they'll prefer that it be moderate).

➤ They'll look at how many other kids you have, and where everybody sleeps.

➤ They'll check out your career obligations.

➤ They'll check whether you have a criminal record.

Sounds awful, doesn't it? Relax! Besides the fact that your life is under scrutiny, the home study is not so bad. It's not an adversarial situation. The social worker is interested in creating, not foiling, adoptions, and the report written should reflect all the wonderful strengths you bring to the child's life.

I Kid You Not!

Here's more about Cinderella's evil stepmom: Cinderella's dad dies, leaving Cinderella an orphan. Her stepmom did not adopt her but kept her on out of pity—and the need for a good housemaid. (It's so hard to get good help these days!) On the other hand, was there stepparent adoption back then?

The Waiting Period

This is a waiting period between the home study and the adoption hearing. In non-stepparent adoptions, the child begins to live with the adoptive parents, and visits are conducted by the adoption agency or by the state. In stepparent adoptions, this period is often waived.

The Adoption Hearing

The adoption hearing is sometimes perfunctory and sometimes waived for stepparent adoptions. In this step, the judge reviews the adoption petition, the home study report, and the name change petition and then signs the papers. You'll get your Final Decree of Adoption, and the child's name will be changed (if that's what you requested). You are now legally the parent! Pop the champagne for you and the sparkling apple juice for your child! (Careful, don't spill them on the newly minted birth certificate.)

Gay Stepparent Adoption

Let's briefly discuss gay stepparent adoption, because it differs slightly from heterosexual adoption in that a gay stepparent is not replacing a parent; he or she is adding another parent of the same sex to the mix.

The general climate for gay adoption is hard but is improving. Only Florida and New Hampshire specifically prohibit lesbians and gay men from adopting, but that doesn't make it easy elsewhere! In some states, the judge can consider the sexual orientation of a parent in the determination of an adoption.

For gay stepparents (or co-parents; see Chapter 20, "Gay Stepparenting"), there's a relatively new way to adopt a child of a same-sex partner without terminating the birth parent's rights. This is called a *second-parent adoption*, and many states honor it. Second-parent adoption recognizes an on-going relationship between the adult and the child, a relationship of "parental quality and duration." That means, if you're in a new relationship, it's wise to wait a while before applying for adoption.

> **Don't Be Wicked**
> Whether you should be open about your sexuality is always a matter of debate, but it's essential that you tell the truth if asked during the adoption proceedings. Lying could make your adoption null and void. Read *The Lesbian and Gay Parenting Handbook* by April Martin (see Appendix A) for advice and additional resources.

The Least You Need to Know

➤ You're not alone; about half of all U.S. adoptions are by stepparents.

➤ Adoption usually terminates the relationship between a child and the other bioparent.

➤ Adoption is permanent, even if the relationship with the child's custodial bioparent dissolves.

➤ You'll need parental consent, or a court order freeing your stepchild, for adoption.

➤ States differ widely in adoption law, and you'll need a lawyer to help you work through the process.

Part 5
Putting It All Together

You're a stepparent, that means you're part of a stepfamily. What would it be like to add a baby to this mix? For some families, it's the best thing they've ever done—but what would it be like for you?

Let's look at steplife a little closer. What does it mean to be a stepparent, especially for you, Stepmom? How about for you, Stepdad? What are your larger concerns?

In this section of the book we look at the future of the stepfamily—your future. We'll check out the realities and hardships of adding a little one, examine the top complaints of stepparents and biological parents, and discuss what's involved in building an extended stepfamily—and bringing it out into the world.

This is where we put it all together.

Hey Sis!

Chapter 25

His, Hers, OURS?

In This Chapter

➤ Making the decision to have a child

➤ Telling the children and your Ex

➤ Half-siblings: objections, reluctance, and excitement

➤ From stepparenting to parenting, in one step

➤ Happy life in the larger family

Okay, Stepparent, I want you ask you a question about a topic as emotionally top-loaded with deep desires and insecurities as a hippopotamus in toe-shoes. Wanna have a baby?

Did you wince? Did your heart flutter? The choice about whether to have children is one of the most important decisions any partnership can make. Whether to bring a new child—a joint child—into a stepfamily is a huge question. There are pros, there are cons, and there are things to watch out for, whatever you decide.

This chapter discusses adding a member—a small but important one—to your stepfamily. We'll go over the decision-making process, the family's reaction to your news, and tips on successfully combining the roles of stepparent and parent.

A New Baby: Why or Why Not?

A new baby, if truly wanted, brings great joy to the stepfamily. Some studies show that there's more happiness and family satisfaction when there is a shared child, and many stepfamilies swear that having a child together is the best thing they ever did for the family. Often, it feels as though a family is born along with the baby.

Stepping Stones Most remarriages happen to people in their 30s and onward, making babies born into stepfamilies the children of older parents. Older parents tend to be wise and patient parents who savor their children. On the other hand, older parents are tired parents!

"We really are family now; we all have relatives who are related to each other, not just by marriage," says Carole, whose son Marcus joined two of her children and one of her husband's to make a family of six. "We all claim the baby. Even when things are rough, now, it's not like strangers fighting. Marcus settled us down."

Though a new baby can bring joy and healing, having one is not a decision to step into lightly. If a new child isn't truly wanted by both partners, resentments can simmer like stew on the stove, with the smell permeating the entire house. It's hard for people who are already parents to start all over again. Adding any family member also has huge financial implications.

A baby is not a quick fix for emotional problems within a family. Don't have a child to solve a problem—it rarely works.

What Do YOU Want, Honey?

For many people, it's the decision that's the killer. Nobody is neutral about having babies (if they are, it's out of pure ignorance of how much a baby impacts lives). For some partners, the decision to have a mutual biological child (or to adopt one together) is easy: a clear "yes, we want one," or "no, we absolutely do not." For the partners who say "yes!" the only decision is *when*, and the only discussions are about how to handle the various complications—other kids' reactions, financial matters, and physical space concerns.

For other lovebirds, the conversations are long and hard. One wants, needs, and demands; the other fights, denies, and refuses. And there are some partnerships where both people feel confused and torn. If one partner has kids and the other does not, the dynamics change again.

As you and your partner discuss the Big Baby Question, it might help to talk about the following issues and determine how they affect your personal situation.

➤ Do you both have biokids? For many couples, the urge to have a mutual biochild is more pressing if only one of you is already a bioparent.

➤ How old are each of you? Are you in the same stage of life? Look at differences in age. A parent with adolescent kids may be reluctant to start over again; a woman approaching 40 might be anxious to settle down and breed.

➤ How old are your stepkids? How old are your biokids? What would it be like for you as parents to have kids with this particular age gap? (What about a 13-year-old and a 2-year-old kid?)

➤ What's driving the baby drive? Do you really want a baby? Insecurity, competition, and a lack of direction sometimes strongly influence people's desires.

➤ How solid does your relationship feel? Having more kids should never be done as an attempt to save a failing marriage. Try to resolve family stuff first.

➤ What's the tension level in the household? Babies rarely allow more sleep. Are you ready to be sleepless and stressed?

➤ What's your financial situation? Money should never be the reason not to have children, but it should be a consideration—and it may affect your timing.

What Are We Arguing About?

You can find many arguments for and against having children. It's impossible to globalize and tell you what your feelings may be (forgive me for trying), but some people find that it helps to look at common reactions to the baby question.

The Reluctant Bioparent

The b`ioparent may love and adore children but feel overwhelmed by the idea of taking on more responsibility. A parent who feels guilty about not seeing enough of her own kids may worry about the impact of a new live-in child on that relationship. A parent still reeling from divorce may be frightened that this relationship won't work either, and that he'll be saddled with another child.

Age concerns are common causes of reluctance, too. My husband Bill had his kids in his early 20s and was fully expecting to be footloose and fancy-free by 40. Instead, he married a younger woman (me!) and found himself in his early 40s contemplating another round of diapers, lunch boxes, and carpooling.

The Deserving Stepparent

Stepparenting is hard and often thankless, and a childless stepparent may feel that after all the work he's put in raising the stepkids, he deserves a child of his own. Being a second wife or husband makes some people feel second class, and not having kids can add to that feeling. Then there's that strong reproductive urge. It's what has ensured the continuation of our species—don't ever underestimate its strength and its effect on people. Most people want to have children of their own.

Mind-Changers

The bioparent may have said, "Of course," while they were courting, but minds change. The stepparent may have thought that stepparenting would be enough, yet a couple of years down the line, her biological urges begin their biological urging, and suddenly she wants a baby. Another stepparent may want kids from the beginning but be willing to sacrifice for love, yet when the initial love-blindness wears off…WAAAAH!

What Will the Kids Say?

Is having a baby fair to the existing kids? Bioparents are concerned and protective of their children's concerns, and rightly so. They may wonder how a child who is already dealing with jealousy (of the new partner and of the new partner's kids) will react to a new baby. Parents and stepparents both may try to figure out how adding a new child to the mix will affect the stepfamily.

It's impossible to predict. You don't know what kind of temperament the new child will have, how the existing kids will react to the new one, and how the family dynamic will change. The only thing that can be said for certain is that the family dynamic *will* change. In many families, the change is for the better. In some it is not. Hey, this is life; there are no guarantees.

A Child for Its Own Sake

The decision to have or have not should not be based on feelings that involve the existing kids any more than decisions about your love life should depend on your kids' feelings. Don't have a baby to score points, to prove something, or to solve a problem. The best and only reason to have a child is because you, as partners, want one.

I Kid You Not!

Lily, a young widow, had two children when she met and married David. David wanted kids—lots of them—and somehow they ended up having three more. Lily loves children, too, and it's a good thing, because all the way through it she was aware that David (in his youth a competitive sportsman) was also (along with enjoying all the babies) trying to one-up her dead ex in terms of reproductivity.

Can't Agree?

Disagreeing on something as fundamental, primal, and emotional as having a child can be very painful for a couple, and if not handled well, it can be very destructive. Counseling can help, both in making the decision and in learning to live with the disagreement. You might want to review the suggestions in Chapter 21, "Stepfamilies in Crisis," for finding a good therapist.

We're Doing It!

Hoorah! You've decided, or you're pregnant, or the adoption papers have been filed. What now? Who tells the ex(es)? How are you going to tell the kids? And how are your kids and stepkids going to react?

Who Tells the Ex?

Don't leave this one to the kids; exes should call exes. Your partner should tell his ex, and you should tell yours. It doesn't matter that you aren't lovers or even friends anymore. No matter how bad the blood is now, the ex's children are about to have a sibling. What affects a child also affects a parent. Consider it a courtesy call to somebody you have a working relationship with, and consider that it will affect the ex emotionally.

A relationship breaking up is one thing, and a repartnering is another, but having a child with somebody else puts a finality to the former relationship. If, for some reason, the ex wanted (or wants) more children and it isn't likely to happen, she or he may have a nasty reaction. As I said before, nobody is neutral about babies.

That all said, the ex doesn't need to be the first person on the list. Waiting until the pregnancy is viable or the adoption papers are in order is always wise.

Telling the Kids

If the kids are old enough to understand, I suggest having the bioparent raise the subject of a new baby before the deed's been done, to get them used to the idea. Once again, this should be done by the bioparent. (Special warning: If you tell the kids you are thinking about having a baby, be prepared for them to tell their other bioparent.)

Bob told his daughters, Stephanie, 14, and Sophie, 10, that he and Katie were thinking about it as soon as they had decided to try for a baby, before she was pregnant. He let them voice their objections (which were many at first) and simply listened. When, a few months later, he came to them with the happy news that Katie was expecting, they didn't go into total shock because they'd already processed the idea.

Prenatal Reactions

Your stepkids and kids may not react at all well at first, or they may be just fine about it. Walter was thrilled when he found out his stepmom was having baby. He began planning immediately how he'd teach it to read and write before it could walk, and he asked his dad if he could take it to school for Show and Tell. Walter's sister Paula, on the other hand, was horrified and devastated that she wouldn't be her Dad's baby anymore: "Well, it better be a boy," she said, and stomped out of the room.

Jealousy and anxiety are common before the baby arrives. Kids may fear being displaced. "Where will we put it, Mom?" 5-year-old Lucy asked anxiously when she heard that her mom was pregnant. "I don't want it to sleep with me!"

Little kids often don't seem to react much to such an announcement. It's too vague, and they can't really understand it. They may, as time goes on, enjoy feeling the baby move in their mother or stepmother's belly.

Kids of all ages tend to get excited as well as anxious (though you may not know it from the blasé expressions many kids wear on their faces). Incorporate them into some of the planning. Solicit their input on names, and help them feel part of the process.

Stepping Stones

Privacy? What's that? Have another kid and the tattered remnants of your privacy are gone (at least for a while). The ex will know if your wife miscarries; the stepkids may be in the delivery room, helping her pant. For private people, this can be hard. Revisit your expectations, establish your boundaries, and release the rest into the clear blue sky.

Postnatal Outcomes

Kids' reactions to the infant are not always warm and welcoming. The eldest child may feel her family position is threatened, as here comes along a new "eldest." The youngest child may mourn his lost position as "family baby" as he moves to a "middle child" position. If handled incorrectly, and if the parents are too wrapped up in their howling little bundle to reassure the older children, a new baby can block up the relationship between kid, bioparent, and stepparent.

Fortunately, the results are usually more positive. Once the baby is born, kids generally relate to their new half-sibling the same way kids always relate to siblings: with a combination of love and hate, interest and disinterest, connection and repulsion.

"It's fascinating to watch them relate," says Paula's stepmother. "Paula is really into the baby. They have their own thing going, and it makes me realize that there's this relationship here that I have nothing to do with." Half-siblings are brothers and sisters to each other. They'll build their own relationships, and they'll have their own pleasures and disappointments with each other. You don't have a lot of control over that.

Have you got a kid or stepkid who's reluctant to warm up to the baby? Don't beg, cajole, or bribe. Let the baby handle it. Babies are brilliant at seduction. The first time a half-sibling encounters a toothless smile, he'll be wooed!

I Kid You Not!

That ubiquitous combination of sibling rivalry and idolatry can exist between half-siblings of any age. Witness the case of Rhonda, 4, and Angela, 24. Rhonda worships Angela; Angela's favorite color is blue, therefore so is Rhonda's. Angela loves to play backgammon with her father when she comes to visit—Rhonda jumps on Angela's back as they play and pulls Angela's hair. Angela complains that Rhonda gets privileges she never had, yet she brings Rhonda fabulous gifts and boasts about her little sister's brilliance to her friends.

Different Surnames

Legally, you can give your new child any last name you want (review the discussion about surnames in Chapter 24, "In Addition, There's Adoption!"), but if you and your partner, or you and your kids, have different surnames, you'll have to decide which one to use. (You can make up your own, too.)

When my daughter Annie was born, we thought long and hard about her last name. I'd kept my own name. What should Annie's be? A deciding factor in giving her Bill's last name (her middle name is my last name) was the fact that his other kids had his last name, and we felt it would help the siblings bond if their last names matched. (In retrospect, a name is just a name, and the kids would have bonded just as well without that similarity.)

His, Hers, and Ours!

It's a baby! It's *our* baby! For many stepfamilies with children from one or both partners, the new baby brings somebody in common to everybody, and a sense of permanence and completion to the family. If you weren't truly combined before, you are now!

Life in the stepfamily with a new baby is no doubt more hectic than before, and it's probably happier. Babies are delightful, winning creatures.

I Kid You Not!

Worried about the effects on the kids from having such a large family? Don't be. As a child, I loved visiting my friends the Faw family: six large, jolly kids and a beaming Ma and Pa Faw (the youngest son was Beau Faw, and that's no faux pas). Kids of all ages like a family scene, and babies thrive on siblings and kid-chaos.

Parenting Is Not Like Stepparenting

If you've stepparented but not parented, you'll be surprised at the depth of your emotional attachment to the new little one. (This isn't to knock your feelings for your stepkids, but the bonding that occurs when you actively parent a child from early on is far more intense.)

Be prepared for some surprises. Many new parents find they change their minds on parenting issues. The disapproving stepparent who felt that their partner was far too lenient on disciplinary issues suddenly lightens up, loosens up, and realizes that kids are not perfect. Stepparents often become better stepparents once they are parents.

Stepparents tend to make good bioparents. They've already had experience with kids, and they are already committed to family life.

Stepparents also commonly find that they feel closer to their stepkids after they've had a child of their own. Sometimes this is because they are more focused in on children—all children. Often a stepparent will fall in love with her stepkids when she sees how much they love and feel close to the baby.

A new baby usually has a positive effect on the partnership as well. Now that you and your Love share something so vital in common, you have more of an equal partnership. For the stepparent who has never parented before, gaining "official" parenthood status can help diminish old power struggles.

The Parent's Reactions to New Parenthood

Though bioparents often fear that having a new child will stretch them too thin emotionally or will interfere with their relationship with their existing kids, in reality, a new baby can lead to a renewed interest in parenting and family life as a whole. This renewed enthusiasm often plays out as more attention paid to the older kids, too—and no, this is not just Parent Guilt talking.

Don't Stop Stepparenting

Okay, so you've got your bouncing biobaby now, and you're finally taking care of a child whose love for you is unconditional and whose feelings are unambivalent. Yes, you can dote on your little one, but this is no time to stop stepparenting. Don't be wicked! Before you go off into Baby Bliss and forget about all this stepparenting stuff, consider a few words:

➤ Your stepkids are an intrinsic part of your family (especially now that you have a biochild of your own who is forever and always related to them).

➤ Watch out that people don't start dividing into teams—his against hers, or the kids from one parent versus the new ones from both. You are all a family. Now might be the time to stop referring to the kids as "James' kids and Minna's kids," or "my stepdaughter" and "his half-brother," and just start calling then "our kids and his brother." Nobody needs to stress on the biological details.

➤ It's normal to fall in love with your new baby, but don't play favorites! A new study shows that both stepmothers and stepfathers are generally more satisfied raising their biological children than their stepkids. For stepfathers, this increased satisfaction comes if and only if they have a new baby with their new partner—and it's their first child. (If both partners have kids and then they have one together, there's no difference.) Watch yourself!

➤ A parent may get so protective of his own kids' interests that he ignores the new little one. Parenting and stepparenting is a delicate balance. Balance requires concentration and relaxation; try for both.

➤ Your stepkids (and your older kids, if you've got them) will need special reassurances from both you and your partner that the baby hasn't replaced them in your affections. They need time alone with their bioparent and their stepparent. Yes, babies need constant attention, but big kids need attention, too.

The Least You Need to Know

➤ Making the decision to have a baby is the hardest step.

➤ Kids may react initially with reluctance and later with joy.

➤ Often it feels as though a family is born along with the baby.

➤ Parenting is not an excuse to stop stepparenting.

So, You're a Stepmom

Remember that statue of Atlas, staggering under the weight of the world? Change Atlas's sex, and you've got a pretty good image of what many stepmothers feel like. Talk to your typical stepmother, and what you'll hear is not a pretty story. Many stepmothers are dissatisfied with their position, frustrated, confused, and struggling with all their might.

"I feel like the biggest witch in the world," says Bonnie, whose two stepkids are in their late teens. "I'm used to thinking of myself as a giving person. But I'm also not used to never being appreciated." Bonnie is not the only one. When I told her that her complaint is common among stepmothers, her eyes filled with tears, "You mean I'm not alone?" Hardly.

According to most experts, stepmothering is the most difficult role in the stepfamily—or at least the most demanding. It's hard to be all things to all people, without being thanked. And the person who usually pays the biggest price for your struggles is *you*.

Though it's not *all* terrible news, I'm not going to pretend things are easy. In this chapter, we'll talk about the realities and discuss ways you can take care of yourself to make your life as a stepmother easier and more satisfying.

The Stepmother and Biofather Complaint Hall of Fame

It helps to know that you're not alone, and it helps to know what biofathers are beefing about, too. Here, then (drum roll, Johnny), are some of the top complaints of stepmothers and their partners, in no particular numerical order. How many match your innermost whining? How many do you hear from your partner?

Top Stepmother Complaints

1. I do all this work, and nobody seems to care. They walk all over me, and nobody says thank you.
2. I want a baby, and he's had enough.
3. Everybody watches me to see how I'm doing. I feel on show all the time.
4. We fight about money. He makes me feel like a stingy, wicked tightwad while I'm just trying to keep to a budget.
5. When the kids are here, I feel left out. He dotes on his daughter like *she's* his lover, not me.
6. My kids are the ordinary, everyday kids to him. When his kids arrive, he drops everything to dote on them.
7. There's absolutely no privacy around here.
8. He expects me to take over and be the mother, to make everything better.
9. He's so scared that his kids will desert him that he won't discipline them, and he buys them anything they want.
10. His ex is a big part of our lives. He still takes care of her. I know they're her kids too, but they communicate far too much. I don't want her negative energy in my household.

Top Biofather Complaints

1. She knew I had kids before she married me, so why is she complaining now?
2. She's so judgmental of my fathering and of my kids. They're not perfect. They're kids!
3. She hates it when I talk with my Ex. I have to—we have to work out details. Besides, we *were* married for a long time. I don't love her, but she's the mother of my children. Plus, when my wife puts down my Ex, she's insulting my kids, too, and insulting my previous choices.

4. The kids come over, and she withdraws.

5. I feel stuck in the middle between her and the kids. I'm always playing mediator, making sure that all sides are okay.

6. She wants a baby, and I already have kids, responsibilities, and financial problems.

7. She gets jealous of the kids, the attention I pay to them, and what I buy them.

8. She tries to be this superwoman. She wants the kids to love her like their own mother, and then when they don't, she's too exhausted to be any good to anybody.

9. She doesn't support me enough. It's all so *hard*, and both she and my kids should be more supportive of me.

10. She just doesn't understand why I parent the way I do, the history between the kids and me, or the feelings I have for my kids.

Stepping Stones

Forget the *hours* of labor giving birth. You're putting in *years* of labor to raise your stepkids. Yes, you deserve more credit. No, you may not get it, at least right now. The trick is finding the joy in the work for the work's sake.

Reality Bites!

Stepmothering may be the toughest task you'll ever take on. You're parenting somebody else's kids, and it can be a big disappointment if they don't accept you. Often, stepkids don't. Here's some more truths:

➤ Stepkids with biomothers in the picture often have such strong loyalty issues that they can't truly engage with their stepmothers. (This is true for stepfathers as well.)

➤ Your stepkids may find you pleasant (they often do), but the emotional connection may go missing. If your marriage breaks up, your relationship with your stepchildren may not last.

➤ Stepmothers tend to play a more limited role in their stepchildren's emotional lives than do stepfathers. (This is beginning to change, though. As more biofathers start to take an active role in parenting, more stepfathers tend to get the emotional shaft as well.)

➤ Studies show that stepmothers have a harder time rearing stepchildren than they do raising biochildren—and it doesn't matter whether the biokids are from the mother's previous marriage or the present one.

➤ Stepmothers tend to be valued by children mostly for their role in the biofather's happiness.

Giving, Giving, Giving

Despite the women's movement and the movement of women into the workforce over the last generation, family roles and expectations have been slow to change. Stepmothers are expected to add parenting responsibilities, active child care, and home maintenance to their other tasks—and to do it gladly. Some of these expectations come from the world at large, and some come from women's partners, who may look to a stepmother to make up for the failings or absence of the biomother. Often the biggest expectations come from women themselves. We *do* expect a lot of ourselves.

Society's Expectations

Beryl, whose stepfamily went through a terrible divorce a couple of years before she came onto the scene, asks, "Why does everybody expect so much from me? People say, 'Wow, you must love kids to take on all those problems.' I feel like I'm being *watched* all the time, like they expect *me* to fix Joe's problems with his kids." The people in Beryl and Joe's community do seem to be hard on her. She overheard one neighbor saying to another, "She'll never get *those* kids on track."

It's hard when other people expect a lot of you and yet don't give you credit enough to believe you'll succeed. As with all expectations, it's vital to *get rid of them.* Dump the "have to's," and try to ignore the neighbors. They don't understand your life or your family. But you do.

The Good News

Okay! Okay! Uncle! Before you jump off a bridge, call the divorce lawyer, or buy a one-way ticket to Rio de Janeiro, let's look at some good news (and not a moment too soon!):

➤ That old wicked witch stereotype? It's probably not coming from your stepchild. (Blame your *own* internalized guilt on that one!)

➤ When stepmothers are not emotionally over-invested in their stepchildren, they make better confidants than do biomothers. Kids can tell their stepmothers private things that would freak out their mothers.

I Kid You Not!

Tasha's stepmother treated her almost like a younger sister: "My mother terrified me, and my stepmother was a lot more accessible," Tasha says. "She's the one who I asked about periods and sex. She listened to my heartbreaks in high school. If I told my real mother anything, she just grounded me."

➤ A stepmother can be an important role model for both stepsons and stepdaughters.

➤ Over time, real friendships can—and often do—develop between stepmothers and their stepchildren.

Improving Your Lot

There is nothing that can't be improved, and the wonderful thing about stepmothering is that you have a tremendous amount of control over the health of your stepfamily relationships. As I've stressed before, communication, lowered expectations, and really working with your partner go a very long way.

Keep Talking!

Resentments can fester if you don't talk about them. Problems rarely go away—they usually just get worse unless they are talked about and resolved. Remember the importance of clearing the air. The rest of your stepfamily may not be good at bringing up problems and issues, so you may be the one who needs to instigate a conversation.

Propose a family meeting (there are tips on how to do this in Chapter 13, "Family Talk"). Or make an appointment with your stepchild to talk one-on-one, step-to-step. Remember to listen actively as they air their dirty laundry. When it comes to your turn, they may need to hear a few points:

➤ You acknowledge and respect that they didn't ask to have another person in their life, let alone another parent.

➤ They can consider you a friend, and you are not trying to be their mother.

➤ Even though you are not trying to mother them, you are one of the adults in the household, and as such, you are in charge of organizing certain things.

➤ You don't want to boss them around or discipline them, but you do expect to be shown some respect. (Review the Family Rules exercise in Chapter 14, "Defying the Discipline Demons.")

➤ You haven't been their stepmother before, and you all need to learn how to do this stepfamily thing together.

➤ You appreciate their input into family life, and you want to know their needs and desires.

➤ They don't have to love you.

➤ You aren't going to push for too much intimacy, but you plan to put energy in, and you hope that someday—not now!—they will want to feel close to you.

➤ You recognize that you all have something big in common: You all love their biodad, and he loves all of you.

I Kid You Not!

Famous stepmothers in the comics: In Garry Trudeau's comic strip *Doonesbury*, Mike Doonesbury's 20-something, hipper-than-thou, Gen-X, "Babe" wife, Kim, is stepmother to his daughter, Alex. Honey, the former Communist Chinese paramour of drug-raddled Duke, is stepmother to Duke's delinquent chip-off-the-old-block.

Revising Your Self-Image

Like many stepmothers, I came to stepparenting reluctantly—so reluctantly that I didn't even admit to myself that I was becoming a stepparent. And this was even though Bill's kids lived with us four days a week, and when we went off to Asia for a year, we planned to have them with us for half the time.

It took time before I was able to revise my self-image enough to claim the title "stepmother." In a social climate where "stepmother" is not a good thing, it's no wonder! Being evil, wicked, and second-place didn't match my self-image. It shouldn't match yours, either.

It was hard for me to claim the role of stepmother. Once I did, I felt a lot better about it. I suddenly had a title for what I was doing: parenting somebody else's children. Claiming the title of stepmother as my own was an important move for me in valuing the role I was playing in Aaron and Rachel's lives. Take a lesson from me. If you don't value and respect what you are doing, nobody else will, either.

I Kid You Not!

Famous stepmother-to-be?: Will Camilla Parker-Bowles ever achieve her life-long desire and become stepmother to the future king of England?

Working with Your Partner

Your partner's position isn't easy, either. (If you don't believe me, go back and read the "Top Biofather Complaints.") As in any stepparenting situation, you and your partner can make it easier on yourselves—and on your stepfamily as a whole—by working together as a team.

Sharon is an unusual stepmother, a woman with few complaints. "I think the secret to my happiness in Donald's family is Donald. He's my total supporter," she says. "If I didn't believe he was totally with me, I don't think I'd enjoy the kids as much. That's not to say he's not on their side, too. I don't know how he does it; he doesn't take sides, but we all feel loved and supported."

Throughout the book, I've stressed the importance of the strength of the couple as the foundation of the stepfamily, but here are a few extra things to keep in mind:

➤ Both stepmothers and biofathers need acknowledgment from their partners of the difficulty of their roles in the stepfamily.

➤ The biofather can help the stepmother by not automatically expecting her to take on his parenting duties.

➤ You, the stepmother, can be a real asset to your partner by making him aware of problems you and other members of the family are having. Many biofathers shut themselves off from problems. When there's a crisis, it's usually the stepmother who makes the first step toward seeking family therapy, if it's needed.

Stepmothers and Discipline

I know, you don't wanna appear wicked. But you don't want to get walked all over, either! And what if you're one of those stepmothers—and there are a lot of them—whose partner is so frightened of losing the kids that he refuses to be the bad guy, or the enforcer of consequences?

Don't let your partner dump the discipline on you!

Discipline is a partnership issue (Chapter 14, "Defying the Discipline Demons," is all about this, so you might want to review it now). Discipline is not about punishment. Instead, it's the daily process of teaching proper behavior. Most teaching comes from modeling the kinds of behaviors you would like to see in a child. Discipline also involves teaching a child that there are consequences—natural or logical—for behavior. As a parent, your partner needs to set reasonable, effective limits and be willing to follow them up with consequences.

When a biofather stops teaching discipline, he's neglecting his role as a father. (Maybe he's suffering from Disneyland Daddy Syndrome—see the glossary.) If your partner is shuffling all the discipline off to you, take some action:

➤ Back off the kids. It is not your responsibility to be the heavy-handed parent—and it's not good for your relationship with the kids, either.

➤ Talk with your partner. Go over Chapter 14 and this section of the book with him. If he shows his kids that he respects them and himself enough to provide strong modeling, set limits on their behavior, and follow through with appropriate consequences, he won't lose them. In the long term, he'll gain their respect.

Stepping Stones
Be flexible in your ideas, your plans, and your tolerances. If you're too rigid, rigor mortis will set in.

The Noncustodial Stepmother

The noncustodial or shared-custodial stepmother (the stepmom whose stepkids don't live with her, or live with her only some of the time) is far more common than the custodial stepmother (whose stepkids live primarily in her home).

Which role is harder, custodial or noncustodial? Well, it depends who you talk to. "I think it's hardest being a noncustodial parent. Nobody takes me seriously as a parent," says Courtney, the stepmother of two kids under 10.

Her friend Louise disagrees, "I enjoy the girls because I don't have to take care of them all the time. I have a letter of medical permission for emergencies (see Chapter 22, "Legal Stuff"), my name is on the school forms, and I'm fine with explaining the situation to people. The key is in not identifying too much with the kids. It's good that they aren't 'mine.' That way I'm not so invested in their successes and failures; they don't reflect on me."

If your stepkids don't live with you, you may feel like a nonentity in their lives when it comes to the outside world. Noncustodial stepmothers often complain about getting very little support from doctors, teachers, lawyers, and other parents. (Try going to a Back-to-School Night with your partner and having the "real" parents treat you like a bimbo who's come along for the free cheese and crackers. Yuck.)

It's hard not to have control over how your stepkids are being raised, especially when you care a great deal, and double-especially when you disapprove of how things are being done in the household of your partner's ex.

You *don't* have control. This is a hard lesson to learn for many people. You may have some influence on the child herself, but you need to disengage from what's happening in that other household. I recommend this for your own sake, for your own emotional survival. Have you ever thought about taking up meditation?

I Kid You Not!

There are no shortcuts to intimacy. Kids have "phony" radar. Don't try to make visits perfect, and don't try to be somebody you're not. You'll risk having the kids respond scornfully, "Who are *you* trying to be? You don't even have kids yourself!" This kind of treatment can hurt your feelings terribly (especially if you *do* want kids and you don't have them). Slack off on trying to be the Mommyest Mom in the world. And don't let them get your goat.

Stomping Out Super Stepmom Syndrome

Stepmothers have a tendency to react to the emotional stresses within the stepfamily by becoming over-involved. You (and the family as a whole) will do better if you take a few steps back from the situation and realize three things:

1. You are not in charge.
2. You cannot change everything.
3. You have influence but no control.

Accepting these points can alleviate a great deal of your stress.

"The limitations of a stepmother's role can be a relief if she will recognize them," says Cherie Burns in *Stepmotherhood: How to Survive Without Feeling Frustrated, Left Out, or Wicked.*

As a stepmother, you can find a certain freedom from worry if you release, relax, and realize, "hey, these aren't my kids!" If Jim doesn't make good grades in math, you can commiserate with him, you can work with him on his quadratic equations, and you can hire a tutor. But you don't need to lie awake nights stressing about how you, as a parent, have failed him. Leave that part of parenting to your partner. Give yourself a break.

> **Don't Be Wicked**
> Some researchers have found that stepmother-stepdaughter relations are worse when the stepmother's marriage is strong. Keep an eye out for jealousy, resentment, and lack of communication. Then talk about it.

Stepmother Survival Tips

Some of these we've talked about before, and some are new. They're the secrets to stepmother survival (and don't say I never gave you anything!):

➤ Don't take over.

➤ Keep your own expectations low. Don't *expect* yourself to feel any particular way about the kids—let yourself feel what you feel.

➤ Be a duck and let society's expectations roll off your back like water. Nobody out there knows the reality of your life.

➤ Don't try to do everything; you'll only fail.

➤ Try to do less, and you'll achieve more.

➤ Use shared activities to build a relationship with your stepchild.

➤ Work to build a connection between your stepchild and you; don't pretend there's a relationship where there's not.

➤ Forget "love"; go for "loving."

➤ Respect your own privacy and the privacy of your stepchildren, and set boundaries about privacy in your household.

➤ Get Zen about it. Don't seek your meaning and purpose in life in the stepfamily; the role of stepmother cannot accommodate such a weight. Get your gratification from your relationship, your job, your other children, your friendships, and your hobbies.

➤ "Care" less and your relationships will be worth more.

➤ Doing everything you can about a hard situation doesn't mean killing yourself— or your spirit or joy of life—over it.

The Least You Need to Know

➤ The role of stepmother is very difficult for most stepmoms.

➤ Society expects a lot of you and yet doesn't believe you can deliver.

➤ Discipline is not your job.

➤ Don't over-invest emotionally in your stepkids. A little distance helps the relationship.

Chapter 27

So, You're a Stepdad

In This Chapter

➤ Top complaints of stepfathers and biomothers

➤ A look at the stepfather's role in the stepfamily

➤ Discipline dos and don'ts for stepdads

➤ All about stepparenting boys and girls

➤ Tips for stepfather survival

Forget about that mythological image of the stepparent as evil stepmother. In fact, forget about the image of stepparent as stepmother at all! The majority of resident stepparents are stepfathers.

This chapter is for you, Stepdad. It's all about the biggest issues for stepfathers: your ambiguous role, discipline, money, respect, and communication problems. How do you gain authority without being authoritative? What's the difference between stepfathering a girl and stepfathering a boy? What's the deal on physical affection? "Inch by inch, row by row, I will make my garden grow," goes the song, and it's especially true for stepfathering. Change takes time. Gather your patience—you'll need it!

Who Is This Man Called "Stepdad?"

You're not the dad, you're more than a pal, and you're not the knight in shining armor. You're not even the king of your own castle. Defining your role as stepfather is sometimes more a matter of figuring out what you *are not* than figuring out what you *are*. No wonder so many stepdads are frustrated by the muddy, murky quality of their family role!

I Kid You Not!

"Neither fish nor flesh, nor good red herring," says an old English proverb from almost 500 years ago. Was the long-lost author talking about stepfathers? I wonder.

As a stepdad, you'll do best if you're able to flex a bit and adjust your role to fit the kids' needs, the times in their lives, and your stepfamily's situation. You're walking a thin line here, trying to be the stepfather your stepkids need while keeping your sense of self intact and making sure your personal needs are met:

➤ Consider how old your stepkids are, and follow the lead of the child. Little kids will easily accept your parenting, even your discipline. Older kids (preteens and teenagers) are going to be far more resistant to any kind of authoritative role that you take.

➤ Start slow. You can be a guide, a buddy, a mentor, a kind and fun uncle, or a psychological father—if you take it really slow. Like maybe next year.

The Stepfather and Biomother Complaint Hall of Fame

What do most stepfathers complain about? What kind of complaints do they hear from their partners? Here are two lists, so you know you're not alone. Read 'em and weep. How many match your own complaints? (How many give you insight into what your partner may be feeling?)

Top Stepfather Complaints

1. Nobody appreciates or respects me for how much work I do for this family. She expects me to help financially, and then I get no credit. I'm just a third wheel.

2. All our decisions about money and vacations have to be cleared with her ex. I want to be head of my own household.

3. I feel lumped in with the kids as something she's taking care of. Where's the romance? When the kids are around, I feel like I have to compete with them for a little attention.

4. The tension when the kids are here is so thick you can cut it with a knife.

5. There's no privacy around here.

6. She relies on me to discipline the kids and then gets angry at me for being too harsh on them.

7. Her ex is never around anymore, and I'm expected to do the parenting without being the dad.

8. When the kids are here, I'm neglected; when the kids are away, I have to comfort her because she misses them so much. When do we just get to be a couple?

9. I'd like a kid of my own, but she wants me to be satisfied with hers.

10. She interferes too much with my relationship with the kids; she wants to be in on everything. We need to solve our disagreements ourselves sometimes, and she's always stepping in the middle.

Top Biomother Complaints

1. He's too harsh on my kids. They're not perfect—they're kids!

2. He wants me to himself and resents the time and energy I put into my kids.

3. He wants to take over. I did just fine when I was by myself.

4. When life is fun, he's in the middle, having fun too. When things get tough, he withdraws, leaving me with all the issues to deal with.

5. He's jealous when I negotiate with my Ex. I have to! He thinks we're out having sex. He doesn't understand how hard these meetings are.

6. He wants the kids to love him like their own father. He shouldn't push so hard.

7. I know he misses his own kids, but he takes it out on mine by not paying attention to them.

8. He wants us to have a kid of our own. I'm not sure I want to start all over again.

9. He's so competitive with my son, and I worry about him with my daughter. Not that I think he'd do anything sexual (he would never cross the line) but I sense this intense attraction/repulsion between them, and I'm not comfortable with it.

10. I feel like this is the United Nations and I'm the simultaneous translator.

Stepfathers and Discipline

For stepfathers, discipline sometimes feels like a no-win situation. Stepfathers tend to blow it by stepping too quickly into the role of disciplinarian. Judith Wallerstein, a specialist in divorce and remarriage issues, speculates that a man might do this in an attempt to make himself more comfortable with another man's children, or to impress his new wife. Often stepfathers become heavy disciplinarians because they don't know how else to react to a lack of respect, or when the kids seem to be in real trouble.

Many moms also make the mistake of expecting their new husbands to step too quickly into the role of "man of the household." Other mothers may resent and be angered by your heavy-duty approach. Yes, they feel that they could use some help, but they don't want you usurping their role as parent. (Mothers don't like to have their roles usurped!)

You will get nowhere by laying down the law, being harsh, raising your voice, demanding action, or applying punishments. Hey, Bub, you're not the dad. Don't try to be. Before you can effectively teach a child discipline, you must gain her trust and respect. (Now might be a good time to go back to Chapter 9, "New Family Structures," and review the steps to gaining authority.)

Don't Be Wicked
Some biomoms assume, now that you're the stepdad, that you should take over as the disciplinarian. Ixnay. You are not the white knight, stepping in to rescue the poor single mom. Don't come on too strong.

But what can you do? Your stepkids may be running wild, out of control. They may be treating you terribly, either with direct antagonism or by ignoring you. When there are disciplinary problems in your stepfamily, take some action:

➤ Understand that many stepkids are used to being independent and doing things by themselves, especially if their mother was a single (and over-stressed) mom for an extended period of time. It's not just you; it's anybody telling them what to do that they resent.

➤ Follow your partner's lead. Have your partner play the heavy. She has biological ties, history, and established love to back her up. She is the mother; your job is to be the man behind the scenes, supporting her efforts. If she has trouble asserting herself, help her privately, but don't step in—it will not work.

Stepping Stones
For step-fathers, the rule is: When the going gets tough, the stepfather gets gentle.

➤ Talk about it with your partner. Discipline must be a mutual parenting decision, so communication between you and your partner is essential.

➤ Take a positive approach to discipline by using regular verbal praise and encouragement, and by showing your respect for your stepkids. You have no idea how many problems you will prevent this way.

Play Fair

If you're in a combined family (if you have kids of your own in the picture), you and your partner need to be extra careful to make sure that the same rules and consequences apply to both sets of kids, both hers and yours.

But Don't Withdraw, Either!

Don't Be Wicked
Don't think of yourself as a knight in shining armor, galloping in to save your stepkids from life in a single-parent family. They may not want to be saved!

Stepfathers tend to be extremists. If things aren't going well, they tend either to come down heavy on the discipline, or they withdraw emotionally. It's hard to stay present when you feel undervalued or unsure of how to react to a hard situation. Don't pull out too early. Try to resist the urge to pull back when things get tough.

Stan was baffled by his three bright and active stepkids. He was unsure about how to deal with their high spirits (he's a quiet sort himself) and was unwilling to come across as "the heavy." The three boys were very close to their mother (the family had weathered their biofather's alcoholism and desertion), and Stan felt left out of the loop and lonely. Unfortunately, his wife Adrienne felt defensive about her tight relationship with the kids, and she refused to talk with Stan about his concerns.

This stepfamily didn't make it. Stan withdrew emotionally to the point where he and Adrienne felt they had nothing in common anymore. Stan couldn't find anything in his relationship with the family to make it worthwhile, so they split up.

Stan is not alone—stepfathers often feel lonely or left out. If you are feeling estranged from your partner, and if problem-solving and active listening don't work, you might want to consider a support group or short-term family therapy to get you back on track. Hey, hang in there. Stay focused, and don't withdraw. It's worth it.

I Kid You Not!

Famous stepfathers in the comics: In Garry Trudeau's long-running strip *Doonesbury*, Zeke, J.J.'s hick, old-hippie boyfriend is de-facto stepfather to cool, pre-adolescent Alex. For Christmas, Zeke gave Alex a stolen Tickle-Me-Elmo, and a can of tuna fish—"the gift of protein." But wait! Rick Redfern, Joanie Caucus's husband, is J. J.'s stepfather. But do you ever see that mentioned?

I Can't Get No Respect!

Respect, unfortunately, rarely comes with the territory—you have to earn it. How is respect earned? Through appropriate, respectful behavior on your part—and a whole lot of patience, because it may take some time. Here's an area where you can help teach your stepkids appropriate behavior. You'll teach it by modeling positive behavior, by respecting your own boundaries without being harsh, and by showing respect to the kids and your partner.

Stepping Stones

Yes, it's hard to work so hard and get no acknowledgment. Patience, Pardner!

Your partner can support your efforts here by letting the kids know, in no uncertain terms, that they don't have to love you (they don't even have to like you), but they need to treat you with decency and respect.

Stepfather: Mr. Moneybags

If you're like most stepfathers, you're making a positive impact on your family's finances. Some statistics say that in the United States, the average stepfather's income is more than twice as high as his partner's and accounts for three-quarters of the family income.

Some other statisticians say that as few as 30 percent of kids receive child support from their biofathers. Even if they are wrong (and I hope they are!), your financial participation is vital. Okay, so why can't you sign a medical consent slip? And how come you can't get any respect?

Arguments about money are far too common in stepfamilies. Money issues are one of the top reasons marriages break up. Too many people equate money and respect: "I'm doing so much for this family, and people aren't treating me very well." And people equate earning power with the power to decide how money should be spent in the household.

Stop. Don't go there. In that direction lies only frustration and bitterness.

Try to separate money, respect, and power. You and your partner will do better if you can see that each of you is contributing equally to the family, not solely in terms of money but rather in energy, effort, and time as well. If you believe that your combined contributions are 50/50, you may be able to ease up whatever tension there is between you about money.

Talk About It

Communication problems are common in stepfamilies, especially between stepdads and their kids. Teenagers, particularly, are terrific at being sullen and silent. And men, as a group, have not been socialized to be as communicative as women. They often have a harder time talking about things that are bothering them.

Take a deep breath and propose a family meeting (go back to Chapter 13, "Family Talk," for tips on how to proceed). A family meeting is a great place to clear the air. (Special alone time with a stepchild can work, too.) If your stepchildren are acting resentful and distant, they may especially need to hear these points:

➤ You're not trying to take over as a father. You are aware that they already have a dad, and he's a fine one. (Okay, you can leave that part out if it's a lie, but don't ever knock Biodad or you'll lose all your credibility, no matter what kind of scumbag he is.)

➤ You haven't been their stepfather before. You all need to learn the ropes together, and you would like their help and input on what they need.

➤ You won't be a bully, but you do need to establish mutual respect. (Review the Family Rules exercise in Chapter 14, "Defying the Discipline Demons.")

➤ You want to build a friendship. You know that it takes time. You're in for the long haul. You aren't going to push for too much closeness, but you are going to put energy in, and you hope that someday—not now!—they'd like to do the same.

Stepfathering a Boy

Stepfathering a boy is different from stepfathering a girl. On the plus side, stepdads tend to have a terrific time with their stepsons. Spending time with their stepsons brings most stepdads tremendous joy. A stepfather can bring a role model, a confidante, and an idol, especially for boys whose biodads have not actively been parenting them.

I Kid You Not!

Famous stepfather in memoir: In Tobias Wolff's memoir, *This Boy's Life*, young Toby's stepfather is a cruel, brutal, and fascinating-to-read-about man. But he's not someone I'd like to meet!

On the minus side, your stepson may have been the "man" of the family, and you are taking his place. You may face a challenge. It's like an animal kingdom thing where the dogs compete for dominance to see who gets to be the Alpha Dog big boss. You know and I know that you are the man of the household now. You're sleeping with the Alpha female, you're in charge financially, and you're older. But the young 'un may not get it. Be prepared to be challenged on everything.

A teenage boy whose biofather is absent may rebel and defy all authority figures, and that includes you. A boy may also try to get rid of you to free his mother so she can reconcile with their biodad. Kids rarely give up the fantasy of their parents getting back together.

This is very tricky business, establishing your position without showing your stepson a lack of respect or putting him down. Here's the most important piece of advice I have for you: Don't ever laugh at him. Stepsons have killed their stepfathers for less.

Stepfathering a Girl

Watch your back, buster! Girls are a real challenge. They'll give you a hard time, and they tend to be distrustful of stepfathers for quite a while.

James Bray, a researcher and clinician in the department of family medicine at Baylor College of Medicine, says that it can take up to two years for girls to feel at ease with their mother's new husband. (Boys, on the other hand, usually take much less time to accept their new stepdad and the relationship.)

Girls often give their moms more post-divorce support than boys do, and as a result, mother-daughter bonds can be very tight. Girls tend to be possessive and protective of their mothers. Stepfathers can feel like the third wheel in a household with all that tightly bonded female energy. Faced with an imposing stepdaughter or two, stepdads tend to either withdraw emotionally from both mother and daughter(s) or be too critical of their stepdaughters—and often too restrictive.

As girls become sexually mature, tensions in the household can grow (go back and reread Chapter 21, "Stepfamilies in Crisis"). It's normal to be attracted to your stepdaughter; there are no biological taboos operating here. But it's not okay to do anything at all about it, no matter how seductive your stepdaughter becomes. You are the adult here. Be one.

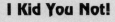

I Kid You Not!

I have a second cousin whose dad has been married six times. Portia has never had a problem with any of her stepmoms (her own mother was wife number one), but life with her one-and-only stepdad has been a constant challenge. Portia complains that her stepdad is jealous of her bond with her mother and tends to step in as a dividing force.

If you've got a stepdaughter, take these steps:

➤ Let your partner be in charge of discipline.

➤ Give your relationship time.

➤ Realize that your stepdaughter's rejecting behavior is not likely to be a reflection on you personally.

Stepfather Survival Tips

Getting through the initial couple of years as a stepfather is hard. Here are a few tips for surviving and thriving.

Don't Touch

Both boys and girls tend to be uncomfortable with physical contact from their stepfathers. By physical contact, we're talking kisses, cuddles, roughhousing, or corporal punishment (which is inappropriate with all kids and especially so with stepkids).

Be verbally affectionate and physically retiring. Touch can be—and often is—misconstrued as sexually inappropriate or brutish behavior.

Nasty Kid Tricks

When a stepchild is angry at his mother, is jealous of you, or is testing the strength of your relationship, he may show it by trying to get you on his side. You may be in for a dose of flattery or other inappropriate behavior. It's time, more than ever, for a strong show of your unified front, your agreed-upon approach. Demonstrate that your stepkid can't come between you or play you off against each other.

The Biomom/Biochild Bond

It's a mistake to think that stepfamilies have to do everything together, and it's vital as a stepfather that you don't threaten the strong relationship between your partner and her children. They'll ally against you if you do. Let her spend time with her kids in much the same way as they've always done.

Frequently, stepfathers feel threatened by their partners' continued closeness with the kids and feel worried that they have no meaning or influence on the kids. You do mean something to your stepkids, and the longer the family is together, the more the relationships will grow.

What About the Biodad?

Many stepfathers have very limited contact with their stepchildren's biofather, simply because he isn't around. If there is no biofather in the picture, particularly if you get your stepkids when they are very young, your role as a stepfather may be more parental than it will be if he's part of your family's weekly life. You may also feel a strong sense of pride for giving your stepchild a life that her absent father never could or would.

More and more, though, biological fathers do play a strong role in their children's lives after divorce and repartnering. A biofather's involvement can affect your authority as a stepfather.

If the biodad is around, it doesn't mean you have no influence in your stepkids' lives. You are important to them, and time will settle most of your (normal!) insecurities about this. You may have more issues to deal with. Your partner may have money hassles, or you may have a beef with him about discipline or other child-rearing concerns. Be aware of a few points:

➤ It's best if you get along, but don't become his pal. Too much closeness between you and your partner's ex can be threatening and confusing to your partner and to your stepkids.

➤ If you're having a disagreement, it's fine to bring it up with him, but it's not worth fighting about. You'll risk tearing up the family. Kids have a hard enough time as it is with loyalty issues. Let your partner handle the vast majority of the negotiations and contacts with her ex. He's her ex, after all.

The Zen of Stepfathering

Just as in the Eastern meditative practices, you'll be a better and more fulfilled stepfather the less you expect and the more you accept.

➤ Expect nothing.

➤ Enjoy the kids for who they are as individuals.

➤ Be patient with the kids and with the situation.

➤ Show and tell your stepkids how much you like, appreciate, and respect them.

➤ Be moderate in your approach, both in discipline and in affection.

➤ Spend special time with your mate. The health of your family is dependent upon the health of your relationship.

➤ Keep a unified front with your partner.

➤ Be fair.

➤ Take your partner's lead in discipline and other parenting issues, and support her actions.

➤ Stay present and conscious. It's hard to be second in your family's affections and not withdraw.

➤ Set your patience flame on slow burn. There's the bait, don't bite!

➤ Apologize when you do bite the bait.

➤ Expect that you will make mistakes, and accept the fact that you are imperfect. Don't try to be Super Stepdad.

➤ Stay patient. Appreciation and love grow.

It's Never Too Late

You may have made many mistakes early in your relationships with your stepkids. Don't despair—most people make mistakes. You're in luck because a relationship is not like a crystal goblet. If it's broken, it can be fixed. Your mistakes can be remedied. Try talking, more talking, and more talking. Don't give up—persistence pays off.

The Least You Need to Know

➤ The majority of stepparents are stepfathers.

➤ Stepfathers tend to leap too quickly and too heavily into disciplining their stepkids.

➤ Stepfathers are often a big support to their stepfamilies. But watch that you don't confuse monetary contributions with control within the family.

➤ Stepfathering boys can be quite different from stepfathering girls.

➤ Stepfathers do better the more they accept and the less they expect.

Chapter 28

Building the Extended Family

In This Chapter

➤ A portrait of the American stepfamily

➤ Extending your stepfamily or combined family

➤ Setting reasonable goals

➤ Being your stepchild's ally and friend

➤ Taking care of yourself

➤ Advantages to life in the stepfamily

Every stepfamily is part of a community. No matter how shy or private you think you are, and unless you're one out of a million families and live on a deserted island with no neighbors, telephones, schools, or relatives, there are other people involved in your lives—and in your parenting.

Imagine your stepfamily standing at a vista point along a beautiful highway. It's the last day of your vacation, and you're taking a family photo. ("Susan, get away from the edge of the cliff!") You have a choice of lenses here: the close-up or the wide-angle.

For most of this book, we've been using a close-up lens to take snapshots one at a time of you, your partner, your stepkid, and your stepfamily. In this last chapter of the book, we're switching lenses. Get out the wide-angle!

Let's look at the larger panorama, the sweeping views, and the terrific scene in which your family stands. We'll look at two questions: "What is the stepfamily's place in this world?" and "How do you, as a stepparent, fit into the larger picture?"

The American Stepfamily Today

What do stepfamilies really look like? How common are stepfamily situations? If you read the books, search the Internet for articles, and talk with the experts, you'll hear enough numbers and statistics to make your head swim. Here's a sample (so our heads can do the breaststroke together). These statistics are collected from reports by the Stepfamily Foundation, Inc., the Stepfamily Association of America, and the U.S. Census Bureau:

➤ Half of all first marriages end in divorce.

➤ About 50 percent of remarriages fail within the first five years.

➤ About 1,300 new stepfamilies form every year.

➤ About 21 percent of American families with children have at least one stepparent.

➤ 15.9 percent of married couple households with kids under 18 in 1990 had a stepparent in the home.

➤ Of kids under 18 living in married couple stephouseholds, 92 percent live with a stepfather.

Don't Be Wicked

Don't be too concerned about statistics. Numbers have their place. They are an important way for social scientists to figure out the trends in our society, and they are vital for establishing funding qualifications for organizations. But statistics don't make a difference in your own family's circumstances. Concentrate on what's going on with *you*, not on how average or unusual your situation is.

Dizzy yet? Impressed? Confused? Distrustful?

Look, it doesn't matter what the numbers say. It's difficult getting accurate statistics, and we all know that numbers can be pushed and pulled like saltwater taffy. These are the important things:

1. No matter what statistics are cited, you are a stepparent, and your experience is *your* experience.

2. You are not alone. There are a lot of stepparents out there. You have a huge pool of people with whom to share experiences and support.

3. Don't ever be frightened of the statistics that cite high failure rates among stepfamilies. They don't apply to you. By reading this and other books, by thinking and planning, and by looking inward and outward for support, you're taking active steps to prevent and improve problems. You are putting yourself in the percentage of families that do make it.

The Extended Family

The shape of the American family is changing for the better, becoming more inclusive, more diverse, and more extended. Shared custody (both legal and physical) is becoming more the norm, and unlike in the past—when many biofathers left the scene—biodads are often very involved in parenting their kids after a divorce. More involvement means more adults in parenting roles and far more well-combined families.

Step-Speak
To extend means both to enlarge and to reach out. An extended family is both larger and more encompassing of other people.

The only problem with this improved state of affairs is that the more people there are involved in any activity, the more time it takes to plan things and to negotiate through differences of opinion. (Hey, as far as I'm concerned, this caffeine-based, gotta-hurry generation could all use a little more slowing down and time-taking anyway.)

The Value of the Extended Family

Children need other people (don't we all?). Kids do best (and parents, stepparents, and families survive intact) when there's a support network of many people, including relatives, adult friends, teachers, and members of the community.

In any community, the people who live there are mostly luck-of-the-draw; you don't get to pick the residents. You don't get to choose your partner's ex, either, or the family of your partner's ex (nor did they get to pick you!). Nonetheless, all of these people are a distinct part of your community now. Recognize that they are part of your stepchild's (and therefore your) support network, and you are part of theirs. The more you're able to see the wider picture and accept the abundance and diversity of this network, the easier it will be for you to rise above individual disagreements.

You can say it's for the sake of the kids, but the sake of the kids is your sake, too. It's nearly impossible for your stepchild to bond with you when your obvious dislike of her other bioparent gets in the way. She'll feel that getting close to you will hurt her biomom or biodad.

Stepping Stones
All generosity—both monetary and emotional—in a stepfamily is ultimately in your own best interest. Some people call this Karma, some call it the Golden Rule, and I call it True. You get as much as you give!

No! You don't have to get all buddy-buddy with the ex now. A working, respectful relationship doesn't mean beer dates, bowling, or heart-to-hearts. Your stepdaughter's soccer coach is also involved in your community, but you don't feel compelled to borrow clothes or tools from her, do you? Work on developing a practical partnership with the ex, not a close friendship.

Take the First Step with the Ex

If things are heating up toward nuclear meltdown, or if the Cold War has been going on for a while, it may be up to you to begin the peace process. Take a deep breath, keep the wide-angle lens open, and begin.

In her book *Cherishing Our Daughters*, Evelyn Bassoff recommends writing a letter to the bioparent to break the ice. (You could do this over the phone or in person, but it's easier and makes more of an impression when it's on paper.) Your letter might say something like this:

➤ You are there for the child, and although being a stepparent has its challenges and may not have been your first-choice role, you welcome the child into your life.

➤ You are not trying to take over her parenting role.

➤ You are committed to doing the best you can to try to be a kind, adult friend to her child.

➤ You would like to put aside disagreements and put the child's interests first.

➤ You are available to talk or correspond any time she has anything to discuss.

Stepping Stones
Combining and extending is fantastic, but it's important to continue to honor the original relationship between bioparent and biochild. If you're a bioparent, too, spend some special time alone with your own kid.

For many people, getting over the initial hump is the hardest. Yes, you run the risk of being snubbed, but your efforts may pay off—and if they do, they'll pay off big-time. Think how much easier your life would be if you didn't have that churning anxiety every time you or your partner had to deal with the ex.

The Cooperation Concept

Cooperation and parenting collaboration with the ex will pay off in more than the money you'll save on antacids and headache relief. You can be a better stepparent if you enlist your partner's ex as a parenting ally. Think of the advantages! You can share information and ideas about problems your stepchildren are having. You and your partner are not as likely to be manipulated by your stepkid. And your stepkids will be happier. They won't feel tension in the air, they'll feel more secure, and they'll accept you sooner and with more grace.

Defeating antagonism takes time. Keep trying—it's worth it.

The Other Relatives

Your partner has broken up with the ex and has found fabulous you! Yet, because your partner has kids, there are still more "other" relatives in the picture besides those Other

Grands. (Remember them—and remember Chapter 17, "Birth Grandparents and Step-Grandparents"). Who else is involved? What about your stepkids' aunts, uncles, cousins, second cousins, and third-cousins-twice-removed? Your partner's ex's relatives may very well be a part of your new family's network.

Here's another opportunity to grow your community and incorporate more concerned adults into your extended family. Once again, it may be up to you to take the first steps, especially if your partner's past relationship crashed, flamed, and burned.

> **Stepping Stones**
> How the family of your partner's ex feels about you will depend, in part, on how and why your partner's previous relationship broke up.

Setting Reasonable Goals

In all your stepparenting endeavors, it's vital to keep your expectations in check and to set reasonable goals for yourself and for your stepfamily.

There's a slogan I keep posted on my office wall: "Perfect is the Enemy of Good." If you try for perfection, you are doomed to fail. Aim your hardest for "good enough." Do the best you can, and be patient. Change takes time. Be kind to yourself.

Defeating Guilt

"Guilt is the gift that keeps on giving," said Erma Bombeck. Used wrongly, guilt can be a destructive force to you and to others. But guilt can be a positive force when it reminds us that we always have the opportunity to improve ourselves and our actions.

> **Don't Be Wicked**
> "You *knew* what you were getting into!" Have you heard that? Don't listen, and don't believe it. You can plan and plan as much as you can, but it's impossible to predict the interpersonal dynamics of a stepfamily. No, you *didn't* know what you were getting into. Nobody does.

It's hard to read an advice book, especially when it points out things that you've done wrong and suggests ways of doing things that you haven't done. Don't let guilt over your past stepparenting practices freeze you in your footsteps. Don't beat yourself up. It's never too late to make changes, and it's never too late to improve your step relationships.

How to Be Your Stepchild's Friend and Ally

The best relationships between stepkids and stepparents come when there is genuine trust and friendship. Remember that these things take time. As the old saying goes, "If at first you don't succeed…." Patience, my friend. Your efforts will pay off in the end.

Here are some strategies for wading through the yuck, right into a positive relationship:

➤ Hang out alone together. Remember the solo outings in Chapter 7, "Instant Parent." Don't stop the bonding process.

➤ Cut your stepkid some slack during transition times.

➤ Keep your promises.

➤ Be generous with your time and your money.

➤ Share your skills, and share your thoughts.

➤ Be honest.

➤ Show unconditional respect.

➤ Teach discipline through modeling and by supporting your partner.

➤ Let your stepchild know that you'll be there for her no matter what she does and no matter what happens.

➤ Stick up for your stepchild when others cut her down.

➤ Don't push for intimacy.

➤ Stay flexible. Go with the flow. Be ready for surprises.

➤ Listen to your stepchild. If you listen hard enough and well enough, he will tell you who he is and what he needs.

Stepping Stones

Celebrate September 16, Stepfamily Day! Twenty-five states—half the nation—have proclaimed it a holiday (no, the banks are not closed...).

Stepping Stones

You're no good to anybody else if you're no good to yourself. Good nutrition, exercise, and a positive outlook affect your stepfamily almost as much as they affect you. Invest in your own well-being.

Looking Inward for Support

Life as a stepparent is very hard. It's hard stretching out your hand toward people you feel (at best) ambivalent or (at worst) antagonistic about. It's hard living in a family stretched tight with tension. It's hard being second banana when you want and need to be loved and cherished as number one. (Don't we all!) You need some support. Some of this support should come from your partner, family, and friends, and some should come from the outside world (remember Chapter 21, "Stepfamilies in Crisis"), but some needs to come from inside yourself.

Big Heart, Tired Heart

Stepparenting is a big job, and big jobs can be exhausting. Most stepparents have large hearts—you need one to take on the care of another person's children. One problem of being a large-hearted person is that you probably overextend yourself emotionally.

Sometimes things aren't working well in your family and you need to make big changes. Other times, life is basically fine and you don't need substantial changes, just a little relaxation and emotional nourishment.

Time, space, and relaxation of your choice are the best medicine after a hard day of stepparenting. (For me it's a hot bath with bubbles, then sushi and time with my husband.)

Relax and Revitalize

Here's a relaxation exercise that can help when things are tense with your stepkids. Take a psychic break from the stresses and strains, and go into the bedroom for 10 minutes or more. You can lie on top of a firm bed or a warm, carpeted floor. As you release tension, you may find that emotions bubble up inside. That's fine. Let them pass through you like a gentle wind along with your breaths.

1. Lie on your back with your legs bent comfortably so your feet are flat on the floor and your arms are by your sides, palms up.

2. Close your eyes lightly and sigh deeply. Breathe deeply and slowly, in through your nose and out through your mouth. As you breathe each breath, count to four.

3. When you've completed 10 breaths, continue breathing.

4. Gently rock your head from side to side. Let it rest in the middle.

5. Feel your jaw drop and relax. Were you clenching your teeth? Feel the lovely relief as you let it go.

6. Relax your forehead. Let your eyeballs sink into their sockets. Feel the skin on the top of your head rest gently against your scalp.

7. Feel how heavy your shoulders are on the floor or bed. As you release them, feel the front of your chest float open and your shoulder blades flatten and widen. Don't force it.

8. Feel your mid-back settle gently against the floor or bed. Breathe.

9. Feel your lower back settle and release. Breathe.

10. Let your buttocks become heavy and flat. Don't force anything—let the breath carry the tension out of your body, and release it into the air.

11. Feel the soles of your feet rest against the floor. Breathe in. Breathe out.

12. Check your body for areas of remaining tension. When you find them, concentrate on inhaling breath into them and letting the tension dissolve with the breath.

Now you're relaxed, so relaxed that you may drift off to sleep for a few minutes. When ready, get up slowly. You'll feel revitalized.

Advantages to Stepfamily Life

Society may scoff, but you'll discover that there are great personal advantages to stepparenting. You have an opportunity to find inside yourself capacities you didn't know you had. Weathering the kinds of difficulties stepfamilies often face bonds families in a profound way and brings couples more intimacy.

You also have a strong opportunity to enhance a child's life. You can be your stepchild's ally and friend. From you, she can learn differences in opinion. From her, you also can learn different ways of living. Perhaps you'll be a role model or a confidante. Your partnership brings security to your stepchild's life and an example of a relationship that works.

Celebrating Your Victories

It's vital to mark milestones, victories, and accomplishments, both large and small.

My friend Ailsa is a professional at this, but I'm not. I tend to take any achievements in stride, barely noticing them, as though just checking them off a mental list. It's hard for me to really acknowledge when things go right. Yet when I tell Ailsa something I've done, she says "Let's celebrate!" A toast at dinner, a bouquet of flowers, a special outing—these small rituals make life joyful, make achievement meaningful, and help us keep troubles in perspective.

In a stepfamily, it's too easy to focus on the things that still aren't perfect and to forget the things that work, that have changed, and that represent real movement.

If you think you may need some help acknowledging how far you've come, take a few moments for the following exercise. In the examples below, I've given you a sample of my own responses. Keep in mind that I've been at this stepparenting stuff for a dozen years now; you may not be as far along. (On the other hand, you may be a much quicker learner than I am!)

How Far You've Come!

1. Make a list of things you appreciate and respect about your stepkids.

   Ericka's answer: I appreciate how Aaron and Rachel accept Annie with unconditional love. I appreciate how they call me on Mother's Day. I appreciate how they respect the members of my family. I appreciate their fierce loyalty to their mother. I appreciate how they accept me as their dad's chosen partner-in-life. I appreciate and respect their intelligence, and how diligently each of them work in their chosen fields.

   Your answer:_____

   _____

   _____

2. Write down what you've have learned about yourself since you've been a stepparent.

   Ericka's answer: I never thought that I could accept another person's children, let alone grow to care about each of them so deeply. I've learned that I'm not perfect, that I'm very often wrong, and that it's okay. I've learned that I'm at my best as a stepparent when I have a balance of private time and social, family time. I've learned, too, that things change over time.

Your answer:_____

_____

_____

3. Write down three things that have changed for the better in your stepfamily since it formed.

Ericka's answer: We've all learned how to be more inclusive and how to accommodate different styles of living. We've grown to appreciate and respect each other more for the individuals that we are. We've learned that we are not in competition for Bill's love, that love is not a limited commodity, and that there is always enough to go around.

Your answer:_____

_____

_____

Enjoy your victories. You've earned them.

Love

All the way through this book, I've asserted that love is not a requirement for stepparents and stepchildren, but that courtesy, caring, and respect are. Nope, I'm not changing my tune now. But love does enter stepfamilies. It's not something to expect or aim for, and it's not a requirement. Love grows, and it cannot be forced. But love cannot grow when you feel threatened. Love can grow only if you open your heart to it. Open your heart!

A Matter of Time

Human beings are very flexible. Think about the variety of climates in which we live, from steamy tropical jungles to the frozen wastelands up north. Now think of the variety of family groupings in which people live: small families, big families, stepfamilies. People have a great capacity to adjust.

In the thick of all the hullabaloo, it's hard to keep your perspective. (Don't stop using that wide-angle lens, now!) It usually takes a year or two for people to get

Stepping Stones Parenting of any kind is hard. But if you back away from the challenges, you'll never reap the rewards.

used to their new situation, but they do adjust. Everybody settles down. With a little time and energy invested in the right places, most stepparenting difficulties are short-lived.

Be pleased and proud that you've taken the time and effort to read this book and to think about these ideas. Look how you've changed already. You've taken a step in the right direction.

The Least You Need to Know

➤ Your stepfamily is part of a larger, important community.

➤ Cooperation and collaboration between you and your partner's ex helps everybody.

➤ It's vital to set reasonable goals and expectations for yourself, and for your stepfamily.

➤ You should use guilt as a wake-up call, not to punish yourself.

➤ There are terrific advantages to stepfamily life. Find them and celebrate!

Glossary

Active listening—Listening to and trying to understand another person's thoughts and feelings by listening silently and then paraphrasing (saying back again as closely as possible without interpretation) what has been said.

Adoption—A legal procedure in which an adult becomes the legal parent of someone who is not his or her biochild.

Ally—Somebody you trust to be there for you, somebody who is on your side. An ally need not be a close friend or even somebody you love.

Alpha Dog—The dominant dog in the dog pack, for whom all the others roll over. In human-speak, the Alpha Dog is the one in charge, the Head Honcho, the Big Kahuna.

Arrearage—An overdue amount of child-support payment. Arrearages are rarely forgiven; if you or your partner can't make a child-support payment, get thee to the courtroom immediately for an adjustment!

Biochild—The natural, biological child of a parent.

Bioparent—The natural, biological parent of a child.

Co-parent—One of two equally responsible, participating parents in a child's life. A co-parent is not necessarily biological. The term is often used to designate one of a child's two parents when the parents are gay or lesbian.

Cohabitation—A legal term that refers to two people of the opposite sex living together and having a sexual relationship. While cohabitation is extremely common, in some states, it is still against the law.

Combined family—A stepfamily with two sets of kids, one provided by each partner.

Consensus—A form of decision making in which everybody must actively agree and any one person has the power to block a decision. Its opposite is dictatorship.

Cross-cultural communication—Communication (written, verbal, or nonverbal) that occurs between people who come from different cultural backgrounds.

Culture—The behaviors and beliefs characteristic of a person's ethnic background, place of birth, religious upbringing, or social class.

Custody—The guardianship, the care of another (usually of a child) that involves making the decisions and being responsible for her well-being.

Dictatorship—Here, a form of family government in which the dictator rules and whatever he or she says, goes.

Discipline—The educational process of instilling values. It is most effective when it incorporates encouragement, praise, trust, and respect for children with firm, wise limits. It teaches kids how to make choices and understand the consequences of their choices. When necessary, it provides related, respectful, and reasonable responses to misbehavior.

Disneyland Daddy Syndrome (D.D.S.)—A condition suffered by a biofather who feels guilty, resentful of his ex, and/or estranged from his children. Its primary symptom is being overly generous to the kids with money and material things. (*See* **Moneybags Mama Syndrome**.)

Empathy—Feeling what another person feels. (*See* **sympathy**.)

Ex—A catch-all term for the ex-partner of your partner (his/her ex), or for your own previous partner (my/your Ex). The ex could be a former lover or a former spouse.

Extend—Both to enlarge and to reach out. An extended family is both larger and more encompassing of other people than a natural family.

Family—A grouping of related people (and how "related" is interpreted is up to you).

FamilyMind—A concept developed by Jeanne Elium and Don Elium that puts the needs of the family as a whole before the needs of any one family member.

Fault divorce—A traditional form of divorce in which one party states mistreatment (such as adultery, desertion, or mental cruelty) as the reason for marital breakdown.

The Grands—The bioparent's parents.

Half-siblings—Kids who share one biological parent, either a mother or a father.

"I" Statement—A statement about your feelings, views, needs, likes, or dislikes that begins with the word "I." "I" Statements tell the listener that you're speaking from your own point of view.

Legal custody—The decision-making authority for a minor child.

Legal guardian—A person appointed by the court to care for a child's personal needs, including shelter, education, and medical care. A legal guardian is not a parent, and (unlike in an adoption) the child's parents retain their rights and financial responsibilities for the child.

Moneybags Mama Syndrome (M.M.S.)—A condition suffered by a biomother who feels guilty, resentful of her ex, and/or estranged from her children. Its primary symptom is being overly generous to the kids with money and material things. (*See* **Disneyland Daddy Syndrome.**)

Natural family—A family in which all the children are the biological offspring of the adults.

No-fault divorce—A divorce where the judge considers nobody at fault, that the marriage, for instance, has broken up because of irreconcilable differences.

Nondominant culture—A culture that lives in a geographical area that is culturally dominated by another culture.

Other Grands—The parents of your partner's ex, who is the other bioparent.

Parent Guilt—An insidious disease characterized by the feeling that you are not giving your child enough love, support, money, sympathy, time, or whatever. It runs rampant among divorced and remarried parents.

Parenting partner—Anybody with whom you share parenting responsibilities on a full- or part-time basis (so that means your Ex, too).

Paternity—The state of being a natural father.

PDA—Public Display of Affection. When your stepkids get into high school, you may see or hear this phrase used as an on-campus no-no.

Physical custody—The right of a parent to have the child live with him or her.

Positive intent—The underlying positive meaning behind any action.

Relative adoption—Adoption by somebody related to the child by blood or marriage.

Regression—Reversion to childish, immature behavior, usually due to emotional distress of some sort.

Semi-combined family—A blended stepfamily in which at least one set of kids lives only part-time in the household.

Shared (joint) custody—An arrangement in which both the care and authority are shared by both parents.

Sole custody—A custody arrangement where the parent has been awarded full legal and physical custody.

Stepfamily—A family in which some members are not biologically or legally related to each other.

Stepparent adoption—Adoption of a marital partner's child.

Stepparenting—Parenting in families with kids who are not biologically related to you.

Stepsiblings—"Sisters" and "brothers" related to each other only by marriage. When parents of unrelated children marry, the children become stepsiblings. There's no biological relationship between stepsiblings.

Step-Grands—The stepparent's parents.

Super Stepparent Syndrome (S.S.S.)—A condition of many overachieving new stepparents who knock themselves out trying to be the best possible parent (or, at least, better than the ex).

Sympathy—The ability to understand and share the feelings of another person.

Visioning—The process of seeing the future with your mind's eye. It's not about magic or prediction; it is, rather, a way of expressing your own hopes and expectations.

Visitation—An arrangement where a person has been awarded the right to spend time with a child but has no decision-making authority.

Temperament—The way a person approaches the world. Temperament is made up of at least 10 characteristics: energy level, regularity, first reaction, environmental sensitivity, adaptability, intensity, mood, persistence, perceptiveness, and physical sensitivity.

Unified front—An agreed-upon approach to an issue. In disciplinary matters, it's best to have at least the appearance of total agreement.

More Good Things to Read

Families and Stepparenting

Adler, Robert. *Sharing the Children*. Bethesda, MD: Adler and Adler, 1988.

Bassoff, Evelyn. *Cherishing Our Daughters*. New York: Dutton, 1998.

Berman, Claire. *Making It As a Stepparent*. New York: Harper and Row, 1986.

Burns, Cherie. *Stepmotherhood: How to Survive Without Feeling Frustrated, Left Out, or Wicked*. New York: Harper and Row, 1985.

Cerquone, Joseph. *You're A Stepparent… Now What?* Far Hills, NJ: New Horizon Press, 1994.

Clurman, Ruth-Ann. *Parenting the Other Chick's Eggs: A Helpful and Entertaining Guide for How to Build a Strong and Loving Blended Family*. Shawnee Mission, KN: National Press Publications, 1997.

Elium, Jeanne and Don Elium. *Raising a Family*. Berkeley: Celestial Arts Publishing, 1997.

Engel, Margorie. *Weddings, a Family Affair: The New Etiquette for Second Marriages and Couples With Divorced Parents*. North Hollywood, CA: Wilshire Publications, 1998.

Furman, Beliza Ann. *Younger Women—Older Men*. New York: Barricade Books, 1995.

Joslin, Karen Renshaw. *Positive Parenting From A To Z*. New York: Fawcett Columbine, 1994.

Lerman, Saf. *Parent Awareness Training: Positive Parenting for the 1980s*. New York: A and W Publishers, 1980.

Keshet, Jamie K. *Love and Power in the Stepfamily: A Practical Guide*. New York: McGraw-Hill, 1987.

Kurcinka, Mary Sheedy. *Raising Your Spirited Child*. New York: Harper Perennial, 1992.

Lansky, Vicki. *Vicki Lansky's Divorce Book for Parents*. Deephaven, MN: The Book Peddlers, 1996.

Poretta, Vicki, and Ericka Lutz. *Mom's Guide to Disciplining Your Child*. New York: Macmillan, 1997.

Rosin, Mark Bruce. *Step-Fathering: Stepfathers' Advice on Creating a New Family*. New York: Simon and Schuster, 1987.

Savage, Karen and Patricia Adams. *The Good Step-Mother: A Practical Guide*. New York: Crown Publishers, 1989.

Cross-Cultural and Gay and Lesbian Stepfamilies

Gardenschwartz, Lee and Anita Rowe. *Managing Diversity*. New York, Irwin Professional Publishing, 1993.

MacPike, Loralee, Ed. *There's Something I've Been Meaning to Tell You*. Tallahassee, FL: Naiad Press, 1989.

Martin, April. *The Lesbian and Gay Parenting Handbook: Creating and Raising Our Families*. New York: Harper Collins, 1993.

Sonnenschein, William H. *The Practical Executive and Workforce Diversity*. Lincolnwood, IL: NTC Business Books, 1997.

Legal Stuff

Family Law Reporter (American Bar Association publication).

Family Law Quarterly (from the Bureau of National Affairs).

(Look through these two journals at your local law library to find announcements of important family law cases all over the country.)

Engel, Margorie Louise and Diana Delhi Gould. *The Divorce Decisions Workbook : A Planning and Action Guide*. New York: McGraw-Hill, 1991.

Estess, Patricia Schiff. *Money Advice for Your Successful Remarriage: Handling Delicate Financial Issues With Love and Understanding*. Cincinnati: Betterway Publications, 1996.

Forman, Deborah L. *Every Parent's Guide to the Law*. New York: Harcourt-Brace, 1998.

Ihara, Toni, and Ralph Warner. *The Living Together Kit: A Legal Guide for Unmarried Couples*. Berkeley: Nolo Press, 1997.

Leonard, Robin and Stephan Elias, *Nolo's Pocket Guide to Family Law*. Berkeley: Nolo Press, 1996.

Mahoney, Margaret M. *Stepfamilies and the Law*. Ann Arbor, MI: University of Michigan Press, 1994.

Ricci, Isolina. *Mom's House, Dad's House: A Complete Guide for Parents Who Are Separated, Divorced, or Remarried*. New York: Simon and Schuster, 1997.

For Stepparents of Teens

Riera, Michael. *Uncommon Sense for Parents with Teenagers*. Berkeley: Celestial Arts, 1995.

Rubin, Nancy. *Ask Me If I Care: Voices from an American High School*. Berkeley: Ten Speed Press, 1994.

Schwebel, Robert. *Saying No is Not Enough: Raising Children Who Make Wise Decisions About Drugs and Alcohol*. New York: Newmarket Press, 1989.

Siegler, Ava L. *The Essential Guide to the New Adolescence*. New York: Dutton, 1997.

Steinberg, Laurence, and Ann Levine. *You and Your Adolescent*. New York: HarperPerennial, 1997.

Stepparent Resources and Support Systems

Support and Information for Stepparents

The Stepfamily Association of America

650 J. Street, Suite 205
Lincoln, NE 68508

402-477-7837
800-735-0329

www.stepfam.org

The Stepfamily Association of America is an educational organization that holds support meetings in chapters all across the country. In addition, the SAA trains and provides professional certification of family therapists in the work of stepfamilies, and maintains a list of organization-approved therapists who have been trained by the SAA or another reputable source. The Stepfamily Association of America Catalog of Stepfamily Resources: Books, Tapes, and Videos is an excellent source of materials. One year membership costs $35.

Step Family Foundation, Inc.

333 West End Ave.
New York, NY 10023

212-877-3244

stepfamily@aol.com
www.stepfamily.org

Since 1975, Jeannette Lofas and The Step Family Foundation, Inc. have provided counseling, seminars for professionals, and information to help create a successful step relationship.

Check out these other web sites:

Positive Steps

www.positivesteps.com

Parent's Place

www.parentsplace.com

Child Abuse Prevention Information and Support

Boys Town National Hotline:

800-448-3000

The Family Violence Prevention Fund:

800-313-1310

Parents Anonymous, Inc.

675 West Foothill Blvd., Suite 220
Claremont, CA 91711

909-621-6184

HN3831@handsnet.org

Parents Anonymous is a national organization that promotes mutual support and parent leadership to any parent in order to build and support strong, safe families. They have affiliates in 30 states who offer Parents Anonymous groups, parent helplines, and advocacy in partnership with parents.

National Domestic Violence Hotline:

800-787-3224

Drug and Alcohol Information and Resources

Alanon-Alateen Information Service:

800-344-2666

Alcoholics Anonymous

Look in your local phone book or write for referrals to local chapters:

General Service Office
Grand Central Station
P.O. Box 459
New York, NY 10163

Marijuana Anonymous World Service Office:

800-766-6779

Nar-Anon Family Groups World Service Office:

310-547-5800

Narcotics Anonymous World Service Office:

818-780-3951

National Drug and Alcohol Treatment Referral Hotline:

'800-662-HELP

National Clearinghouse for Drug and Alcohol Information:

301-468-2600

Other Helpful Family Resources

American Association of Retired Persons (AARP):

202-434-2296

The Grandparent Information Center, a division of The American Association of Retired Persons, puts out a newsletter called Parenting Grandchildren: A Voice for Grandparents.

The American Anorexia/Bulimia Association:

212-891-8686

Centers for Disease Control National AIDS Hotline:

800-342-AIDS

Children's Rights Council (CRC)

300 I Street NE, Suite 401
Washington, DC 20002

202-547-6227

The Children's Rights Council is concerned with the healthy development of children of divorced and separated parents. They work for custody reform by minimizing hostilities between parents, substituting conciliation and mediation for adversarial litigation, providing equitable child support, and strongly advocating a child's access to both *parents as well as the extended family. The CRC has a wealth of available information and holds annual conferences.*

The National Association for the Advancement of Psychoanalysis:

212-741-0515

This association can provide referrals to therapists in your area.

National Center for Lesbian Rights

870 Market Street, Suite 570
San Francisco, CA 94102

415-392-6257

The National Center for Lesbian Rights provides adoption information for gays and lesbians, as well as sample co-parenting agreements.

Parents, Families, and Friends of Lesbians and Gays (PFLAG)

202-638-4200

PFLAG has chapters and support groups all across the country.

Planned Parenthood Federation of America

Look in your phone book for a local clinic, or contact the main office:

810 Seventh Avenue
New York, NY 10019

212-541-7800

San Francisco AIDS Foundation Hotline:

415-FOR-AIDS

Tips for Resolving Family Conflicts

This appendix offers some general tips for resolving conflict:

- ➤ Use "I" statements. ("I see things this way...." "This is how I feel about....")
- ➤ Stay in the present. No dredging up the past.
- ➤ Stay specific; don't speak in abstracts.
- ➤ No globals (always, never, all, should).
- ➤ No taboo subjects or hitting below the belt.
- ➤ Don't interrupt. At times you might really have to bite your tongue, but do it so that the speaker can finish before you respond.
- ➤ Ask questions to clarify, but stay away from "why." ("Why do you need to lose your temper all the time?") "How" is a better choice. ("How can I act so that you don't lose your temper as often?")
- ➤ Request specific behavior changes only, not a whole change in personality. Keep your requests very specific.
- ➤ Listen as much, or more, than you talk.

Fighting a Fair Fight

Fighting is not always a negative thing. When done fairly, a good fight can clear the air and resolve family problems. Here's a template for use in a conflict between two people within the family. It can be particularly useful if you find your fights wandering off subject into wild digressions, or bringing up past issues. This template is fast and it's effective, but it only works if both people involved want to try it and are willing to follow the rules.

1. Schedule the fight. Tell the person with whom you have a conflict that you want to talk about a specific issue. Ask that person for an appointment to sit down together and work it out.

2. Plan a time and a place where you won't be disturbed. Allow enough time (half an hour won't do it), enough emotional space (fighting with John about the dishes the night before John's chemistry final is not a good plan), and the right space (a room at home where you can be alone is better than a formal restaurant).

3. Either one of you may begin. Person 1 describes the events or problems as she sees them. Person 2 practices active listening, which means listening thoroughly, not arguing (Person 2 will get his chance in a moment!), and then paraphrasing to Person 1's satisfaction.

4. Then it's Person 2's turn to state his version of the situation! Person 1 listens actively. Person 2's version may be similar to or very different from Person 1's. It may begin and end at a different point in time. Person 2 now paraphrases Person 1's story.

5. Don't stop here! Just discussing the issue and events is not enough, even if you've cleared up misunderstandings. Part of fair fighting includes resolving feelings.

6. Person 1 describes her emotional reactions to the situation. Person 2 listens actively and then paraphrases what Person 1 has said she feels. Now it's Person 2's turn to describe his emotional reactions while Person 1 listens and then paraphrases.

7. Each person states what she or he would like to see happen in the future. In a situation where one person has behaved badly or injured the other, the injured party should provide a way for the other person to make it up to him. If both people are equally at fault, you can use this opportunity to reaffirm your commitment to having a good relationship, and celebrate the end of the tensions.

8. Finish with a nonverbal acknowledgment of the resolution, such as a handshake, a hug, or a kiss.

When the Kids Are Fighting

When your kids and/or stepkids are fighting, you may be called upon to help resolve their conflicts. Here are some tips to make life a bit more serene:

➤ Stop the fight.

➤ Give the kids a cool-down period (this may need to be enforced through time-outs). The cool-down period is not punishment, and it should be enforced equally.

➤ Encourage kids to resolve the issue themselves.

➤ If they are unsuccessful, you or your partner should step in as mediator. If you are mediating, keep your partner "in the loop" by requesting information and feedback about the situation, as well as about your behavior as the mediator.

➤ Emotionally remove yourself as a participant in the conflict, and take on the role of mediator. This may mean a change in attitude. Imagine yourself standing far away from the fray. You are not on either child's side.

➤ To mediate, lead the kids through steps 3, 4, 5, and 6 in the Fighting a Fair Fight exercise.

➤ Help mediate a discussion on step 7. It may help to write down each person's resolution.

➤ Kiss and dismiss. Your eventual goal is to teach the kids to mediate their own disputes.

A Clean Room!? What's Your Expectation?

Many stepfamily conflicts occur because people from different families have differing ideas about how the household should be run. When you ask your stepdaughter to clean her room, what do you mean by that? Does that include simply getting all the toys on the shelf and the clothes in the hamper, or do you expect her to vacuum, dust, and make sure all surfaces are clear? If you don't spell it all out, you may find yourself with more conflict in the household than you desire.

Here's a way to reduce the arguments over household chores: Define your expectations!

Creating a chore checklist for each job helps the entire stepfamily. You'll know that your expectations have been clearly stated, and your stepchild will know what is expected of him. He'll have a reminder sheet to follow, and you'll have an easy way to check that he is doing what you've both agreed upon.

Below is a list of possible tasks. Look through the list, and write those that you feel are appropriate in the spaces below. Always take your child's age into consideration! (A 4-year-old may not be able to fold her own clothes, but she can help put them away. An 8-year-old probably isn't doing his own laundry, but he can dust.) The chore checklist should be modified as the child matures. Keep in mind that these are only examples of what you can choose.

POSSIBLE ROOM CLEANING CHORES

Clothing

- ❏ Fold clothes
- ❏ Put clothes in appropriate drawers
- ❏ Hang up coats
- ❏ Hang up dresses
- ❏ Hang up blouses or shirts

- ❏ Organize closet by clothes type
- ❏ Put all shoes and slippers in closet
- ❏ Launder clothes
- ❏ Put dress-up clothes in dress-up trunk
- ❏ Put dirty clothes in hamper (check under bed and in closet)

Surfaces

- ❏ Take objects off dresser, dust, and return objects neatly
- ❏ Take objects off bedside table, dust, and return objects neatly
- ❏ Take objects off shelves, dust, and return objects neatly

Toys

- ❏ Put game pieces back in their boxes
- ❏ Put toys back on shelf/drawers/bins

Music and Computer Programs

- ❏ Make sure all tapes, CDs, and disks are in their cases
- ❏ Put cases on appropriate shelf

Books

- ❏ Put books back on shelves
- ❏ Put library books in pile by door to return

Schoolwork/Desk

- ❏ Organize desk so homework and books are accessible
- ❏ Throw away old clutter and scrap paper
- ❏ Empty wastepaper basket in the outside trash can

Bed

❑ Remove sheets and pillowcases ❑ Put dirty sheets in the hamper

❑ Remake bed with clean sheets ❑ Wash sheets

Walls

❑ Scrub bad spots off walls with spray and rag

❑ Make sure all posters are still securely attached

Floor

❑ Move furniture aside and vacuum

❑ Vacuum dust from under bed

YOUR LIST

❑ _____ ❑ _____

❑ _____ ❑ _____

❑ _____ ❑ _____

❑ _____ ❑ _____

How to be Good to Yourself

Being a stepparent is hard. Throughout this book, I've encouraged you to take care of yourself and to treat yourself with respect, encouragement, and a little pampering (you'll need it!). I know from experience, though, that when you feel bad, you often feel *bad*, and it's hard to even remember what makes you feel good!

Fill out this worksheet when you are in a good mood. Then, when times get tough, you can refer back to it for inspiration and ideas on ways to make yourself feel better. For each statement, I've provided a few starter ideas (these are things that make me feel good) and have estimated how much time each activity takes. Feel free to use or adapt my ideas, if they fit you. I encourage you, though, to make up your own. The only one who truly knows what you like is you. Be selfish! You spend a lot of time in your life doing the "right" thing and taking care of other people. This is a pamper list for you!

Once you have your list, use it.

I feel calmer when I:

_____

_____

_____

Erica's Answers:

     Take a bath: 45 minutes

     Read a novel: 30 minutes or more

     Work in the garden: 1 hour

     Play a card game with Bill: 20 minutes

     Take myself out for sushi: 1 and a half hours.

I feel happier with myself when I:

_____

_____

_____

Erica's answers:

> Call my grandmother(s): 10 minutes
>
> Complete old thank-you letters: 30 minutes
>
> Cook and eat a wonderful meal: 2-3 hours

I feel better about my body when I:

_____

_____

Erica's answers:

> Stretch: 5 minutes
>
> Take a walk: 20 minutes to 2 hours
>
> Take a dance class: 2 hours
>
> Put on attractive clothes: 5 minutes

I feel excited by life when I:

_____

_____

Erica's answers:

> Eat a square of really good dark chocolate: 2 minutes
>
> Work on my novel: 2-5 hours
>
> Take a nature walk: 1-3 hours
>
> Do something I've never done before: 5 minutes to 2 years.

Index

G

gay/lesbian couples, *see* lesbian/gay couples
generational differences
 cross-cultural, 202, 205
 values, conflicting, 189
gift-giving
 combined families, 216
 holidays/celebrations guidelines, 215-217
girlfriends
 cohabitation, 42-44
 evaluating as potential stepparents, 31
graduations, guidelines, 217
grandchildren, name preferences, 186-187
Grandparent Information Center (AARP), 193
grandparents
 alliances against stepparents, 188
 becoming Step-Grands, 193-194
 children living with, 193
 conflicts, resolution advice, 191-192
 legal rights, 192
 name preferences, 186-187
 Other Grands (other grandparents)
  defined, 186
  legal rights, 192
  level of involvement with children, 190-191
 relationships, developing, 187-188
 roles, 192-193
 Step-Grands (step-grandparents)
  defined, 186
  inheritance clauses for stepgrandchildren, 192
  legal rights, 192
  negative behaviors by stepchildren, 190
 values, generational conflicts, 189
grief
 remarriage emotions, 59
 resolution, 68-72
Growing Up Again, 67
guardianship, 250
 versus adopting stepchildren, 272

guilt
 Disneyland Daddy Syndrome (D.D.S.), 266
 emergence, 68-69
 feelings, interference with spousal privacy, 95-96
 manipulation
  children, 122
  comparing households, 267
 Moneybags Mama Syndrome (M.M.S.), 266
 noncustodial parents, 96
 overcoming, 317-318
 Parent Guilt, 263-266
 remarriages, disloyalty to children, 92-93

H

half-siblings, 282-284
 conflicts, resolving, 285
 privacy, lack of, 286
 stepchildren/stepparents relationship, effect on, 288-289
 stepsiblings, 288-289
  after birth of baby, 286
  feelings prior to birth, 286
  reactions, 284-285
 surnames, 287
 see also, babies, having
Hansel and Gretel stepmother myth, 17
harmony, unrealistic expectations, 9
hearings, adopting stepchildren, 276
holidays/celebrations, 211-212
 adult stepchildren, 214
 alternative plans, 213, 218
 cross-cultural stepfamilies, 205
 custody agreements, 213
 exclusion, 217-218
 expectations, 210
 family events, guidelines, 217
 gift-giving
  coordinating with ex-spouse, 216
  guidelines, 215-217
 gracious behavior, 218
 guilt, children, 214

loneliness, 214
loyalty issues, children, 214
memories, 210-211
new holidays, creating, 213
personal special days, 214-215
problem-solving, 212
refusing invitations, 218
rituals/traditions, 211
splitting time between families, 213
stepsibling rivalry, 213
weddings, 217
winter holidays, 210
home studies, 275-276
homes
 accidents, 114
 children
  adjustment period with new stepparents, 112
  decorating decisions, 113
  private space, 114
 claiming new territory, 112
 combined families, 114
 existing versus new, 110
 finances, combined families, 110-111
 furnishings, 112-113
 mortgage affordability, 110-111
 moving, effects of, 111
 off-limits area designations, 112
 organizing, stepfamilies, 67
 Post-Move Letdown Syndrome (PMSL), 111
 room cleaning chores, 340-341
 rules, 115
How to Talk So Kids Will Listen and Listen So Kids Will Talk, 138
humor, 73
 cross-cultural stepfamilies, 198

I - J - K

"I" statements, 325
 as element in conflict-resolution, 150-151
in-laws, 188-189
incest, 237-238
income conflicts
 ex-spouse, 264-266
 stepfamilies, 263-264

L

T